FAMILIES AND SOCIAL NETWORKS

NEW PERSPECTIVES ON FAMILY

NCFR Published in cooperation with National Council on Familiy Relations

Series Editor: **Maximiliane Szinovacz**
University of Illinois, Urbana—Champaign

Series Editor-Elect: **Linda Thompson**
Virginia Polytechnic Institute & State University

Books appearing in New Perspectives on Family are either single- or multiple-authored volumes or concisely edited books of original articles on focused topics within the broad field of marriage and family. Books can be reports of significant research, innovations in methodology, treatises on family theory, or syntheses of current knowledge in a subfield of the discipline. Each volume meets the highest academic standards and makes a substantial contribution to our knowledge of marriage and family.

SINGLES: Myths and Realities, *Leonard Cargan and Matthew Melko*

THE CHILDBEARING DECISION: Fertility Attitudes and Behavior,
Greer Litton Fox, ed.

AT HOME AND AT WORK: The Family's Allocation of Labor,
Michael Geerken and Walter R. Gove

PREVENTION IN FAMILY SERVICES: Approaches to Family Wellness,
David R. Mace, ed.

WORKING WIVES/WORKING HUSBANDS, *Joseph H. Pleck*

THE WARMTH DIMENSION: Foundations of Parental Acceptance-Rejection Theory,
Ronald P. Rohner

FAMILIES AND SOCIAL NETWORKS, *Robert M. Milardo, ed.*

In press:

FAMILIES AND ECONOMIC DISTRESS: Coping Strategies and Social Policy,
Patricia Voydanoff and Linda C. Majka, eds.

Other volumes currently available from Sage and sponsored by NCFR:

THE SOCIAL WORLD OF OLD WOMEN: Management of Self-Identity,
Sarah H. Matthews

SEX AND PREGNANCY IN ADOLESCENCE, *Melvin Zelnik, John F. Kantner, and Kathleen Ford*

FAMILIES AND SOCIAL NETWORKS

EDITED BY

RobertM. Milardo

Published in cooperation with
the National Council on Family Relations

SAGE PUBLICATIONS
The Publishers of Professional Social Science
Newbury Park   Beverly Hills   London   New Delhi

For information address:

SAGE Publications, Inc.
2111 West Hillcrest Drive
Newbury Park, California 91320

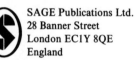

SAGE Publications Inc.
275 South Beverly Drive
Beverly Hills
California 90212

SAGE Publications Ltd.
28 Banner Street
London EC1Y 8QE
England

SAGE PUBLICATIONS India Pvt. Ltd.
M-32 Market
Greater Kailash I
New Delhi 110 048 India

Printed in the United States of America

Library of Congress Cataloging-in-Publication Data

Families and social networks.

(New perspectives on family)
"Published in cooperation with the National Council on Family Relations."
1. Family—United States. 2. Social networks—United States. I. Milardo, Robert M. II. National Council on Family Relations. III. Series.
HQ536.F3335 1987   306.8′5′0973   87-20462
ISBN 0-8039-2643-X
ISBN 0-8039-2644-8 (pbk.)

Contents

Series Editor's Foreword
Maximiliane Szinovacz   7

Preface   9

1. **Families and Social Networks: An Overview of Theory and Methodology**
Robert M. Milardo   13

2. **The Influence of the Interactive Network on Developing Relationships**
Catherine A. Surra   48

3. **Social Networks and the Transition to Motherhood**
Kathryn McCannell   83

4. **Precious Moments with Family Members and Friends**
Reed W. Larson and Nancy Bradney   107

5. **Changes in Social Networks Following Marital Separation and Divorce**
Marylyn Rands   127

6. **Individual Development and Intimate Relationships in Middle and Late Adulthood**
Rosemary Blieszner   147

7. **Relationships Among Family Members and Friends in Later Life**
Colleen Leahy Johnson   168

8. **Loneliness: A Life-Span, Family Perspective**
Daniel Perlman   190

9. **Healing Members and Relationships in the Intimate Network**
Carlfred B. Broderick   221

About the Contributors   235

Series Editor's Foreword

The themes of social affiliation and integration—how individuals and groups relate to other individuals as well as to informal or formal groups—have been central to sociology and social psychology since their beginnings. We have learned that the specific characteristics of their social ties have important consequences for the individual and the larger societal structures.

Among these ties, interactions with and supports from relatives and friends have been and continue to be of primary importance. Whatever impact industrialization and urbanization may have had on nuclear families, they have not erased the social support functions among kin. Recent studies show, for instance, that the quality of individuals' and families' social networks influences such divergent behaviors as adjustment to parenthood, use of physical violence against children and spouses, marital task allocation or the burden experienced by family caregivers of the elderly.

Robert Milardo and his coauthors provide us with insights into the most recent advancements in social network analysis as it pertains to families and other intimate relationships. Taking a social psychological perspective, the authors address issues in conceptualization and measurement as well as a variety of theoretical, empirical, and applied topics. The chapters cover families at different stages of the life cycle and refer to different types of network qualities.

This variety and the rigorous scientific standards applied throughout the volume render it a valuable contribution to the NCFR-Sage Monograph Series. Family scholars should find the book useful in pursuing the many as-yet-unanswered questions in family network analysis, and clinicians should find in it guidelines for applying insights from network analysis in their work.

—Maximiliane Szinovacz

Preface

The importance of friends and family in the life-course is elementary and indisputable. Few matters are more central to our lives as the relationships in which we find ourselves. And yet, few scholars have systematically examined the interconnections bonding families to their social environments of kin, friends, neighbors, coworkers, and acquaintances.

Family sociologists traditionally have examined the interrelations of kinship and the internal character of families, both psychologists and medical sociologists have examined the social support available from kith and kin and its relationship to the psychiatric and physical well-being of individuals, social psychologists have investigated the fields of interpersonal attraction and more recently the development of personal relationships, and still other social scientists have explored collectives of personal relationships usually termed social networks as they relate to the particular status of individuals—for example, class standing, age, or gender. This broad array of contributions from a number of perspectives forms the underpinnings of the present volume.

The analysis of families and social networks can assume essentially two forms. We may examine the local structure in which family relationships are embedded. A network's size, composition, or interconnectedness of members are all examples of indices of "local structure." Structural characteristics have important consequences for the initiation, maintenance, and dissolution of pair relationships. A second and complementary approach to the study of families and social networks centers on what individuals actually do for and with one another as well as how they personally evaluate their relationships. The chapters in this volume are organized around this dual focus on the analysis of network structure and interaction, with some emphasizing one perspective over another and others addressing questions of both a structural and interactional nature. There are undoubtedly other ways to conceptualize networks or to phrase questions concerning networks and close relationships (many of which are reviewed briefly in Chapter 1), but this volume is limited to specific aspects of networks, their affects and consequences. Issues pertaining to race and ethnicity, geographic and social mobility, and other classical themes are mentioned only briefly.

[9]

The intention in preparing this book was to encourage the systematic and integrated study of personal relationships, some intimate and enduring, others rather ordinary and brief, in addition to examining the structures that these relationships create. Throughout, several theoretical and methodological perspectives are presented. In each contribution, the authors address issues concerning families and social networks, although their views differ as a function of their own theoretical perspectives.

The first chapter provides an overview of theory and research on families and social networks. A framework is developed for conceptualizing several distinct types of networks, and the measurement strategies available for identifying network members are scrutinized closely. Important distinctions are drawn between the analysis of network structure and the analysis of multiple social relationships, and the implications of each type of analysis are illustrated.

Chapter 2 by Catherine Surra examines how social networks influence the patterns of interdependence between romantic partners. Surra challenges the long-standing assumption that the development of close relationships is uniform with linear increases in pair interdependences. The properties descriptive of the interdependences of network members are reviewed. Surra provides a penetrating analysis of prototypical networks that vary in selected structural properties, such as density, clustering, and overlap. These prototypes are then used to generate hypotheses concerning the differential effects of network structure on the developmental course of pair relationships. Network properties influence, for instance, such diverse causal conditions as the propinquity of partners, their expectations concerning relationships, their feelings and knowledge about partners, and the availability of alternative associations.

Kathryn McCannell in Chapter 3 examines shifts in social relationships that occur during the transition to motherhood and the role networks play in easing postpartum adjustment. She details findings from her longitudinal study of the social and personal consequences of mothering, adding insight to our understanding of the social processes surrounding this passage as well as useful suggestions for the design of interventions.

In contrast to the emphasis on structural analyses presented in the first chapters, Reed Larson and Nancy Bradney focus on the momentary experience of family members in their interactions with each other, their kin, and friends. The chapter addresses fundamental questions, for example: "When do individuals experience enjoyment and absorption in their social activity or boredom, pain and anxiety?" Larson and Bradney remind us of an important distinction between interactions with their constituent momentary subjective states and personal definitions of relationships that are viewed as derivative of interactions. A unique methodology for sampling contemporary personal and social events is employed, with samples representing three age groups. These data reveal striking continuity across the life span in the power of friends to generate enjoyment, to permit transcendence of the usual preoccupations of everyday life, and to redirect attention toward new ideas, to play and to other people.

Marylyn Rands in Chapter 5 provides a systematic and theoretically based framework for analyzing changes in the social networks of former spouses following separation and divorce. Her study is unique in both its design and in the variety of detailed information gathered. This inquiry questions the implications of network stability and turnover, supportive versus interfering networks, and the development of new social bonds on the personal experience of men and women following divorce. The study provides strong support for the connection of network structure and interaction with personal well-being following marital dissolution.

Chapter 6 by Rosemary Blieszner and Chapter 7 by Colleen Johnson provide us with analyses of the variations in social participation that accompany the later stages of the life course. Blieszner examines issues pertaining to individual development and the impact of intimate relationships among spouses, friends, and kin, with particular attention drawn to the interplay of marriage and close ties with friends in middle and late adulthood. She examines how the socialization experiences of husbands and wives result in divergent developmental concerns and perceptions of marriage and friendship.

Colleen Johnson concentrates on the dimensions of pair relationships that are associated with the provision of social support. Comparisons of marital, parent-child, friendship, and kinship dyads are examined in order to identify those relationships that facilitate supportive behavior. Are, for example, relationships with kin and friends interchangeable, or are they specialized, with some providing emotional support and others providing instrumental aid? Findings are presented from a longitudinal study of posthospitalized elderly and their contact with network members. Changes in relationships with family and network members are identified as individuals make the transition from relatively good health to illness and dependency. Three dimensions of relationships emerged from variations in the responses of network members to the changing health status of one member. These dimensions are: the degree of normative regulation specific to the relationship, the type of reciprocity underlying the exchange of aid, and the changing power structure brought about by changes in dependency needs.

Social psychologist Daniel Perlman in Chapter 8 analyses the experience of loneliness and its connection to social isolation, the absence of network relationships. Perlman argues that loneliness occurs when there is a mismatch between an individual's actual social relationships and the individual's needs or desire for social affiliation, but that the experience of loneliness is not necessarily synonymous with social isolation. This basic prescription is then expanded and applied to questions concerning variations in loneliness across the family life cycle, or across major transitions such as parenthood or widowhood. Comparisons are drawn between intimate and nonintimate bonds with network members and the relative contribution of each to the experience of loneliness.

Analyses of social networks have important consequences for the design and implementation of family therapy as well. In Chapter 9, Carlfred Broderick develops a fourfold typology of networks based on the concepts of cohesion and flexibility, and he notes how each type of network is apt to support or impede therapeutic efforts directed at a particular member or family unit. Throughout, Broderick argues persuasively that a thorough knowledge of an individual's or family's social network, including both its structure and dominant value system, will enlighten interventions strategies.

The support, advice and encouragement of several colleagues and friends moved this book from the abstract to the accomplished. Mike Johnson and Ted Huston were important in this way. Cathy Surra provided critical commentary and support throughout. My colleagues at the University of Maine, especially Marc Baranowski and Steve Marks, shared their expertise and advice, and the Maine Agricultural Experiment Station provided financial support (MAES Pub. No. 1154).

I am grateful to the authors of this volume for their extraordinary insights, patience, and enthusiastic participation. Finally, a special thanks goes to Maxi Szinovacz, Editor of the National Council on Family Relations Monograph Series of which this book is a part, and two anonymous reviewers. Maxi understood the purpose of the volume and her advice was always rewarding.

To Jennifer, my family, and friends this book is dedicated.

—Robert M. Milardo

1

Families and Social Networks: An Overview of Theory and Methodology

Robert M. Milardo

An individual human being has no significant separate existence, but is the product of a complex and elaborate system of interactions with other individuals [David R. Mace, 1985, p. 81].

The relationships we maintain with other individuals, some close and of long standing and others ordinary and brief, are among the most important features of life. They are the raw materials by and through which personal biography, family and social structure are framed and constructed. When asked, individuals will rate personal relationships as a central feature of their lives (Berscheid & Peplau, 1983) and they invest a considerable amount of time and energy maintaining ties with kin and nonkin alike (see Larson & Bradney, this volume).

Curiously, in many ways we know very little about the character of personal relationships, either in terms of basic descriptive information, their internal dynamics, or the more global patterns of social structure. Few theoretical models in the social sciences formally recognize relationship properties, as distinct from properties of individuals, and fewer still acknowledge the role of local structure in the development of personal relationships, although there are exceptions (Kelley et al., 1983). Yet, families live in an elaborate system of interactions where they create ties of varying complexity and strength with a broad array of other individuals, other families, and larger social collectives. Families are profoundly influenced by this web of ties and they are active agents in modifying and adapting these communities of personal relationships to meet ever-changing circumstances.

By centering on the social context in which relationships unfold, endure, and sometimes deteriorate, this volume draws on recent advances in the analysis of social networks.[1] In the following pages, I briefly trace critical developments in network analysis. This review will help to illuminate how social networks have been conceptualized as a means to examine the fabric of social structure, and it will help to illustrate and distinguish the focus of this volume from other equally important applications of network analysis. Following this discussion, I examine in greater depth how personal social networks have been conceptualized and I critically evaluate the methods used to identify members. In doing so, three distinct types of networks are defined, namely, psychological, exchange, and interactive networks, and the importance of linking research interests with network type, as well as methods appropriate to each type, is emphasized. The significance of theoretical clarity in the definition and measurement of social networks seems fundamental, an important bridge to the remaining chapters and to future efforts to establish causal interconnections between families and their social networks.

CONCEPTUALIZING SOCIAL NETWORKS

The concept of social networks applied to human groups appears in the early writing of several sociologists and social anthropologists. Initially, the use of the network concept was largely metaphorical and did not identify specific characteristics or dimensions useful in depicting particular networks (Mitchell, 1969). In his investigations of a Norwegian parish community, Barnes (1954) employed the network concept in a more analytical sense by suggesting that social structure is revealed in the connectedness of individuals in a community. Further refinements were developed subsequently, providing a means by which several features of social networks could be specified with the intention of quantifying the social structure of a community (Boissevain, 1974; Mitchell, 1969).

Quite apart from the work of British social anthropologists, several social psychologists in the United States had employed the network concept, but for very different purposes. Moreno (1934) and his associates were concerned with the affective bonds of small groups, usually schoolchildren. The friendship choices of groups of people provided the basis for describing networks graphically. Various graphic techniques were developed so that structural characteristics of the group could be identified visually based on each member's choice of friends. Individuals most often chosen as friends (stars), or subgroups of individuals who choose each other as friends (cliques) were located (Moreno, 1934). Sociograms and related graphic techniques soon proved too cumbersome, and more sophisticated applications of matrix algebra were developed where each cell contained a potential tie linking one member of the network with another (Festinger, 1949). This technique was later refined extensively and multivariate data reduction techniques were developed, such as cluster analyses which locate bunches of individuals who are linked to one another but have few ties with others (e.g., Salzinger, 1982), and block modeling which aggregates individuals based on the structural equivalence of their social ties (White, Boorman, & Breiger, 1976; Winship & Mandel, 1983; Wu, 1983).[2]

One legacy of this early work is the current interest in the structural analysis of social systems, an area with a rapidly advancing arsenal of analytical procedures (see Burt & Minor [eds.], 1983; Marsden & Lin [eds.], 1982). Network analysts are concerned with explanations of behavior based upon the patterned interconnections of members, rather than the independent effects of personal dispositions or dyadic relationships. They avoid explanations of behavior based on normative beliefs or categorical memberships like gender, race or class, because such explanations are inherently astructural. Aggregating people into groups based on discrete properties of individuals inadvertently destroys "structural information just as centrifuging genes destroys structure while providing information about composition" (Wellman, 1983, p. 166).

The structural analysis of social networks has taken a variety of forms, although nearly all are concerned with issues of social integration and the normative rights and duties that prescribe the activities of bounded groups (for reviews see Blau, 1982; Wellman, 1983). For example, anthropologists and sociologists alike have attended to the effects of migration from rural areas to urban centers and the ways people maintain traditional values through elaborate networks of personal relationships. One result of this work is that social mobility is not only governed by network ties in that individuals typically use pathways developed by kin and village members who have migrated earlier, but that traditional solidarities are maintained through these pathways and relationships within homogeneous ethnic groups (Wellman, 1983).

Still others have expanded the application of the network concept to analyses of social structure that are centered primarily on how patterns of ties influence social behavior, including the diffusion of resources and the integration of individuals in large-scale social systems. Network analysis differs from the traditional sociological frameworks of Durkheim, Marx, Parsons, and Levi-Strauss, theorists that share an interest in social integration and structure, by focusing on the specific pattern or distribution of social positions and relations among networks of individuals or organizations, and by providing precisely defined concepts coupled with rigorous analytical methods for documenting "social integration," "mobility," or "resource allocation," and for comparing the structure of one network with that of another. Investigators, for example, have examined how network structure influences cultural factors as in the diffusion of information in youth culture (Granovetter, 1983), political thought and social policy (Erickson, 1982; Knoke & Laumann, 1982), or how ties linking organizations influence the prominence of metropolitan areas (Ross, 1987). Several illustrative applications of network analysis are depicted in Table 1, and although a comprehensive review of this material is beyond the present scope, classical sociological themes such as social integration, anomie, stratification and class relations are clearly important in contemporary network theory and research.

In light of the objectives of this volume, the analysis of network structure has several important, and largely unrealized, applications to the study of family relationships. For instance, consider the interaction of a couple who maintain a variety of network ties with network constituents who know and interact with one another regularly independent of this couple. In this case, the network members have the potential to coordinate their support of the target couple in times of need. Such support might be relatively formal and ritualized, as in the case of an anniversary party, or it might be relatively informal, as in the case of occasional visits following the birth of a child. In contrast, if the network members are relatively unknown to one another, the coordination of support is prevented.

In a loosely structured network, knowledge of the need for support is

TABLE 1
Illustrative Sociological Applications of Network Analysis

Topic	Network Unit	Theme
Organizational sociology (Ross, 1987)	Corporate headquarters and manufacturing units	Metropolitian prominence is dependent on characteristics of the area (e.g., its population size) and characteristics of its industries such as the number of corporate headquarters located within the area relative to the industrial production facilities located elsewhere.
Social integration and the diffusion of scarce resources (Granovetter, 1983)	Organizational and personal networks	The diffusion of ideas and information among individuals, innovations within large-scale organizations, and cohesion in complex social systems results from the unique function of weak ties to bridge divergent network segments that otherwise would be isolated from one another.
Social stratification and the origins of elite groups (Moore & Alba, 1982)	Leading executives in large public or private organizations	The relations of political power to other aspects of social stratification are examined in terms of the influence of social origins (e.g., class) on elite recruitment and the prestige and influence of individuals within elite networks.
Local integration of urban neighborhoods (Greenbaum & Greenbaum, 1985)	Personal networks in bounded communities	The basic structure of personal networks, degree of social participation, and intimacy of relationships are influenced by residential proximity, ethnic homogeneity, and involvement in local institutions.
Belief systems and political ideologies (Erickson, 1982)	Personal networks	Structural characteristics such as density, interconnected cliques, and the structural equivalence of social positions facilitate social comparisons and the formation of similar attitudes, belief systems and ideologies. Thus, belief systems are derivative of patterns of social relations and in the Durkheimian tradition guide essential processes like conflict, negotiation and social exchange.
The interdependence of relations of paid labor, domestic labor, and personal communities (Wellman, in press)	Personal networks	The position of individuals in social hierarchies influences internal relations of power and dependency within households and the development, form and content of ties with network members, while simultaneously households and network ties create and sustain labor markets. Involvement in domestic and paid labor affects and is affected by the structure of personal networks and the degree and type of social participation of individuals.

[17]

severely inhibited, and knowledge of the target couple must be communicated directly to each network member by one spouse or the other. A tightly structured network, on the other hand, facilitates shared knowledge, and by virtue of their knowing one another network members could communicate information about the target couple. In this example, the availability, type, amount, and timing of social support or interference is a function of the structure of the social network. The effect of local structure is quite independent of the precise nature of the personal relationships that compose a particular network. Local social structure is the primary determinant of the personal choices, opportunities, and constraints framing the development of all social relationships (see chapters by Surra and Rands, this volume).

A distinct advantage of network analysis lies in its ability to specify attributes of local social structure influential in the formation and development of personal relationships. Structural analyses rest on the premise that networks have a reality of their own in much the same way individuals and relationships do. Properties of network structure, therefore, are irreducible. The influence of network structure cannot be reduced to the simple effects of normative constraint, personality attributes, or the cumulative effects of multiple interacting dyads.

Elizabeth Bott (1971) was among the first to recognize the link between the internal character of a relationship and the structure of a network by arguing that the conjugal roles adopted by spouses depend on the connectedness of their friendship networks. Bott observed that families in which spouses complete household tasks separately and engage in leisure pursuits separately maintain interconnected networks such that the members tended to know and interact with one another independently of the spouses. In contrast, spouses who share household duties and spend leisure time together have dispersed networks in which the members are unknown to one another.

Bott hypothesized that closely knit or highly dense networks would exert informal pressure upon members to help one another and to validate a common system of beliefs and values. This community of mutual expectations and reciprocal aid had clear implications for spouses: "Each will get some emotional satisfaction from these external relationships and will be likely to demand correspondingly less of the spouse. Rigid segregation of conjugal roles will be possible because each spouse can get help from people outside" (p. 60). In this way, the degree of social support derived from network members, and expected by members from spouses, explains the segregation of marital roles.

Since the original publication in 1955 of Bott's study of 20 London families, a wide variety of attempted replications and criticism has followed (for reviews see Bott, 1971, pp. 248-330; Lee, 1979; and for recent tests see Gordon & Downing, 1978; Morris, 1985; Richards, 1980; Rogler & Procidano, 1986). A thorough review of this work is beyond the scope of the chapter; however, scholars have identified a number of key issues, including how the distinction is drawn between the separate and joint networks of spouses and how the internal structure of these networks may best be revealed (Lee, 1979). Several important advances in the conceptualization of network types, their structural properties, and the assessment of each will add clarity to this area; these advances are reviewed in detail in a later section.

In addition to the affects of network structure, kin, as well as friends, coworkers and other associates, have an important direct and personal influence on family relationships. The availability of friends, in particular, is associated with personal feelings of well-being and expressed satisfaction with marriage (Willits & Crider, 1986), although this relationship is apt to be curvilinear, with extensive contacts with others interfering in the maintenance of optimum family functioning (Broderick, this volume; Holman, 1981). Friends also serve as an important conduit of information about one's spouse and children. Bott (1971) noted that the friends of spouses "ensure that each person learns about the other's activities" (p. 94). Information and advice flowing within families and between network members and spouses or children is not always in agreement, however.

Kemper (1968), for example, examined the ways in which family members prescribe the behavior of husbands/fathers in nonfamilial settings (e.g., work), as well as the extent to which employers and coworkers prescribe the behavior of husbands/fathers in family settings. The results demonstrate that wives, children, and parents of spouses were actively involved in both familial and nonfamilial settings through their prescriptions of appropriate role behavior for husbands. In a complementary fashion, members of the work setting, especially colleagues, offered prescriptions for the behavior of husbands/fathers in nonfamilial and familial settings. At times the prescriptions of wives and work colleagues concerning the appropriate action of husbands/ fathers were not in agreement.

The internal dynamics of family relationships are influenced not only through the activities of the participants themselves but also through the activities of spouses, and their children, with other individuals. Although it is often useful to restrict the scope of an inquiry, addressing a singular relationship to achieve a depth of investigation, it is also useful to consider what family members do with other individuals within the wider tracings of kith and kin.

Two themes, then, guide the composition of this chapter and those that follow: the analysis of network structure and the analysis of multiple personal relationships. To be sure, other applications of network analysis to family studies are possible and in fact ongoing. Researchers have examined differences in the affiliations of people in urban and rural communities (Fischer, 1982; Wellman, 1979), life-cycle variations in networks (Dickens & Perlman, 1981), and, more recently, the effects of parents' social participation with kin, friends, and acquaintances on the sociability of their children (Homel, Burns, & Goodnow, in press). Others have examined the influence of kin on mate selection, conjugal roles, power and decision making, and marital adjustment, as well as the influence of kin on migration and the economic stability of family units (for an excellent review, see Lee, 1979). Although much of this work, particularly in regard to kinship, does not identify specific structural properties of networks and tends to use normative explanations where structural explanations are likely to be more appropriate, it is suggestive about how network properties are linked to marital outcomes. The focus of this volume on the structure and content of personal social networks is but one of many ways to study networks. Nonetheless, each of these applications requires clearly defined concepts paired with valid and reliable measurement techniques, a requirement that until recently has received but cursory attention.

In the following pages, a theoretical framework is presented by which networks may be defined both conceptually and operationally. Doing so is important, because the way we define a network determines in large part the value other structural features take on, such as the density or overlap of a network. Generally, networks defined narrowly will evidence a tighter structure (e.g., higher density) than networks defined more broadly.

SOCIAL NETWORKS DEFINED

Personal social networks typically are defined as a collection of individuals who know and interact with a particular target individual or couple (compare, Fischer, 1982; Laumann, 1966, Lee, 1979). The network members may know one another or they may not. How well individuals need to know another or how frequently they must interact are left unspecified by the definition. Close friends of long standing and mere acquaintances could be considered network members, and closeness and frequency of interaction need not be highly intercorrelated (Jackson, Fischer & McCallister-Jones, 1977; Walker & Thompson, 1983).

When networks are defined rather broadly in terms of those individuals who are known by name and with whom respondents have had a degree of personal contact, regardless of how superficial or intimate, then networks are in fact quite large. In an intriguing program of research, Killworth, Bernard, and McCarty (1984) provided the first empirical examination of the range of people known to respondents. Each participant in this study was given a dossier on each of 500 target individuals. The dossiers on targets were fictitious but realistic, and included a name and location in addition to information on age, sex, occupation, organizational affiliations, and hobbies. Targets represented a range of ages, statuses and so on, and were distributed world-wide. The task for participants was to get a message to each target individual. To do so, participants were asked to nominate someone they knew who might know the target or at least pass the message along to another person who might know the target. Only people who were acquainted with one another would be allowed to pass on the message. For example, given a dossier on Marcelina Catalan from Buenos Aries, a female age 46 who worked as an accountant and enjoyed swimming, respondents indicated their choice of an individual who would be most able to get a message to Marcelina.

The number of distinct choices generated by a respondent ought to represent an index of that respondent's total social network. In general, respondents identified an average of 134 distinct choices, i.e., network members. Because the number of different choices increases rather rapidly for the first few targets and much more slowly thereafter, Killworth et al. (1984) argue a curve representing the number of distinct network members elicited from a given set of targets would "eventually become asymptotic to a constant value" (p. 384). This "constant value" would represent the average size of a network for a contemporary citizen of the United States. Extrapolation suggests a mean of approximately 250 network members. Less than 10% of the total number of network members were identified as kin, while a considerable majority were considered friends (86%) known through a variety of contexts.

Clearly, some individuals are more socially active than others. Killworth et al. (1984) report considerable variation in the size of the network generated through the reverse small world procedure described above. Although the mean number of network members is 134, the standard deviation is 65. Studies of individual differences in network size have yet to be accomplished, because research has centered on differences in averages between groups (e.g., young and old individuals) rather than on variations between individuals within groups. Nonetheless, a number of factors may account for some of this variation, including levels of education, occupation and income (Belle, 1982; Fischer, 1982), physical attributes such as attractiveness (Reis et al., 1982), relatively stable personal dispositions (Perlman, this volume), the complexity of social skills (Burns & Farina, 1984; Cook, 1977; Fischer & Phillips, 1982) and stage of dating or the family life-cycle (Dickens & Perlman, 1981; Johnson & Leslie, 1982; Surra, this volume).

Of course, it would be utterly impractical in most research to identify all the network members of a particular individual or family. The question becomes one of generating an adequate sample from the larger population of network constituents. Essentially three types of networks are defined, each associated with a particular measurement strategy and each with certain advantages and disadvantages associated with their use. The types—(1) networks of close associates or significant others, (2) exchange networks, and (3) interactive networks—are defined below, and several criteria useful in judging the adequacy of each sampling technique are suggested.

Networks of Close Associates

Networks of close associates are collectives of people who are considered important and perhaps intimate "friends" by target individuals. Johnson and Milardo (1984), for instance, defined networks as "those people whose opinions of your personal life are important to you" (p. 895). Alternatively, several researchers have operationally defined networks simply in terms of one's closest associates outside the household (e.g., Fischer et al., 1977; Leslie & Grady, 1985; Riley & Cochran, 1985; Shulman, 1975; Wellman, 1979). Typically this name-eliciting procedure limits the maximum number of network members identified, usually from 6 to 15 individuals.

Defining networks in terms of people considered close to respondents has several advantages. The assessment procedure is rather straightforward and cost-effective, in that a minimum amount of time is required to generate a list of names. Such a network also represents the individuals judged significant or important in accord with the perceptions of respondents. Paradoxically, however, there may be little correspondence between those individuals considered important and those individuals with whom interactions occur on a routine basis (Jackson, Fischer & McCallister-Jones, 1977; Shulman, 1975; Wellman, in press). It is likely that networks of significant others are composed of both active and passive ties; in other words, ties based on considerable face-to-face interaction and ties based on affective bonds with irregular or infrequent interaction.

Active and passive ties are important because of their potential impact on target individuals, but they tend to operate in distinguishable ways. Ties with active significant others include routine interactions which may involve the exchange of direct aid, advice and criticism, support and interference. Passive ties with significant others involving infrequent interaction may be equally supportive, or at least influential to the degree that target individuals express that they are more or less supported by a network member or believe such support or influence would be forthcoming should the need arise. On the other hand, passive ties may be hallmarked by an absence of expected support rather than by its presence, and a confusion of normatively defined role expectations with actual supportive exchanges (McCallister-Jones & Fischer, 1978).

The method of identifying networks of close associates is limited for several reasons. By focusing solely on intimates, this method omits other important sectors of the total network. Intermediate friends, neighbors, coworkers, and other acquaintances are apt to be omitted from a list of intimates, but these individuals provide crucial reference points through which people make social comparisons enabling the development of personal beliefs and values. Through relationships with these individuals, however superficial, we share information, goods, and services, as well as positive and negative regard.

Individuals with whom interactions are typically negative, hostile or conflict habituated are omitted as well, such as former paramours or spouses, kin relations or professional rivals, but even these relationships may serve as important sources of social comparison, support, and interference. A young father, for instance, may find himself in constant disagreement with his coworkers regarding appropriate child-rearing strategies, but through such negative exchanges his own beliefs become solidified (compare McCannell, this volume). On the other hand, interference and conflict by and with network members can have entirely deleterious consequences (Bott, 1971, p. 94; Broderick, this volume; Tolsdorf, 1981).

Interpretations of closeness or intimacy are apt to vary widely across individuals and consequently invite systematic measurement error (McCallister-Jones & Fisher, 1978). Considerable variation in the interpretation of closeness or intimacy has been found across gender (Bell, 1981; Peplau & Gordon, 1985; Weiss & Lowenthal, 1975), stage of the life-cycle (Dickens & Perlman, 1981), ethnicity and culture (Johnson, 1977; 1982), and historical periods (Degler, 1980; Gadlin, 1977; Scanzoni, 1979).

In a study of the social activity of college students (Milardo, Johnson, & Huston, 1983), a respondent reported interacting with 64 different people over 10 days and of these network members 16 were nominated as close friends by the respondent. Another student, who was representative of the sample as a whole, reported interacting with a total of 26 different people, of whom 6 were considered close friends. We cannot assume the two respondents, with such radically different levels of social activity, were interpreting close friendship in a similar manner. If we simply requested each respondent to list a maximum of 6 close friends, their answers would have appeared similar, when in fact their levels of social participation with close friends and others were quite divergent. The interpretation of close friendship undoubtedly varies both phenom-enologically, in terms of the respondent's personal definition of closeness, and socially, in terms of the actual content of interaction.

The interpretation of closeness also varies systematically across gender, influencing the identification of significant others by women and men. Although both sexes tend to nominate network members based on how well they know people, women may employ a more stringent criteria for assessing a relationship's intimacy than men. Hammer (1984) reported that half of the network members identified by women and a fifth of those named by men were judged as people known well. Possibly men know people on average less well than women and this accounts for the differences in network composition; in fact, there is some evidence to support this explanation (Hill & Stull, 1981; Rands & Levinger, 1979). But regardless, if women and men identify network members based on different criteria, other analyses will reflect this differential bias. In other respects, however, the networks of women and men are comparable. Both use perceptions of frequency and recency of contact, especially in combination, as selection criteria (Hammer, 1984).

In addition to variations between individuals in their personal definitions of close friendship, considerable variation in close friendships can be expected because the friendships of adults are often specialized, each serving a particular function. Although ideally one may define a close friend as someone who serves many roles—for example as social companion, confident, and source of material or symbolic rewards—in practice it is likely that such friendships are exceptional. McCallister-Jones and Fischer (1978) found great diversity in the functions served by close friends. We might expect sharing intimacies to typify close friendships, and yet their research demonstrates that among adults only 18% of the close friends identified were later nominated as people whose judgments the respondent would rely on, only 34% were nominated as people they would consult about personal matters, and surprisingly, only 45% of the people identified as *best* friends were later called "especially close." A significant proportion of these relationships (35%) are purely affective ties with little if any contemporary social exchange.

In a study of variations in friendship across the life-course, Lowenthal and her associates (Weiss & Lowenthal, 1975) found that close friendships tend to serve a variety of specialized functions. For instance, a middle-aged woman described one friend as "[like me] in some ways because we have both chosen to retreat from life," another as "a good person ... not wise ... but good ," and a third as "my fun friend ... we go to horse races" (p. 59). A similar heterogeneous pattern emerged when respondents were asked to evaluate their closest friendship using a variety of descriptive categories (e.g., understanding, dependable, likable, trustworthy). Of the descriptors mentioned, a mere 5% were attributed to all three of the closest friends, whereas approximately 75% of the descriptors were unique to a particular friendship.[3]

Yet another problem in developing a valid and reliable measure of a network constituency is illustrated when considering the demand characteristics associated with nominating one's closest associates. The question implicitly assumes that respondents have close associates, and enough of them to satisfy the needs of a social scientist. Requesting a respondent to provide a list of people considered important or close carries with it unnamed guidelines concerning who should be included and a certain demand that some number of network members be identified. We may expect social isolates to be prone to exaggeration and to confuse actual closeness based on social exchanges with normative expectations commensurate with certain role relations. For example, "He is my brother, therefore we must be close" (McCallister-Jones and Fischer, 1978). Similarly, we may expect a significant association of age with the nomination of purely sentimental ties (e.g., nieces, grandchildren), particularly among the elderly (Fischer, 1982; Johnson, this volume).

Sampling a network constituency based on a singular criterion of significance or closeness has the advantage of being a relatively cost-effective procedure, representative of respondents' personal attributions of importance, and it is a widely used procedure. On the other hand, it fails to distinguish active ties from those of a purely affective or sentimental importance, selectively omits members of other important network sectors, neglects systematic interindividual variations in the attribution of closeness, assumes equivalence and reciprocity across all close relationships when in fact such relationships among adults tend to be highly specialized and asymmetric, and places excessive demand on respondents to produce socially desirable responses. In short, the method employs a univariate criterion to represent the inherent multiplexity of personal relationships.

Exchange Networks

A promising approach to the study of personal networks by survey method has been developed by Fischer and his colleagues (McCallister-Jones & Fischer, 1978; Fischer, 1982). The procedure targets a subset of the total network for potential nomination, including people with whom the probability of rewarding exchanges is high. This criterion has been broadened by several researchers to include individuals with whom the probability of unrewarding exchanges is high, e.g., conflict-habituated relationships (Barrera, 1981).[4]

The identification of network members proceeds in two stages. The first stage employs a highly structured interview schedule that presents respondents with a set of social settings (e.g., personal household, work) in addition to several categories of individuals defined specifically in terms of the probability of rewarding exchanges. Prototypes include a spouse, or dating partner if the respondent is unmarried, as well as people on whom the respondent may rely as confidants, for their judgment or for personal favors, including home care, child care, or other symbolic or material resources. For instance, concerning work respondents are asked:

> Some people never talk with anyone, either on or off the job, about how to do their work. Other people do discuss things like decisions they have to make, work problems they have to solve, and ways to do their work better. Is there anyone you talk with about how to do your work? [If yes] Who do you talk with about your work? [Fischer, 1982, p. 324].

In essence, a broad pool of potential network constituents are specified based on a set of explicitly defined criteria for their inclusion.

The second phase of data collection permits respondents to supplement the list of core network members with the names of people who are considered important. The latter people are typically kinfolk; relationships with them appear passive, of an affective or sentimental nature, and without the inclusion of frequent interaction or the regular exchange of goods or services. Once respondents have identified a network constituency, follow-up questions are designed to elicit descriptive information on selected members. This set of follow-up questions would vary to suit the needs of a particular research program, but might include sex of the network member, relationship to the respondent, and perhaps queries concerning the identification of separate friendships or those held in common by both spouses, the origin of friendships and so on.

The use of approximately 10 specific name-eliciting questions rests on the assumption that sampling a wide variety of social exchanges and social settings that typify the lives of most individuals produces a more representative sample of a network constituency than simply examining one specific class of close relationships, and it improves generalizations about other structural features of the network. This latter issue is particularly important when interest is in linking attributes of local social structure to opportunities or events in target families or individuals. For example, linking a network's density to the availability of social support requires a reasonably sound measure of density that in turn requires the accurate identification of a sample of network members. All measures of network structure are contingent on the adequacy of the sample and reliability of the name-eliciting procedure. It makes little theoretical sense to describe the networks of families as highly dense when the measure of density rests on a narrowly and perhaps unreliably defined set of network members.

Secondly, rather than defining the criteria for inclusion in an abstract and ambiguous form such as "significant other" or "close friend," a more veridical sample results from clearly defined standards for inclusion of network members. Finally, rather than require participants to make decisions regarding who they consider important, in the Fischer procedure this decision is made essentially by the researcher. The importance of network members rests on what they actually do for and with the respondent—for instance, who provides emergency child care, or help at work.

The psychometric properties of the procedure are better understood than that currently available for procedures designed to identify the network of close associates. Barrera (1981) reported a test-retest reliability of .88 over a two-week period when total network sizes are correlated. The correspondence of names elicited at each occasion of measurement was also quite high, in that 74% of the network members named in one session were named in both. The procedure is perhaps best viewed as a means to sample various sectors of the total network and not as an exhaustive name-eliciting procedure capable of identifying all network members, an outcome that would be unnecessarily cumbersome and in many cases would yield an exceedingly large sample of names. The procedure is well documented and easily exported with adaptations to suit particular needs (see Rands, this volume).

Interactive Networks

The social participation of family members with their kin, friends, and acquaintances forms an important but grossly understudied area of research. As with each of the name-eliciting procedures detailed earlier, the essential task is to identify a network constituency based on the people with whom family members interact on a somewhat routine basis. Clearly, it is necessary to decide a priori what constitutes a routine interaction, although frequently measures of the interactive network fail to do so. Once a constituency is identified, we may proceed with an analysis of multiple relationships, as in their supportive and interfering function, or with analysis of network structure, as in the linkage of network interconnectedness with marital quality. Unlike other comparable methods for generating network data, typically researchers are as interested in how often and how much people interact with one another as they are in specifying the identity of interactants. For this reason, this section proceeds by examining the accuracy of methods designed to identify a network membership as well as to estimate other parameters of social participation such as the frequency and duration of interactions.

The methods developed for identifying interactive networks include questionnaire items and diaries of social episodes completed by respondents. A critical analysis of each method is based on two theoretical notions: immediate versus retrospective accounts of social activity, and the seat of responsibility for the aggregation of data (Milardo, 1983).

Social activity may be reported by respondents immediately following the occurrence or retrospectively for a particular period of time (e.g., over a week, month, or year). Second, respondents may be required to provide aggregate measures of social activity (e.g., the frequency of interaction with a friend over the last week), or the responsibility for aggregation may be assumed by the researcher. For instance, based on some documentation of social interactions, the researcher may calculate a measure of frequency of interaction.

Measures of network attributes based on contemporary accounts of social activity are preferred over retrospective accounts. Very often respondents are required to answer questions of the type "With whom have you interacted over the last week, month, or year?," or "How often do you interact with kin, friends, or acquaintances? Frequently, seldom or never?" Responses to these questions are both retrospective and respondent-aggregated. Consider, for example, the name-eliciting procedure employed by Cohen and Sokolovsky (1978) in their investigation of the social participation of former psychiatric patients. Respondents were asked to nominate "all links [relationships] within the preceding year with a frequency [of interaction] of a least once a month" (p. 549). Such a seemingly innocuous question requires the recall of information in the distant past as well as some rather complex mental arithmetic, particularly when relationships may involve considerable interaction, perhaps several episodes per week, over a short period of time, such as a few months. Several lines of inquiry suggest that these prototypical measures yield unreliable and less veridical data when compared to accounts of social participation based upon "immediate" sources of data later aggregated by the researcher.

Bernard, Killworth, and their colleagues investigated the accuracy of informants in their reports of social network data (for a review see Bernard, Killworth, Kronenfeld, & Sailer, 1984). Through a series of experiments with a variety of naturally occurring groups, in which interactions among group members were unobtrusively monitored, participants were consistently unable to recall with any degree of certainty with whom they interacted. Bernard et al. (1984) expected individuals who typically maintained records of their interactions (e.g., ham radio operators) to be more accurate in their recall; they were not. Office personnel who were aware that their interactions were being monitored were no more or less accurate than those groups being monitored with less obtrusive methods. Encouraging respondents to become more cognizant of their interactions over time, and hence more accurate later on, also yielded no appreciable increase in accuracy. In general, respondents were able to recall fewer than half of their actual communications either in terms of frequency or duration, they were unable to rank order group members in terms of frequency, and queries concerning who they liked produced nearly the same results as queries about who they talked to (compare Burt & Bittner, 1981; Romney & Weller, 1984).

One of the seven experiments conducted by Bernard, Killworth and Sailer (1982) was based on frequent users of a computer-conferencing system who could freely send and receive messages to and from one another. This study is notable for several reasons. The actual behavior of participants was known, having been monitored electronically by the experimenters, thus permitting the direct comparison of recall with behavior. The windows over which recall was solicited varied systematically from 0 to 60 days (i.e., the number of days over which respondents were asked to report on their communications). And the lag time between the end of a window and interview was varied (from 0 to 60 days). Although a variety of measures of accuracy were derived, the results are surprisingly uniform across each measure. Put simply, recall data is rarely a valid proxy for behavior. For example, while respondents actually interacted with an average of 6.0 users, they reported interactions with 2.5 people on average and of those recalled about one-third were *not* communicated with at all. Similarly, users were unable to correctly identify the person communicated with most often or the top 5 more than half of the time. Bernard and his colleagues (1984) conclude on the basis of their empirical work that "what people say about their communications bears no useful resemblance to their behavior" (p. 5).

If individuals are unable to accurately recall with whom they interact or provide aggregate indices of activity, then the question remains whether reductions in the required recall and aggregation of data would increase accuracy. In theory, the production of veridical data requires a narrowing of the time frame between the occurrence of a social episode and its reporting, thus minimizing the effects of memory loss or distortion. Second, it requires minimizing the need for participants to aggregate data.

In line with this reasoning, Bernard et al. (1982) found that questions concerning interactions over the previous 24 hours produced more accurate data than questions concerning interactions that occurred a week or more in the past. With a window and lag of one day, respondents were able to recall about 70% of the people to whom they sent messages and an equivalent percentage of the people from whom they received messages. Accuracy decreased rapidly as either the window or especially lag time increased.

Additional investigations directly comparing self-reports of interactions completed immediately following the occurrence of an event (i.e., a lag of 0) with a questionnaire measuring aggregate summaries of interpersonal events clearly demonstrates the superior accuracy of contemporary reports (Conrath, Higgins, & McClean, 1983). In the contemporary self-report data, respondents concurred approximately 50% of the time on the occurrence of interactions across all individuals with whom they spoke. The comparable estimate of reciprocity for the questionnaire data is about 25%. Methods have been developed to monitor social participation and produce network data with concomitant gains in accuracy, and several are reviewed below.

Self-report interaction records. One method designed to generate contemporary reports of social activity required research participants to report on their social activity daily for 10 consecutive days (Milardo, 1982; Milardo, et al., 1983). Social interaction report forms were provided for this purpose, and participants were instructed to complete one interaction record for each voluntary social episode over ten minutes in length (compare Nezlek, Wheeler & Reis, 1983). Each record included data on all individuals present during an interaction, their sexes and relationships to the respondents, for example. Additional indices might be included in the records as needed.

Social interaction records have several advantages and disadvantages associated with their use. The records provide a relatively objective definition of the network constituency. All people present during interactions are de facto members of the respondent's network. Subjective definitions of network membership are avoided, and participants are not burdened with recalling precisely who is significant or with whom interactions occurred in the distant past.

Interactive measures of network membership additionally allow the researcher to determine the significance of particular members or groups of members (cliques) based on empirically derived composites of the interaction records. As an example, judgments of significance may be based on indices of the frequency or duration of interactions, contemporary ratings of the intimacy of interactions, or descriptions of exchange content (e.g., the exchange of material or symbolic goods or services or demonstrations of affection).

The accuracy of the method is contingent on a number of factors but appears considerably higher than questionnaire items of the sort reviewed earlier. When asked, respondents report failing to record approximately 5% of their interactions, indicate they update their records 1.5 times per day on average, and estimate accuracy on a seven-point scale at about 2.5, where high accuracy is equivalent to the low end point of the scale (Milardo et al., 1983; Nezlek et al., 1983). A more objective index of accuracy has been derived by comparing the interaction records of roommates. Intraclass correlations of the number of times roommates reported interacting with one another ranged from .76 to .81 in separate studies (Nezlek et al., 1983).

The quality of interaction records is contingent on well-designed training sessions, particularly with regard to the definition of an episode of interaction, as well as regular monitoring of participants during data collection in order to provide necessary guidance. Report forms need to be concise and to require minimal time for completion, as longer forms requiring more than five minutes to complete greatly diminish accuracy (Conrath et al., 1983). The objectivity of the events being monitored plays an additional role in determining the accuracy of records. All things being equal, events that are concrete and easily defined with clear boundaries yield more accurate recall. Spouses, for example, tend to agree on their independent reports regarding the occurrence of sexual activity, a relatively objective event with clear boundaries, but they are less apt to agree on the amount of time invested in conversation or recreation, or simply whether an argument occurred in the previous day, events that are relatively subjective and difficult to define (Christensen, Sullaway, & King, 1983).

These findings suggest that data regarding who was present during an interaction will probably be more accurate than estimates of the duration of an interaction or the provision of supportive behaviors. Such predictions are supported in a study of social contacts among personnel in public agencies (Fraser & Delewski, 1985). Respondents in this study nominated a pool of professional colleagues who were subsequently interviewed, thus allowing a direct comparison of the responses of subjects with those of network members. All network members confirmed relationships with subjects, but little agreement surfaced with regard to less concrete areas, such as the frequency of contact or other qualities of social involvement.

Interaction records via telephone interviews. A second method for generating contemporary records of social interaction employs a time-sampling procedure in which respondents are interviewed by phone concerning their social activity with network members during the previous 24 hours (Huston, 1982). This method shares all of the advantages of the use of interaction records completed by respondents, but has several additional advantages. Interviewing respondents by telephone virtually guarantees the completion of records on a daily basis, while if respondents complete the records, daily compliance may only be approximated (Huston & Robins, 1982). More important, telephone interviewing can be designed to collect data far more efficiently and perhaps more accurately. Interview protocols may be entered into portable microcomputer terminals, thus producing more uniform and complete interviews. At the same time, responses to queries concerning interactions may be entered directly onto disk or tape storage; data are available for immediate analysis. The use of micro-computers results in considerable savings in cost, because the need for preparing large pools of data into machine-readable form is eliminated.

Any method designed to document social interactions is apt to generate a considerable amount of data. For example, in a longitudinal study of close romantic relationships, respondents reported on well over 4,000 separate interactions in the first wave of data collection; each interaction was recorded on a separate form (Milardo et al., 1983). These raw data had to be entered into machine-readable form and then aggregated for each respondent to yield summary indices for later analysis (e.g., computations of each respondent's average frequency and duration of interaction per day). With the use of an interactive computer, both the data entry and aggregation are performed at the time of the interview, resulting in significant reductions in direct and indirect costs. A variety of safeguards may be build into the procedure, virtually eliminating incomplete interviews or miscoded data (compare Shanks, 1983).

Sampling momentary social experience. Larson and his coworkers (this volume) developed a method for sampling current social experience and momentary subjective states. With this method, research partici-pants are signaled electronically over a period of time. Respondents then complete interaction reports when paged at random times during the day. These reports may index the nature of the current activity, other individuals present if any, or reports on momentary subjective states. The method provides an opportunity to examine data that were previously unavailable for scrutiny, data that form the essential elements of social relationships. Emotional states, in particular, are subject to considerable fluctuation and reinterpretation over time, and, as noted earlier, the accuracy of recalling the identity of interactants deteriorates rapidly over time. The experience-sampling method, because it is based on present-time reports of activity or affective state in its most elementary form, is perhaps the most accurate means of acquiring contemporary network data, and perhaps the only method for generating reports of emotional states as they are experienced during routine daily experience.

Comparing Interactive and Exchange Networks

Although a variety of methods have been developed for identifying network constituencies, the most fruitful methods are based on clearly defined criteria for the nomination of potential members designed to sample from a variety of network sectors. Traditional survey methods based on a single name-eliciting question are admirable in their simplicity, but generally do not compare well with more comprehensive methods using a variety of name-eliciting questions that sample specific social settings and role relationships. Researchers interested in identifying either the network members with whom routine interactions occur or indices of social participation clearly should abandon questionnaire-based methods in favor of contemporary methods designed to generate daily or momentary reports of social participation.

Several questions remain to be addressed, however, including the convergence or degree of overlap between networks generated by divergent methods. Geographic separation or extensive obligations to career and family may preclude interacting with network sectors considered important or significant to respondents. Under this condition, time-sampling procedures would be incapable of identifying significant others seen infrequently. On the other hand, there is little reason to presume that measures of the network of significant others or exchange networks represent the actual level of social activity, at least in terms of the identity or absolute number of people with whom routine interactions occur.

To examine the question of the overlap between exchange and interactive networks, we analyzed pilot data from 25 wives and their husbands (Milardo, 1986a). Each individual was interviewed using a revised version of the aforementioned Fischer procedure. This version includes 12 name-eliciting questions and yields an average of nearly 23 network members. Fischer (1982), using a much larger sample and slightly fewer questions, found an average network size of 18.5.

Following the face-to-face interviews, 42 spouses from 21 couples were interviewed by telephone on 7 nonconsecutive days. During these calls, respondents indicated with whom they had interacted over the previous 24 hours. On average, spouses reported interacting with 15.8 individuals over the 7 days; on average 9 of those interactants were unique, i.e., not previously identified in the exchange network.

In both procedures we gathered information on the name, gender, and relationship to the respondent of each network member. This information allowed us to identify those individuals present in both networks or only one. Our measure of convergence in the exchange and interactive networks represents the proportion of network members who were identified in both networks relative to the size of the total combined network. The combined network size is a nonredundant total in which each particular individual is counted only once. The degree of overlap averages 24.6% (SD = 11) across all respondents. In short, there appears to be very little convergence between the methods. The exchange network, based on questionnaire items, and the interactive network, based on contemporary reports of social activity, produce distinctly different networks. Moreover, there is little relationship between the size of each network, whether total sizes ($r = .14$, $p = .19$) or exchange network size is correlated with the number of unique interactive members ($r = .05$, $p = .38$). Individuals with large exchange networks do not have correspondingly large interactive networks, and so too for those with modest exchange networks. The size of the exchange network simply fails to predict the size of the interactive network.

As the procedure for generating measures of contemporary social activity is rather time-consuming for respondents, we were reluctant to require more than 7 telephone interviews. Nevertheless, questions remain concerning the impact of windows greater than 7 days on the degree of overlap or the size of the interactive network. Would the degree of overlap have increased significantly if 14 days had been monitored? And at what point would network size begin to reach an asymptote? To clarify these issues the nonredundant cumulative size of the interactive network was plotted over time. At day 1, respondents identified an average of 3.2 network members, at day 3 a cumulative total of 7.9 different interactants, and at day 5, 12.8 interactants. The increases in network size over time are substantial; new members are added to the network at a rate of approximately 2.4 per day for the first 5 days. This highly significant linear trend appears to level off towards the end of the data-collection period, but not by much. During the last few days of monitoring, approximately 1.5 new members are added each day. These analyses suggest that increasing the window over which respondents report on their social activity would increase the size of the interactive network.

Whether the degree of overlap would increase substantially over windows greater than 7 days seems doubtful, because the potential size of the interactive network is unlimited, or nearly so, while the size of the exchange network tends to average 20 or so members, and increasing the number of name-eliciting questions included in a survey instrument beyond 10 to 12 questions tends to yield redundant information (McCallister-Jones & Fischer, 1978).

The exchange and interactive networks are clearly tapping unique aspects of an individual's life space. This suggests that each network type has a theoretical and substantive significance that goes well beyond the explicit issue of methodological refinement. The networks may have very different, possibly uncorrelated, structures. This issue is important, since a variety of individual and relationship properties, such as the availability of social support or the stability of a marriage, have been linked to network structure (see Milardo, 1986b; Surra, this volume). It is quite possible that each network type functions in unique ways serving distinctly different purposes. If, for example, interactive networks tend to be loosely structured and largely composed of "weak ties," we might expect them to function differently than exchange networks that virtually by definition are composed of "significant others" and typically include a large proportion of kin (about 40% to 50% on average—Fehr & Perlman, 1985; Milardo, 1986b). Because kin tend to know one another, exchange networks may be highly interdependent relative to interactive networks. Further developments in theory and research may be realized when the psychological and social significance of network types is clearly recognized and methodologies appropriate to specific interests are applied.

NETWORK STRUCTURE AND
RELATIONSHIP OUTCOMES

All investigations of families and social networks fundamentally rest on the premise that individuals exist within a social context that is both directly and indirectly defined by the individual and is in turn influential in personal and social life. Analyses of the social context of families may feature the investigation of multiple personal relationships or they may focus on local social structure. Investigations, for example, have centered on supportive and nonsupportive relationships with network members as they influence family relationships (Fehr & Perlman, 1985), and clinicians have noted the effects of relationships with kin, neighbors, friends, and coworkers in determining family dynamics and as facilitators or impediments to successful interventions in distressed families (Broderick, this volume).

An analysis of network structure, on the other hand, would focus on the network's collective influence upon the coordination, degree, form, and timing of social support as each parameter is determined by the interdependence of network members. In highly interdependent networks where people know one another, members may share knowledge of another's need, and if necessary coordinate aid or interference. Thus the potential support available is a function of the collective interdependence of network members, and this effect is entirely independent of the quality of any particular pair relationship between the target individual (or couple) and network member. Incidentally, when family scholars in research or clinical settings speak of a family's "enmeshment" in a kinship system, or of the extended family's "togetherness," they are often referring to network structure. As will be noted shortly, conceptualizing the degree of interdependence linking network members in terms of structural attributes provides a means to clearly define structure and to quantify the degree of enmeshment or togetherness (compare Broderick, this volume; Olsen & McCubbin, 1983).

Analyses of network structure, as it mediates relationship outcomes and personal dispositions, have been neglected, perhaps reflecting the "free will" tradition of American social science to over emphasize the role of personal choice to the neglect of social constraint (Johnson, 1985; Wellman, 1983). The value of structural analysis may be illustrated in a number of ways; the issue of friendship choice, and more particularly mate selection, are briefly considered below (compare Surra, this volume).

Individuals choose their friends freely, and thus directly influence the structure of their networks, at least in terms of size. But the choice of a friend, and as a consequence the structure of the network, is best thought of as a matter of personal choice operating within certain environmental contingencies beyond individual control. For instance, although individuals demonstrate a preference for socially similar others, the relative proportion of friends of similar background is largely a function of both the opportunities and constraints imposed by the environment. Individuals residing in a neighborhood dominated by a particular class are more likely to develop friendships from that class, regardless of their own class membership (Huckfeldt, 1983).

Personal choice and environmental condition interact in other important ways as well because the very choice of a friend has structural implications. When individuals choose each other as spouses, they adopt one another's kinship network, a local social structure over which they have little control and one that is apt to profoundly influence the spouses throughout their lives, particularly if children are born into the marriage. Friendship choice is one instance of the way in which individuals create the very social structures that constrain them (Salzinger, 1982).

The direct influence of network structure on the initiation, maintenance, or termination of a personal relationships may be illustrated in a variety of ways. Two individuals may choose to become friends (or spouses) not simply because of a mutual attraction, but because they each have many friends in common who also know and interact with one another (i.e., highly interdependent networks). The network members may introduce the two individuals and encourage them to become friends. Of course, family sociologists have long recognized the importance of situational conditions like propinquity and homogamy as they influence relationship development. However, the great value of network analysis is the specificity gained in documenting the strength and pathways of structural effects.

In contrast to the initiation of a personal relationship, two individuals who wish to cease their relationship (or marriage) may find it highly costly or even impossible if they share many network members who know one another. Highly interdependent networks may have a stabilizing influence on dyadic relationships among members. Although the stabilizing influence of network structure has yet to be examined fully, Ackerman (1963) found that spouses who maintained joint networks tended to have more stable marriages than those with separate networks. Among friends, members of highly structured networks, such as clique members, are far less likely to either lose or gain friends over time in comparison to members of loosely structured networks (Salzinger, 1982).

The structure of a network may have a profound influence on the intensity of constituent personal relationships as well. Friends have a greater opportunity to learn about one another if the constituencies of their respective networks are similar, that is, overlapping. Much of what we know about our friends is not necessarily the result of direct communications (self-disclosures), but results from what others tell us about our friends. Interdependent networks increase the potential for learning about friends indirectly through communications with third parties. In this way, the intimacy of a particular relationship is determined not only by what pair members share directly with one another, but also by the proportion and absolute number of friends they have in common (i.e., the degree of structural interdependence) and what pair members intentionally or unintentionally reveal to the network members. These events may increase the intensity of a pair relationship and the diversity of knowledge on which that relationship is based. The effects of structure on closeness or intimacy are considerable and independent of dyadic factors, such as a target couple's mutual attraction, personal commitment, evaluation of social exchanges, or comparisons with available alternatives.

A variety of measures have been developed to quantify network structure and differentiate the form of one network from that of another (for reviews see Milardo, 1986b; Surra, this volume). Density, cluster or clique structure, and overlap are major examples of structural attributes and generally each measure provides a slightly different manner of documenting the presence or absence as well as the organization of pair relationships among network members. Density, for instance, refers to the degree to which network members know one another apart from their ties to ego. Clique structure refers to the presence of highly interconnected subsections of the network. Networks may have equivalent sizes and densities but yet have entirely unique clique structures (Friedkin, 1981).

The measures of density, clique structure, and overlap are frequently considered nonequivalent and irreducible properties of networks. They are nonequivalent in the sense that each measure is uniquely defined, at least operationally, and each captures a unique element or characteristic of a network's latent structure. This nonequivalence may be rather trivial from a theoretical standpoint, however. They are irreducible and distinct qualities of networks in the sense that knowledge of individual members of a network, including personal attitudes and so on, as well as knowledge of the pair relationships of members, including the frequency of interaction or patterns of communication, would reveal nothing about the social structure in which those individuals are a part.

Density, clique structure, and overlap are conceptualized herein as unique, but probably intercorrelated, operational definitions of a common underlying feature of social networks, namely structural interdependence. The conceptual meaning of structural interdependence hinges upon the placement of pair relationships within the network, including both the simple presence or absence of pair relationships (e.g., density) as well as the overall pattern of those relationships (e.g., clique structure). In contrast to measures of structural interdependence, other measures of network structure focus on the placement of individuals in terms of the overall number of members (i.e., size) or the patterning of members in particular groups (i.e., network composition or homogeneity). This distinction is important because the collective influence of a network on an individual results from the relationships between network members and not simply from the direct bonds linking the target individual to each network member. In the following chapter, Surra examines some of the ways in which structure influences the initiation and development of personal relationships.

SUMMARY

This introductory chapter reviewed the initial applications of the concept of social networks to the study of social systems and highlighted how the analysis of personal networks and close relationships can be integrated. Essentially two unique types of networks were examined: the cognitive, or psychological, network and the behavioral, or interactive, network. Empirically based comparisons suggest very little overlap between the types.

Psychological networks are conceptualized as networks of significant others, and as exchange networks. Each of the cognitive networks is generated by retrospective survey methods, with the exchange network including a broader array of role relationships and identifying both intimate as well as nonintimate ties. In contrast, measures of the network of significant others are cost effective but generally do not compare well with techniques for identifying exchange networks, as the latter techniques tend (a) to elicit constituents from a larger sampling frame, (b) to specify the criteria clearly for the nomination of constituents, and (c) to produce more reliable data.

Interactive networks have been sampled with both retrospective survey methods and contemporary accounts of daily social activity. I have argued that contemporary methods for identifying members of the interactive network or other indices of social participation are clearly preferred over retrospective methods because individuals are unable to accurately recall their interactions over the distant past. It should be noted that perceptions of social activity are certainly important determinants of behavior. However, the actual direct influence of network members on the thoughts and actions of individuals is inescapable, is apt to be far more consequential, and has yet to be investigated, with few exceptions (Larson & Bradney, this volume).

The concept of structural interdependence was introduced to underscore the close theoretical ties between a number of commonly applied structural attributes (e.g., density and clustering), in addition to providing a theoretical basis for linking network structure with specific relationship outcomes. I have argued here that the development, maintenance, and stability of marital relationships, in addition to other forms of close personal relationships, are influenced by network structure, and particularly by the degree of structural interdependence. Analyses of network structure provide a powerful means to supplement analyses that attribute cause to inner psychological or social psychological (dyadic) events or conditions, and yet avoid the inherent lack of specificity common to traditional social structural models of family dynamics. Network analysis identifies the pathways by which social structures influence personal relationships, and the concept of structural interdependence provides the means to quantify those pathways.

NOTES

1. There are undoubtedly many other ways to examine the social context of families. One interesting and underutilized approach has been developed by Garbarino and Sherman (1980). By operating within an ecological model (Bronfenbrenner, 1979; Garbarino, 1977) these researchers defined the social context of families in terms of neighborhoods, and spouses were requested to provide information concerning the physical attributes, subjective evaluations, and local involvements of themselves and others in neighborhood activities.

2. Much of the now-classic work in the development of network analysis is reprinted in Leinhardt (1977), including papers by Heider, Cartwright and Harary, Radcliff-Brown, Barnes, Bott, Granovetter, Holland, and so on.

3. The tendency to maintain specialized friendships does not appear to characterize the entire adult life-course. Men in the preretirement years demonstrate an increasing interest in developing close, intimate friendships with peers, and these friendships tend to be complex and multifaceted (Blumstein & Schwartz, 1983; Brown, 1981; Weiss & Lowenthal, 1975). In comparison to men, women demonstrate greater interest in friendship, including more complex relationships, throughout the adult life-course, an interest which may decline somewhat with age (Blieszner, this volume).

4. In some ways the emphasis on *rewarding* exchanges is unnecessarily narrow. Individuals routinely find themselves engaged in relationships which are decidedly unrewarding, perhaps even adverse. To identify these individuals we have employed the following name-eliciting question after Barrera (1981):

All things considered, nearly everyone has associates with whom they have disagreements. For example, we sometimes have disagreements with friends or neighbors, with people at work, or even parents, in-laws or other relatives. Are there people that you can expect to have some unpleasant disagreements with or people that you can expect to make you angry and upset? [Probe] Anyone at work? In your neighborhood? Any friends? Or parents, in-laws or other relatives?

In our pilot work, 25 wives and their husbands who were married an average of 8 years separately nominated an average of 2 people in response to this question (cf. Barrera, 1981). Of the 102 names elicited, well over half (57%) were nominated solely in response to this question and no other; 27% of the nominees were blood kin, 18% in-laws, 29% coworkers, 9% neighbors, and 17% "other."

REFERENCES

Ackerman, C. (1963). Affiliations: Structural determinants of differential divorce rates. *American Journal of Sociology, 69,* 13-20.

Barnes, J. A. (1954). Class and committees in a Norwegian island parish. *Human Relations, 7,* 39-58.

Barrera, M. (1981). Social support in the adjustment of pregnant adolescents: Assessment issues. In B. H. Gottlieb (Ed.), *Social networks and social support* (pp. 69-96). Newbury Park, CA: Sage.

Bell, R. R. (1981). *Worlds of friendship.* Newbury Park, CA: Sage.

Belle, D. E. (1982). The impact of poverty on social networks and supports. *Marriage and Family Review, 5,* 89-103.

Bernard, H. R., Killworth, P. D., & Sailer, L. (1982). Informant accuracy in social-network data V. An experimental attempt to predict actual communication from recall data. *Social Science Research, 11,* 30-66.

Bernard, H. R., Killworth, P. D., Kronenfeld, D., & Sailer, L. (1984). On the validity of retrospective data: The problem of informant accuracy. *Annual Review of Anthropology, 13.*

Berscheid, E., & Peplau, L. A. (1983). The emerging science of relationships. In H. H. Kelley, E. Berscheid, A. Christensen, J. Harvey, T. Huston, G. Levinger, E. McClintock, L. Peplau, & D. Peterson, *Close relationships* (pp. 1-19). NY: W. H. Freeman.

Blau, P. (1982). Structural sociology and network analysis: An overview. In P. V. Marsden & N. Lin (Eds.), *Social structure and network analysis* (pp. 273-279). Newbury Park, CA: Sage.

Blumstein, P. and Schwartz, P. (1983). *American couples.* New York: Morrow.

Boissevain, J. (1974). *Friends of friends.* Oxford: Basil-Blackwell.

Bott, E. (1955). Urban roles: Conjugal roles and social networks. *Human Relations, 8,* 345-383.

Bott, E. (1971). Family and social network (2nd ed.). New York: Free Press.

Bronfenbrenner, U. (1979). *The experimental ecology of human development.* Cambridge, MA: Harvard University Press.

Brown, B. (1981). A life-span approach to friendship: Age-related dimensions of an ageless relationship. In H. Lopata and D. Maines (Eds.), Research on the interweave of social roles, Vol. 2: Friendship. (pp. 23-50). Greenwich, CT: J.A.I. Press.

Burns, G. L. & Farina, A. (1984). Social competence and adjustment. *Journal of Social and Personal Relationships, 1,* 99-113.

Burt, R. S., & Bittner, W. M. (1981). A note on inferences regarding network subgroups. *Social Networks, 3,* 71-88.

Burt, R. S., & Minor, M. J. (Eds.). (1983). *Applied network analysis: A methodological introduction.* Newbury Park, CA: Sage.

Christensen, A., Sullaway, M., & King, C. (1983). Systematic error in behavioral reports of dyadic interaction: Egocentric bias and content effects. *Behavioral Assessment, 5,* 131-142.

Cohen, C. I., & Sokolovsky, J. (1978). Schizophrenic and social networks: Expatients in the inner city. *Schizophrenia Bulletin, 4,* 546-560.

Conrath, D. W., Higgins, C. A., & McClean, R. J. (1983). A comparison of the reliability of questionnaire versus diary data. *Social Networks, 5,* 315-322.

Cook, M. (1977). The social skill model and interpersonal attraction. In S. W. Duck (Ed.), *Theory and practice in interpersonal attraction.* New York: Academic Press.

Degler, C. (1980). *At Odds.* New York: Oxford University Press.

Dickens, W. J., & Perlman, D. (1981). Friendship over the lifecycle. In S. Duck & R. Gilmour (Eds.), *Personal relationships 2: Developing personal relationships* (pp. 91-122). London: Academic Press.

Erickson, B. H. (1982). Networks, ideologies, and belief systems. In P. V. Marsden & N. Lin (Eds.), *Social structure and network analysis* (pp. 159-172). Newbury Park, CA: Sage.

Fehr, B., & Perlman, D. (1985). The family as a social network and support system. In L. L'Abate (Ed.), *Handbook of family psychology and therapy: Vol. 1* (pp. 323-356). Homewood, IL: Dorsey Press.

Festinger, L. (1949). The analysis of sociograms using matrix algebra. *Human Relations, 2,* 153-158.

Fischer, C. S. (1982). *To dwell among friends: Personal networks in town and city.* Chicago: University of Chicago Press.

Fischer, C. S., & Phillips, S. L. (1982). Who is alone? Social characteristics of people with small networks. In L. A. Peplau and D. Perlman (Eds.), *Loneliness: A Source of current theory, research, and therapy* (pp. 21-39). New York: Wiley Interscience.

Fischer, C. S., Jackson, R. M., Stueve, C. A., Gerson, K., & Jones, L. M. (1977). *Networks and places.* New York: Free Press.

Fraser, M., & Delewski, C. H. (1985). *Self-reports of social network contacts: Caution is warranted.* Manuscript submitted for publication.

Friedkin, N. E. (1981). The development of structure in random networks: An analysis of the effects of increasing network density on five measures of structure. *Social Networks, 3,* 41-52.

Gadlin, H. (1977). Private lives in public order: A critical view of the history of intimate relationships in the United States. In G. Levinger and H. L. Raush (Eds.), *Close relationships* (pp. 33-72). Amherst: University of Massachusetts Press.

Garbarino, J. (1977). The human ecology of child maltreatment: A conceptual model for research. *Journal of Marriage and the Family, 39,* 721-735.

Garbarino, J., & Sherman, D. (1980). High-risk neighborhoods and high-risk families. *Child Development, 51,* 188-198.

Gordon, M., & Downing, H. (1978). A multivariate test of the Bott hypothesis in an urban Irish setting. *Journal of Marriage and the Family, 40,* 585-594.

Granovetter, M. (1983). The strength of weak ties: A network theory revisited. In R. Collins (Ed.), *Sociological theory: 1983* (pp. 201-233). San Francisco: Jossey-Bass.

Greenbaum, S. D., & Greenbaum, P. E. (1985). The ecology of social networks in four urban neighborhoods. *Social Networks, 7,* 47-76.

Hammer, M. (1984). Explorations into the meaning of social network interview data. *Social Networks, 6,* 341-371.

Hill, C. T., & Stull, D. E. (1981). Sex differences in effects of social value similarity in same-sex friendships. *Journal of Personality and Social Psychology, 41,* 488-502.

Holman, T. B. (1981). The influence of community involvement on marital quality. *Journal of Marriage and the Family, 43,* 143-150.

Homel, R., Burns, A., & Goodnow, J. (in press). Parental social networks and child development. *Journal of Social and Personal Relationship.*

Huckfeldt, R. F. (1983). Social context, social network, and urban neighborhoods: Environment constraints on friendship choice. *American Journal of Sociology, 89,* 651-669.

Huston, T. L. (1982). *The topography of marriage: A longitudinal study of the changes in husband-wife relationship over the first years.* Paper presented at the International Conference on Personal Relationships, Madison, WI.

Huston, T. L. & Robins, E. (1982). Conceptual and methodological issues in studying close relationships. *Journal of Marriage and the Family, 44,* 901-925.

Jackson, R. M., Fischer, C. S., & McCallister-Jones, L. (1977). The dimensions of social networks. In C. S. Fischer and associates (Eds.), *Networks and places* (pp. 39-58). New York: Free Press.

Johnson, C. L. (1977). Interdependence, reciprocity and indebtedness: An analysis of Japanese-America kinship relations. *Journal of Marriage and the Family, 39,* 351-363.

Johnson, C. L. (1982). Sibling solidarity: Its origins and functioning in Italian-American families. *Journal of Marriage and the Family, 44,* 155-167.

Johnson, M. P. (1985). *Commitment, cohesion, investment, barriers, alternatives, constraint. Why do people stay together when they really don't want to?* Paper presented at the annual meetings of the Theory Construction and Research Methodology Workshop, National Council on Family Relations, Dallas, TX.

Johnson, M. P. & Leslie, L. (1982). Couple involvement and network structures: A test of the dyadic withdrawal hypothesis. *Social Psychology Quarterly, 46,* 34-43.

Johnson, M. P., & Milardo, R. M. (1984). Network interference in pair relationships: A social psychological recasting of Slater's (1963) theory of social regression. *Journal of Marriage and the Family, 46,* 893-899.

Kelley, H. H., Berscheid, E., Christensen, A., Harvey, J. H., Huston, T. L., Levinger, G., McClintock, E., Peplau, L. A., & Peterson, D. R. (1983). *Close relationships.* New York: W. H. Freeman.

Kemper, T. D. (1968). Third party penetration of local social systems. *Sociometry, 31,* 1-29.

Killworth, P. D., Bernard, H. R., & McCarty, C. (1984). Measuring patterns of acquaintanceship. *Current Anthropology, 25,* 391-397.

Knoke, D., & Laumann, E. (1982). The social organization of national policy domains: An exploration of some structural hypotheses. In P. V. Marsden & N. Lin (Eds.), *Social structure and network analysis* (pp. 255-270). Newbury Park, CA: Sage.

Laumann, E. O. (1966). *Prestige and association in an urban community.* Indianapolis: Bobbs-Merrill.

Lee, G. (1979). Effects of social networks on the family. In W. R. Burr, R. Hill, F. I. Nye, & I. L. Reiss (Eds.), *Contemporary theories about the family: Research based theories, Vol. 1* (pp. 27-56). NY: Free Press.

Leinhardt, S. (Ed.). (1977). *Quantitative studies in social relations.* New York: Academic Press.

Leslie, L. A., & Grady, K. (1985). Changes in mothers' social networks and social support following divorce. *Journal of Marriage and the Family, 47,* 663-673.

Mace, D. R. (1985). The coming revolution in human relationships. *Journal of Social and Personal Relationships, 2,* 81-94.

Marsden, P. V., & Lin, N. (Eds.), *Social structure and network analysis.* Newbury Park, CA: Sage.

McCallister-Jones, L., & Fischer, C. S. (1978). *Studying egocentric networks by mass survey.* Working Paper No. 184, Institute of Urban and Regional Development, Berkley, University of California.

Milardo, R. M. (1982). Social networks in developing relationships: Converging and diverging social environments. *Social Psychology Quarterly, 45,* 162-172.

Milardo, R. M. (1983). Social networks and pair relationships: A review of substantive and measurement issues. *Sociology and Social Research, 68,* 1-18.

Milardo, R. M. (1986a). *Comparing the exchange and interactive networks.* Paper presented at the annual meetings of the National Council of Family Relations, Dearborn, MI.

Milardo, R. M. (1986b). Personal choice and social constraint in close relationships: Applications of network analysis. In V. Derlega and B. Winstead (Eds.), *Friendship and social interaction* (pp. 145-166). New York: Springer-Verlag.

Milardo, R. M., Johnson, M. P., & Huston, T. L. (1983). Developing close relationships: Changing patterns of interaction between pair members and social networks. *Journal of Personality and Social Psychology, 44,* 964-976.

Mitchell, J. C. (1969). The concept and use of social network. In J. C. Mitchell (Ed.), *Social networks in urban situations* (pp. 1-50). Manchester, England: Manchester University Press.

Moore, G., & Alba, R. D. (1982). Class and prestige origins in the American elite. In P. V. Marsden & N. Lin (Eds.), *Social structure and network analysis* (pp. 39-60). Newbury Park, CA: Sage.

Moreno, J. L. (1934). *Who shall survive: A new approach to the problem of human interaction.* New York: Beacon.

Morris, L. (1985). Local social networks and domestic organizations: A study of redundant steel workers and their wives. *The Sociological Review, 33,* 327-342.

Nezlek, J. B., Wheeler, L., & Reis, H. T. (1983). Studies of social participation. In H. T. Reis (Ed.), *Naturalistic approaches to studying social interaction, 15,* San Francisco: Jossey-Bass.

Olsen, D. H., & McCubbin, H. I. (1983). *Families: What makes them work.* Newbury Park, CA: Sage.

Peplau, L. A., & Gordon, S. (1985). Women and men in love: Sex differences in close heterosexual relationships. In V. E. O'Leary, R. K. Unger, and B. S. Wallston (Eds.), *Women gender, and social psychology.* Hillsdale, NJ: Lawrence Erlbaum.

Rands, M., & Levinger, G. (1979). Implicit theories of relationship: An intergenerational study. *Journal of Personality and Social Psychology, 37,* 645-661.

Reis, H., Wheeler, L., Spiegel, N., Kernis, M., Nezlek, J., & Perri, M. (1982). Physical attractiveness in social interaction II: Why does appearance affect social experience? *Journal of Personality and Social Psychology, 43,* 979-996.

Richards, E. F. (1980). Network ties, kin ties and marital role organization: Bott's hypothesis reconsidered. *Journal of Comparative Family Studies, 11,* 139-151.

Riley, D., & Cochran, M. M. (1985). Naturally occurring child rearing advice for fathers: Utilization of the personal social network. *Journal of Marriage and the Family, 47,* 275-286.

Rogler, L. H., & Procidano, M. E. (1986). The effect of social networks on marital roles: A test of the Bott hypothesis in an intergenerational context. *Journal of Marriage and the Family, 48,* 693-701.

Romney, A. K., & Weller, S. C. (1984). Predicting informant accuracy from patterns of recall among individuals. *Social Networks, 6,* 59-77.

Ross, C. O. (1987). Organizational dimensions of metropolitan dominance: Prominence in the network of corporate control, 1955-1975. *American Sociological Review, 52,* 258-267.

Salzinger, L. L. (1982). The ties that bind: The effect of clustering on dyadic relationships. *Social Networks, 4,* 117-145.

Scanzoni, J. (1979). Social exchange and behavioral interdependence. In R. L. Burgess and T. L. Huston (Eds.), *Social exchange in developing relationships* (pp. 61-98). New York: Academic Press.

Shanks, J. M. (1983). The current status of computer-assisted telephone interviewing. *Sociological Methods and Research, 12,* 119-142.

Shulman, N. (1975). Life-cycle variations in patterns of close relationships. *Journal of Marriage and the Family, 37,* 813-821.

Tolsdorf, C. (1981). Social networks and families of divorce: A study of structure-content interaction. *International Journal of Family Therapy, 3,* 275-280.

Walker, A. J., and Thompson, L. (1983). Intimacy and intergenerational aid and contact among mothers and daughters. *Journal of Marriage and the Family, 45,* 841-849.

Wellman, B. (1979). The community question: The intimate networks of East Yorkers. *American Journal of Sociology, 84,* 1201-1231.

Wellman, B. (1983). Network analysis: Some basic principles. In R. Collins (Ed.), *Sociological theory 1983* (pp. 155-200). San Francisco: Jossey-Bass. Wellman, B. (in press). Domestic work, paid work, and net work. In S. Duck and D. Perlman (Eds.), *Understanding personal relationships: An interdisciplinary approach.* Newbury Park, CA: Sage.

Weiss L., and Lowenthal, M. F. (1975). Life-course perspectives on friendship. In M. F. Lowenthal, M. Thurnher, and D. Chiriboga. *Four stages of life* (pp. 48-61). San Francisco: Jossey-Bass.

White, H. C., Boorman, S., & Breiger, R. (1976). Social structure from multiple networks: I. Blockmodels of roles and positions. *American Journal of Sociology, 81,* 740-780.

Willits, F. K., & Crider, D. M. (1986). *Well-being at midlife.* (Bulletin 863) Pennsylvania State University Agricultural Experiment Station, University Park, PA.

Winship, C., & Mandel, M. (1983). Roles and position: A critique and extension of the blockmodeling approach. In S. Leinhardt (Ed.), *Sociological methodology 1983-1984* (pp. 314-344). San Francisco: Jossey-Bass.

Wu, L. (1983). Local blockmodel algebras for analyzing social networks. In S. Leinhardt (Ed.), *Sociological methodology 1983-1984* (pp. 272-313). San Francisco: Jossey-Bass.

2

The Influence of the Interactive Network on Developing Relationships

Catherine A. Surra

In her memoir of her parents, Margaret Mead and Gregory Bateson, anthropologist Mary Catherine Bateson (1984) wrote of her mother's death:

> A parent dies and one gropes for a certain knowledge of the person who is gone. More and more, it has seemed to me that the idea of an individual, the idea that there is someone to be known, separate from the relationships, is simply an error. As a relationship is broken, or a new one developed, there is a new person. So we create each other, bring each other into being by being part of the matrix in which the other exists [p. 117].

One irony in Bateson's observation is that even those of us who study relationships often are so concerned about understanding friendship, romance, or marriage that we forget about the matrix of associations in which individuals and any one of their relationships are embedded. We

AUTHOR'S NOTE: Preparation of this chapter was supported in part by a grant from the Agricultural Experiment Station, University of Illinois at Urbana-Champaign, Project Nos. 1-6-53543 and 1-6-53694.

forget that the romance, for example, may be one of two or more romances; that the relationship with the lover is one of several relationships with casual acquaintances, friends, and kin; and that yesterday's friendship is today's romance and today's romance is tomorrow's friendship. The actual flow of alliances in day-to-day life involves the definition and redefinition of relationships and of the self in relation to others. As Bateson suggests, to attempt to understand someone or any one of their relationships separate from the social matrix is misleading.

Social network analysis is one tool for conceptualizing and measuring the social matrix. The intent here is to examine one facet of this matrix, the interactive social network, and its effects on developing relationships. Although the focus is on heterosexual involvements, much of what is said applies to other close relationships.

The interactive social network is defined in terms of those people with whom an individual engages in face-to-face interaction (Milardo, 1983, this volume). The term "interactive network" is described more fully below, and two ways it influences developing relationships are delineated. First, the interactive network is viewed as a set of separate dyadic relationships, including the relationship between romantic partners and between each partner and another individual, such as a parent or friend. Each of these relationships is described in terms of the pattern of interdependence between the members of the dyad. The influence of interdependence in dyadic relationships with network members on premarital involvements is then examined.

Second, the impact of the interactive network as a whole is considered by specifying properties that are used to characterize the interconnectedness of the entire network and the effects of variation in these properties on developing relationships. Throughout the discussion, the interplay between changes in interdependence in the premarital dyad and in the network is addressed. To lay some groundwork for the discussion, a model of the developing relationship is presented that will aid in defining a relationship and in examining social networks as one cause of change in relationships.

THE DEVELOPING RELATIONSHIP: CHANGES IN THE PATTERN OF INTERDEPENDENCE

Social networks influence the development of relationships because they are partial determinants of the pattern of interdependence between partners. According to Kelley et al. (1983), interdependence can be defined as the mutual influence of the observable behaviors performed by one partner (P) on the other (O). Huston (1983) defined influence as the cognitive, affective, or behavioral change occurring in O as the result of P's actions, and argued that, to understand influence, it is necessary to observe the influence sequence. An influence sequence is the effect of P's action on O, in combination with the subsequent effect of O's action on P. By linking together the influence sequences that occur during interaction, interdependence can be represented as a series of causal interconnections between the affective, cognitive, and behavioral responses, or events, occurring in P and O (Kelley et al., 1983).

Events and the interconnections between them are the "basic data" of relationships (Kelley et al., 1983, p. 27). By accumulating information about recurrent patterns of influence sequences, any relationship can be characterized in terms of its *properties* of interdependence. Some of the more salient properties that can be used to distinguish among different kinds of relationships (e.g., personal from impersonal), or to characterize one kind of relationship at different points in its development, include the frequency, pattern, strength, diversity, and symmetry of interconnections between P and O; the degree to which the behaviors done by P facilitate or interfere with O's events; and the duration of the interaction or the relationship. A *close* relationship is one that has frequent, strong, and diverse interconnections that occur over a relatively long period of time (Kelley et al., 1983).

When it comes to the evolution of premarital relationships, it is generally assumed that the frequency, strength, and diversity of interconnections increase as relationships become more involved and that the reverse is true of relationships that become less involved. Although such an assumption seems intuitively obvious, little research has been done to verify it. The assumption that interdependence in relationships increases with depth of involvement carries with it the corollary that the increase is normative, that is, it applies to most couples. Yet studies of marital relationships show that there is considerable variation across couples in at least one dimension of interdependence, the extent to which spouses perform activities together, both within and outside the home (see Surra, 1980, for a review). A classic example of variation in marital patterns in Bernard's (1964) distinction between interactional marriages, in which companionship is high, and parallel marriages, in which spouses usually carry out activities separately.

Surra (1985) examined whether similar differences occurred in the amount of interdependence during premarriage and whether these differences were linked to the way relationships moved toward marital commitment. Retrospective data on courtship were gathered from newlyweds, who graphed changes in commitment from the day they met until they wed and provided information on the extent to which they did various activities with their partners. The results showed that the sample of 50 couples fell into four types of courtship and that partners in the types differed on changes in the amount of interdependence from casually dating to early marriage. Partners in two of the types had relationships that moved quickly and rapidly to marriage. Interdependence for these partners was high and increased throughout courtship. Partners whose relationships evolved to marriage at a slow pace became increasingly interdependent, but to a lesser extent than those in rapidly developing relationships. Finally, partners whose courtships moved at an intermediate pace showed, on average, little evidence of increasing interdependence during courtship. Consequently, they were less interdependent at marriage than those in the remaining types.

The work on courtship types suggests that the assumption of developmental increases in interdependence holds for some, but not all, couples. What accounts for developmental changes in interdependence and for variation in developmental change? Kelley and his coauthors (1983) used the term *causal conditions* to denote factors responsible for stability and change in patterns of interdependence. Because other authors have discussed the identification of causal conditions (Huston & Robins, 1982; Kelley et al., 1983), here it is necessary to note only that the existence of a cause is inferred by examining whether a change in a presumed cause elicits a corresponding shift in the property of interdependence in question. This criterion is equivalent to the "covariation principle." It must also be demonstrated that the effect changes after a change in the cause (temporal precedence), and alternate causal explanations need to be eliminated.

To show, for example, that social networks bear upon developing interdependence, it must be demonstrated that some occurrence that originates in the social environment has an effect on either or both partners, which, in turn, impinges on the interconnections between them. The impact of this socially derived occurrence must be apparent consistently and generally across persons to infer the existence of a causal condition (Kelley et al., 1983). Hence, in order to demonstrate that parental opposition to relationships causes changes in interdependence, it must first be established that, when opposition increases, in the form of such behaviors as parents' criticizing the partner, imposing sanctions against seeing the partner, or engaging in activities to separate the pair, the frequency of interaction between partners subsequently decreases. In addition, the evidence must show that other plausible causal conditions, such as increases in either or both partners' ambivalence about becoming involved or decreases in the rewards derived from interaction, are not responsible for, or do not independently contribute to, the observed reduction in frequency of interconnections.

This example illustrates the way social networks might directly impinge upon developing interdependence; however, the influence of the social network can be indirect, mediating changes in interdependence by means of its action on other kinds of causes. To simplify the complexities of causal analysis, the various kinds of causes that bear upon interdependence can be organized according to their origin (Kelley et al., 1983). Causal conditions are located in the personal attitudes, skills, beliefs, or traits of an individual partner; in the social or physical environment (e.g., social support or climate, respectively); in the relation between a particular partner and the environment (e.g., an illness that is brought under control in certain climates); or in the relation between the partners. The latter type of causal condition comprises factors that exist by virtue of a particular combination of P and O characteristics or the interaction between P and O. Examples of these so-called P × O causes are the degree of similarity between partners on attitudes or interpersonal norms and agreements (e.g., "We are compatible") that emerge from interaction.

When this framework for causal analysis is used as a guide, causality is a multifaceted, multidirectional process. Causes from different levels of analysis and different causes from the same level are assumed to interact to determine whether interdependence grows, deteriorates, or stabilizes. From this perspective, interactive networks affect interdependence actively and directly through the behaviors of network members, as well as indirectly, by effecting change in other causes. Instead of acting directly on the frequency of interaction between partners, for instance, parental opposition may affect interdependence through its influence on one partner's beliefs about compatibility, which then alters the amount of time partners spend together. Similarly, such economic and social causes as changes in businesses and migration in and out of communities may affect the composition of the interactive network and, therefore, the pool of available partners (Davis-Brown, Salamon, & Surra, 1987).

The interactive network is a force in developing relationships because it represents a web of real associations with others. As such, it limits opportunities for interaction with others and helps to shape the character of that interaction. Study of the interactive network, however, is uninformative about the psychological influences of present and past social relationships. These kinds of influences include such phenomena as the effects of norms held by network members (Ridley & Avery, 1979), the impact of socialization on internalized beliefs about romantic relationships, and attributional and social comparison processes (Surra & Huston, 1987). Although the premise of this chapter is that the interactive network influences developing relationships, there are equally powerful influences not described here that stem from other ways of defining "social network."

TOWARD A CONCEPTUAL AND OPERATIONAL DEFINITION OF THE INTERACTIVE NETWORK

A social network is usually thought of as the set of persons with whom an individual is associated. The analysis of social networks is concerned with the linkages among persons in the set, and focuses on the connections between any two persons in the set and among all persons in the set. A more concrete way to conceive of P's social network is to think of P as the hub of an irregularly shaped wheel that has spokes emanating from it to various points along the rim of the wheel. Some of the spokes represent the linkages between P and the other persons in the network, who are the points along the rim. Other spokes connect the people along the rim of the wheel to each other, some of whom are directly connected to P and others who are connected to P only through their tie to another person.

Because the interconnections among the persons in the set are compelling to study, scholars often move directly to that topic, ignoring problems of definition. Even from the general definition of networks just provided, clearly the picture of the network that results depends upon the way "linkage" is defined (Milardo, 1986). The definition of linkage determines, for example, whether a tie exists between P and another person, the number of different people in the network, and the amount of interconnectedness among members of the whole network. The remainder of this section is devoted to a more precise description of the interactive network.

Defining the Interactive Network

The interactive network is determined by actual contact among persons. As a result, its theoretical significance lies in the bounds it imposes on the people and relationships within it. The behaviors transacted between individuals are sources of constraint and opportunity for network members in two ways. At the dyadic level of analysis, the amount and kind of interaction P has with O affects the amount and kind of interaction P has with X, where X is a member of P's network. Likewise, the kinds of information and other resources exchanged between P and X potentially become the substance of interaction between P and O, as is the case when parents lend their married daughter money for the down payment on a home for her and her husband. In this way, the pattern of interdependence between any two partners in the network influences the pattern in any other dyad.

To carry the example one step further, the configuration of interdependence within the network as a whole can influence the relaying of any resource from one individual to another. Because the interactive network is a group of individuals who may or may not interact with each other and who, if they do interact, do so in varying degrees, the nature of the linkages among the individuals can also be analyzed for the entire group. Milardo (1986) observed that to comprehend the collective influence of networks on individuals it is necessary to single out properties that describe the kind and degree of interdependence within the network.

Considerable attention has been given to identifying the properties of interdependence in interactive networks at both the dyadic and network levels of analysis. Nevertheless, the distinction between the two levels is blurred when they are considered from a developmental perspective. Over time, changes in interdependence in dyads will result in changes in networks. Specifically, the pattern of network interdependence will change as previously unacquainted members begin to interact and those who once interacted stop doing so. As shown below, the idea that changes in dyadic and network interdependence are interconnected through time has ramifications for the kinds of methodologies useful for studying relationship development.

Shown in Table 1 are properties of dyadic interdependence which derive from analysis of the interaction between any P and O or between any P and X. Theorists generally agree about the kinds of properties and their meanings, regardless of whether the interest is primarily in dyads

TABLE 1
Properties of Interdependence in Dyads

Property	Definition	Example
Content	The kind of events that interconnect P and O	The types of behaviors or activities performed by P and O; the types of resources exchanged
Diversity	The degree of variety in the events that interconnect P and O	The different kinds of behaviors or activities performed by P and O; the variety of role relationships that connect P and O
Frequency	The number of interconnections between events in P and those in O	Frequency of contact between P and O; frequency of exchanges between P and O
Duration	The length of time P and O are interconnected	The length of the relationship between P and O; the amount of time spent in interaction
Strength	The intensity with which events in P are connected to events in O	The magnitude or regularity of P's influence on O
Symmetry	The degree of similarity between P's connections to O's events and vice versa	The reciprocity in behaviors exchanged between P and O; the relative dependence of P's behaviors on O's
Interference	The extent to which P's behaviors facilitate or interfere with the goal-directed sequence of events in O	The meshing of P's and O's behaviors; the compatibility between events in P and events in O

(Hinde, 1979; Huston & Burgess, 1979; Kelley et al., 1983) or in networks (Boissevain, 1974; Fischer et al., 1977; Mitchell, 1969; Ridley & Avery, 1979; Milardo, 1986). Because the definitions of properties of interdependence given by Kelley et al. (1983) are the most general and inclusive of other definitions, those in Table 1 are based primarily on their work.

The term *structural interdependence* (Milardo, 1986) refers to properties that reflect the degree and patterning of linkages among network members. Properties of structural interdependence describe the "placement of pair relationships within the network, including both the simple presence or absence of pair relationships . . . as well as the overall pattern of those relationships" (Milardo, 1986, p. 157). The operational definitions of properties of structural interdependence are summarized in Table 2. The properties are useful for identifying that portion of influence on developing relationships that is uniquely contributed by the network. Of the properties listed, density, clustering, reachability, and overlap are the most fundamental for describing structural interdependence. Although the properties in Table 2 are quite similar to those identified in Milardo, there are some differences. According to Milardo, density, clustering, overlap, and interconnectedness (i.e., the average number of connections each person has with other network members) form the foundation of structural interdependence. I added the property of reachability or centrality to Milardo's list because it has been shown to be associated with developmental changes in pair relationships within the network (Hammer, 1980; Hammer & Schaffer, 1975). The property of interconnectedness was deleted because it is less generally recognized. Even though Milardo argued that network size is more a measure of the placement of individuals in the network than an indicator of interdependence, I included it here because it is correlated with other structural properties (Friedkin, 1981).

Although the properties of structural interdependence—like those of dyadic interdependence—are believed to be intercorrelated, each conveys distinctive information about linkages within the network. For this reason, and because the topic of developing relationships requires analysis of the properties of both P's and O's networks, they are considered separately here.

Density is a measure of the extent to which the possible connections among network members do, in fact, exist. Shown in Figures 1 through 6 are examples of networks of P and O with varying densities; in all cases, P is treated as a member of O's network and vice versa. In Figure 4, P's network and O's network have equivalent densities of 50% because in each network there are 3 actual ties out of 6 potential ties. Although density is a heavily studied characteristic, its application is problematic for a number of reasons. The overall size of the network constrains the values of density that are likely to be obtained. As size increases, members of larger networks will have to maintain a greater number of contacts than those in smaller networks in order to achieve networks of equal density (Boissevain, 1974; Milardo, 1986). Friedkin (1981) used a Monte Carlo procedure to examine the interrelationship among the structural features of networks of varying size, and found that larger networks showed higher levels of structural cohesion on measures of

TABLE 2
Properties of Interdependence in Social Networks

Property	Definition	Source
Size	The number of different individuals with whom a person interacts	Boissevain, 1974; Milardo, 1986; Milardo et al., 1983; Mitchell, 1969; Ridley & Avery, 1979
Density	The ratio of actual connections each person has to the maximum number of potential connections, excluding the connections between the target person and other network members	Boissevain, 1974; Milardo, 1986; Mitchell, 1969; Ridley & Avery, 1979
Clustering	The extent to which the network has subgroups of high density; members of clusters have a large number of connections with each other relative to the number of connections they have with persons outside the cluster	Boissevain, 1974; Milardo, 1986; Salzinger, 1982
Reachability, distance, or centraility	The distance between one network member and another measured as some function of the number of connections from one network member to another	Boissevain, 1974; Fischer et al., 1977; Friedkin, 1980, 1981; Hammer, 1980; Hammer & Schaffer, 1975
Overlap	The extent to which individuals who are members of one person's network are also members of another's; the proportion of network members held in common by two individuals who are connected	Hammer & Schaffer, 1975; Huston & Burgess, 1979; Milardo, 1982, 1986

reachability and clustering at lower densities than did smaller networks. Even though density values are instructive as an indicator of average numbers of connections, they are uninformative about the configuration of subgroups within the network (Salzinger, 1982).

Clustering is used to describe the existence of cliques within the network. Salzinger (1982) defined a cluster as a group of three or more individuals who are connected to at least one person in common and who have more ties with each other than they do with others. Triadic clusters are believed to be especially significant in networks because of the tendency toward *transivity*, or triadic closure, whereby P's ties to both O and X eventually foster a tie between O and X (Granovetter, 1973, 1983). Although Friedkin (1981) showed that clustering, measured as the average number of triads in which a person is involved, is positively related to density, network size mediates this relationship: high levels of clustering are achieved at lower levels of density in large networks than in small. Milardo (1986) observed that within two networks of the same size and density the clique structure can vary dramatically; high density can stem from a large number of interconnections spread throughout the whole network or from the concentration of many ties within one subgroup.

The property of reachability has to do with the distance separating network members from one another. It is usually measured in terms of the length or number of different paths needed to connect individuals to one another (Friedkin, 1981; Hammer, 1980; Hammer & Schaffer, 1975). In his Monte Carlo study, Friedkin found that at low densities most persons are directly connected to one another, while at high densities more pairs are joined only by means of their mutual ties to another. As the size of the network increases, greater reachability is obtained at lower densities. Because this property taps the degree of access network members have to one another, it is especially salient when it comes to characterizing the flow of information and other resources through the network.

Whereas the properties of size, density, clustering, and reachability are indicators of structural interdependence in one person's network, the property of overlap is inherently a dyadic measure. Overlap is a measure of the extent to which two individuals have the same networks. Because overlap is applicable to the dyad as a unit, it may be the most useful structural property for explaining how social networks affect dyads. This is because of the relationship between overlap and other properties discussed so far. The amount of overlap between P's and O's network places constraints on and provides information about the remaining properties. The greater the amount of overlap between the interactive networks of two individuals, the more similar their networks are on other dimensions of structure. In the ideal case in which P and O have exactly the same networks, or 100% overlap, all of the other properties will also be equal. Conversely, when overlap is low there is a greater possibility for discrepancy between the other characteristics of

P's and O's networks. In this way, overlap can be an especially efficient measure of network structure.

Amount of overlap, like other structural properties, is moderated by network size. The amount of overlap possible is limited by the size of P's network relative to O's such that the smaller of the two constrains overlap (Friedkin, 1980).

Overlap is a measure of the structural cohesion because, within any one interactive network, the greater the number of connections held in common by any two members of the network, the greater the structural interdependence (Hammer, 1980; Hammer & Schaffer, 1975). For any two persons in any one interactive network, the tendency toward transivity or triadic clustering described earlier translates to a tendency toward overlap. More generally, individuals who are members of the same cliques in interactive networks are more likely to have highly overlapping networks. Of course, two individuals may also be members of nonoverlapping clusters (see Figure 4). As with the other properties, clustering and overlap are related, but each provides unique information about structural interdependence.

THE IMPACT OF THE INTERACTIVE NETWORK ON DEVELOPING RELATIONSHIPS

The Influence of Interdependence in Dyads

How does the nature of interdependence in one type of relationship in the network affect changes in interdependence in another? To focus the answer to this question on the development of relationships, three different dyads need to be considered: the target dating relationship between P and O; P's relationship with a particular network member (X); and O's relationship with a network member (Z). According to the ideas about causal conditions presented earlier, changes in interdependence between P and X or between O and Z may directly alter the behaviors, thoughts, and feelings that connect P and O. Johnson and Leslie (1982), for example, argued that because available time is limited, P's interaction with O will constrict P's with X. In terms of the properties listed in Table 1, if the frequency, diversity, and strength of P's interaction with O increases, there may be subsequent decreases in these properties for P and X (or for O and Z). If interdependence between P and X continues to decrease, eventually their tie will be severed completely, thereby reducing the interconnectedness of the entire network. The same arguments apply to the effects of P-X interdependence on P and O. Alternatively, changes in interdependence in a particular network relationship may mediate P-O interdependence by their impact on other causal conditions, as in the case where a woman's establishing a new acquaintance with a man alters her long-term partner's perception of her trustworthiness. This shift in a P × O causal condition may change the amount of time he spends with her.

Researchers who study developing romantic associations have examined some of the possible connections between interdependence in the target dyad and that in association with third parties. Empirical work has concentrated on the property of interference; specifically, how P or O is affected by opposition or support from third parties. Second, research has examined corresponding shifts in the amount of interdependence between P-O and P-X, depending upon the nature of the P-X relationship (i.e., kin, friends, or acquaintances).

Support and interference from third parties. Research has addressed the impact of interference and support on subjective conditions such as love; on multiple measures of involvement (e.g., love and probability of marriage); on changes in stage of involvement (e.g., the movement from serious dating to engaged); and on the stability of the P-O relationship. Predictions about the association between the amount of interference and romantic involvement are varied. Some investigators have hypothesized that the relationship is negative and linear (Parks, Stan, & Eggert, 1983); others that it is positive and linear (Driscoll, Davis, & Lipetz, 1972); and still others that it is curvilinear, such that the direction of the association changes with stage of involvement (Johnson & Milardo, 1984). More surprising than the variety in predictions is that each has obtained some empirical support. The discrepancies in the findings that pertain to the interference-support question can be explained, in part, by variations in the methods used in different studies; however, presuppositions about the nature and influence of interference and support have molded the kinds of questions asked and the means used to ask them.

Leslie, Johnson, and Huston (1986) looked at the connections between behaviors performed by parents to show approval and disapproval of their children's dating choices and behaviors performed by children to try to influence their parents' opinions of their dates. Children's influence attempts included, for example, "talking to parents about my partner's good points" and "talking about how partner treats me"; examples of parental behaviors are "asking how partner is doing" and "talking about others to date." Influence attempts and parental approving behaviors covaried, and both were more likely when dating relationships were deeply involved. The pattern of results for parental disapproving behaviors was similar, though weaker. Parental approval and disapproval were weakly related to developmental change in stage over a 4-month period. It appears that some parents and children simply have high levels of interaction about dating and that the more serious the romance, the more they exchange information about it.

When more global, self-report ratings are used to assess interference-support, researchers are more likely to find a connection with developmental change in dyads (Driscoll et al., 1972; Johnson & Milardo, 1984; Parks & Adelman, 1983; Parks et al., 1983). Consistent with the so-called "Romeo and Juliet effect," Driscoll et al. found a positive correlation between changes in romantic love and interference. Cross-sectional data supported Johnson and Milardo's prediction that interference would be low at the earliest stages of romantic involvement, highest at the midstages, and low again at later stages. Longitudinal analyses revealed that high interference at the start of the study increased the likelihood of relationship deterioration during a 1-year period.

Parks et al. (1983) found strong positive associations between support from own as well as partner's network and involvement. Opposition from the partner's network, in contrast, was associated with less involvement. In a related study, Parks and Adelman (1983) found that high support was associated with relationship stability.

The findings from research on interference and support are inconclusive about how they affect developing relationships. Although some results from *longitudinal* studies that measured daters' global perceptions of interference indicate that it is related to relationship growth and deterioration (Johnson & Milardo, 1984; Parks & Adelman, 1983; Parks et al., 1983), studies that employed behavioral self-report measures of parental approval and disapproval (Leslie et al., 1986) failed to find much evidence of a longitudinal connection between opposition and developmental change. Explanations for these inconsistencies arise from both methodological and substantive issues. With regard to the latter, it is useful to draw on the assumptions described earlier about the workings of the interactive network. In this situation, these assumptions imply: (a) that interference and support are behaviors expressed by network members that block or facilitate, respectively, the execution of partner's individual goals and behaviors regarding relationships (see Table 1; Kelley et al., 1983); (b) that interfering or supportive behaviors influence the interdependence in the dating relationship itself; (c) that parents, friends, and other people take an active role in dating relationships; and (d) that interference and support may influence developmental change in dyads by acting on other causal conditions.

The study by Leslie et al. (1986) comes closest to examining the mechanisms of interference and support from the interactive network with a suitable methodology for testing them; yet the findings provided little indication that parental inference operated in developmental change. One reason is that studying the interactive network, with its emphasis on the direct intervention of parents and friends in dating choice, conveys a limited picture of network influences. Except under conditions in which partners are seriously involved with someone who is considered a "bad match" by family members or friends, the influence of network members is likely to be indirect, shaping such things as partners' beliefs about suitable dating choices and marriageable relationships (Leslie et al., 1986; Surra & Huston, 1987). Sussman (1953) interviewed parents to find out about their role in mate selection. Their major concern was that their children form endogamous unions; active opposition to marriage was greatest when children married exogamously. Parental efforts to shape children's mate choices were most often indirect, occurring *throughout* the child's lifetime, as parents chose places of residence, planned social activities, and socialized children to make appropriate mate choices.

Studies of perceived interference and support may find that degree of "opposition" is influential because they tap global *expectations* for how others *might* react, as well as *perceptions* of others' behaviors. The implicit influences of networks, which stem from parental socialization, observations of the romantic relationships of close associates, and one's own past romances (Surra & Huston, 1987), may be more powerful than direct intervention by third parties.

Regarding measurement of the interactive network, separate reports obtained from each person in a couple and from third parties are needed to carefully study interference and support. This is because different levels of support may be wrought by different parties; parents may actively disapprove of a relationship, while friends may encourage it. Similarly, to the extent that daters from the same couple have different interactive networks, they may be the recipients of different amounts of support. Up to now, interfering and supportive behaviors have been studied only from the viewpoint of the targets of the behaviors and not the actors, making it difficult to substantiate the reliability or validity of reports. Finally, given the lack of correspondence between the composition of networks of interactants and of significant others (Milardo, this volume), research that assesses interference from significant others (e.g., Johnson & Milardo, 1984; Parks & Adelman, 1983; Parks et al., 1983) probably provides an invalid characterization of interference from interactants.

Because the research on interference and support has relied upon homogamous college-student samples (Johnson & Milardo, 1984; Leslie et al., 1986; Parks & Adelman, 1983; Parks et al., 1983) and because active opposition is likely to be greatest when involvements are serious and exogamous, the degree of opposition from the interactive network probably has been underestimated. In fact, no research has reported much opposition from network members. Parks et al., for example, found that opposition was strong for only 2% of one network sector, partner's friends. Variation in opposition and support is likely to be maximized in nonacademic settings and contexts, where individuals with heterogamous characteristics are likely to meet (cf. Kerckhoff, 1974).

Frequency and duration of interaction with third parties. Researchers who study the social context of developing relationships have also been interested in the phenomenon of social withdrawal. The withdrawal hypothesis is that as dating partners become more deeply involved with each other they become less involved with their networks. The processes believed to be responsible for social regression are varied. Because such resources as time and emotional energy are limited, partners will progressively isolate themselves from others as they draw closer to each other. In addition, withdrawal is thought to be a function of setting boundaries to establish the unity of the pair. (See Johnson & Leslie, 1982, for a review of the mechanisms involved in social regression.)

Milardo and colleagues (Milardo, Johnson, & Huston, 1983) observed changes in network size and in the frequency and duration of interaction with different network members to test their hypothesis that withdrawal over the course of dating relationships would be greatest from third parties who were least close. Cross-sectional comparisons clearly showed that less-involved daters interacted more frequently and longer with close and intermediate friends and acquaintances than more-involved daters. No such differences were found for kin. Longitudinal tests showed that, for daters who regressed in stage of involvement, interaction with the total network and with intermediate friends and acquaintances increased, but no changes were found for interaction with close friends and kin. Cross-sectional analyses also showed that total network size was greatest for least-involved partners, though the size of the kin network was larger at engagement. Longitudinal analyses showed no changes in size according to whether relationships advanced, stabilized, or regressed in stage over three months. The researchers interpreted their results to mean that withdrawal occurs from all network sectors (i.e., it does *not* depend on closeness to third parties) and that the length of the study was too short to detect longitudinal changes in interaction with close friends and changes in network size.

Before the phenomenon of social regression takes an immutable hold on the minds of scholars, it might be useful to consider the possible limits of withdrawal and some alternate interpretations of these findings. One possibility is that selection effects operated in the cross-sectional data such that persons who maintained larger networks or more frequent and longer interactions with close friends were more apt to break up during earlier stages. Another question is whether the length of the study period was too short to longitudinally verify cross-sectional results (also, see Leslie et al., 1986). The answer to this question depends, in part, upon the numbers of persons who changed stage during the study period, and whether these numbers give sufficient power to detect changes statistically. A related issue is whether time, change in stage, or both are important dependent variables. Because the data from most studies suggest that stage of relationship is a more sensitive indicator of developmental change than is chronological time (e.g., Milardo, 1982; Parks & Adelman, 1983; Parks et al., 1983), studies that are long enough to detect changes in stage are probably long enough to detect its correlates.

The question "how long is long enough?" masquerades as a merely methodological one, however. The most definitive evidence indicates that withdrawal may indeed be confined to intermediate friends and acquaintances and to certain network properties, namely, the frequency and duration of interaction. The idea that withdrawal is pervasive runs counter to other changes in social participation, whereby individuals whose relationships progress incorporate members of the partner's network into their own (Milardo, 1982). Making the formal transition from engagement to marriage, in particular, carries with it the task of taking on new affiliations, especially with kin (Surra & Huston, 1987). Thus, declines in the *kin* network can be expected to be nil for persons whose relationships progress, as the available data show (Milardo et al., 1983). Furthermore, as "advancing" partners take on some new network members and drop off others, the net decline in size may be zero.

The extent to which partners withdraw from close friends, kin, and others probably depends upon the strength of the tie between P and O. The research on the courtship types (Surra, 1985) showed that, in general, partners who became the most interdependent with each other withdrew more from their networks whereas those who reported little increase in dyadic interdependence withdrew less from the network. These findings indicate that assessments of corresponding changes in the pattern of interdependence between P-O, P-X, and O-Z might be informative about the wide variation in withdrawal that has been observed (Johnson & Leslie, 1982; Milardo et al., 1983; Surra, 1985).

In addition to the strength of the tie between P and O, the structural interdependence of the network itself probably plays a major role in accounting for variation in withdrawal. It is generally true that the more interdependence there is in the network as a whole, the more cohesive are the separate dyads within it. Therefore, withdrawal is likely to be greatest when the degree of network interdependence is low. Conversely, when network interdependence is high there will be pressure from members to maintain the status quo, and withdrawal can be expected to be less. Variation in withdrawal depends upon the relative connectedness of P's network versus O's; the sector of the network in question; the property of the network under consideration; and the degree of P-O interdependence. Each of these issues is taken up in more detail in the next section.

The Influence of Structural Interdependence in Networks on Developing Relationships

To my knowledge, of the properties of structural interdependence defined in Table 2, only overlap has been studied in connection with developing romantic relationships (Milardo, 1982). However, a body of knowledge about how the properties of interactive networks affect other kinds of relationships, such as friendships or coworkers, and about other kinds of networks (e.g., the network of significant others) is rapidly accumulating. By drawing on these data, predictions can be made about the impact of structural interdependence on developing relationships. In addressing this problem, the properties of P's network must be considered in tandem with those of O's to make predictions about the effects of social structure on the dyad. In the analysis that follows, some degree of interdependence between P and O is assumed so that P is always a member of O's network and vice versa, except where relationship initiation is discussed.

Because each network property conveys unique information and because the unit of analysis is the network of an individual (P or O), the social structure within which the P-O relationship develops can vary tremendously. To accommodate this variety, six ideal types of network structure are examined (see Figures 1-6), in which varying degrees of density, overlap, and clustering are represented. The types of structure depicted in the figures are ideal for several reasons. Despite the fact that network size is an important variable, it is held relatively constant in all cases, at 4 or 7 members. For purposes of illustration, the types are based on extreme values of network properties. Nevertheless, there is evidence that each structure exists in reality, although the real structures may not be as pure as those in the figures.

The analysis demonstrates that each structure has differential effects, depending upon the developmental stage of the P-O relationship. In addition, it becomes apparent that some structures have more important ramifications for the network itself than for the target dyad.

Case 1. In the first kind of structure (see Figure 1), the interdependence of one partner's network, as indicated by density, clustering, and distance, is high compared with the other's, and the overlap of their two networks is comparatively low. In Figure 1, the density of P's network is 100% but that of O's is 29%.[1] The overlap between their networks is 50% (3/6). Although P is directly connected to A, B, and C, the distance between P and D, E, and F is two links because P is connected to these persons only through O. Both P and O are enclosed in a fully-saturated clique; however, O maintains separate contact with D, E, and F, who are unconnected to P and to each other.

Studies of patterns of spousal networks indicate that similar configurations do, in fact, exist in reality. Both Bott (1971) and Jones (1980) found a pattern of what I will call "intermediate" network interdependence, in which partners maintained some separate and some shared connections and density was variable (*n* = 9 of 20 families in Bott's study and *n* = 11 of 24 in Jones's). It is easy to imagine situational factors that might bring about the pattern in question; for example, when one

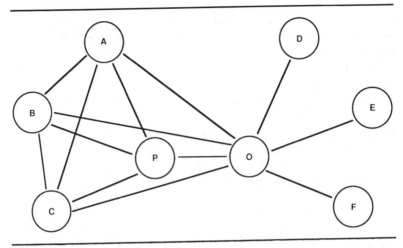

Figure 1.   Case 1

partner (O) moves to a new location, work situation, or school, maintains some old ties, but comes into contact with P's already established network.

Both Bott (1971) and Jones (1980) reported that networks of intermediate interdependence were associated with more flexibility in the P-O relationship than were more tight-knit structures, but not as much flexibility as more loose-knit networks. In the Bott study, the degree of segregation in conjugal roles was positively related to the degree of network interdependence. The division of labor between spouses in the intermediate pattern was less separate than for spouses who had more highly connected networks. Jones found that an intermediate network structure permitted spouses the supportive benefits of some shared, close associations as well as the freedom and individuation derived from the maintenance of some separate associations.[2]

Several predictions derive from the analysis of networks of intermediate interdependence. The configuration in Case 1 is likely to have a stabilizing effect on the P-O relationship and to enhance P-O interdependence. The structure of O's network is probably highly changeable, especially as the amount of interdependence between partners increases. Salzinger (1982) investigated the connections between clustering and friendship formation among college students, who provided retrospective information about changes in friends over a 3-month span of time. Members of clusters were less likely to gain and lose friends than were nonmembers; 58% of cluster members reported no changes in friendships whereas 90% of nonmembers reported some change. In addition to the findings that within-cluster relationships were more stable, the alterations that did occur in the friendships of cluster members generally involved making friends with people who were in the cluster to whom they had not been previously tied and dropping off those people who were not cluster members. Similarly, Hammer (1980) showed that the likelihood of a tie between two network members at Time 2 was a direct function of the *distance* between them and the number of connections they shared in common (i.e., overlap) at Time 1.

The available data support what is becoming a general proposition in social network analysis: Networks of *moderate* interdependence become more so over time, and serve to bolster the stability of dyads within them (see Hammer, 1980; Hammer & Schaffer, 1975; Milardo, 1986; Salzinger, 1982). Predictions for Case 1 follow directly from this proposition. The embedment of the P-O dyad in a dense clique is apt to enhance the stability of their relationship; however, O's relationships with D, E, and F presumably will deteriorate or become incorporated into the existing cluster. Hence the density, clustering, reachability, and overlap of O's network are likely to increase.

These changes will be mediated by the strength of the interdependence between any two dyads in either network. Granovetter (1973, 1983) theorized that the amount of overlap in the networks of any two persons is a function of the strength of the tie between them. When the tie between P and O is weak, overlap will be low; the converse is true for strong P-O connections. Tests of Granovetter's hypothesis supported the prediction. Transivity, or triadic closure, was much more likely for strong ties than for weak, which tended toward intransitivity (Friedkin, 1980; Weimann, 1983). Hammer (1980) found that stronger ties between two persons were associated with more dramatic increases in network interdependence over time. With regard to dating partners, in particular, the amount of overlap in their separate networks increases as partners become more involved (Milardo, 1982).

In view of its focus on the links between network properties and the strength of dyadic ties, Granovetter's (1973, 1983) work and its supporting data have implications for the study of developmental change in dyads. The effects of the structure in Case 1 on relationship initiation can be examined by assuming that no tie exists between P and O but that all other ties remain the same. The resulting structure would undoubtedly be conducive to the formation of an association between P

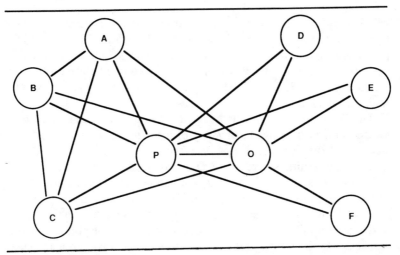

Figure 2.   Case 2

and O. Because of the tendency for nonexistent ties within cliques to be formed and because of O's ties with other members of P's cluster, P and O have a strong likelihood of meeting in the first place. The loose-knit character of O's network probably means that the ties to D, E, and F are relatively weak. Consequently, the P-O relation is apt to thrive within a social environment optimal for relationship formation and maintenance: a ready source of strong social embedment, on the one hand, and freedom of movement with low probability of opposition, on the other.

Case 2. Figure 2 illustrates a situation in which P has contact with O's associates, O has contact with P's, and some of their associates know each other, but others do not. In terms of network properties, overlap is 100%, and, therefore, the density of each network is the same, 43%. Although this level of density is moderate, Friedkin (1981) showed that high network interdependence can be obtained with densities below 50%. This indeed is the situation in Case 2, where both P and O are in a completely interconnected cluster with A, B, and C. P and O also have ties to individuals who are not in the cluster and who are unconnected to one another (D, E, and F).

As in the previous case, this structure exhibits an intermediate degree of network interdependence (Bott, 1971; Jones, 1980). Even though Bott reported a high degree of variation on marital role segregation within the intermediate pattern, she described one identifiable subset of spouses who maintained shared networks that had factions, some of which were more closely interconnected with others. These spouses had tightly connected kin networks, similar to A, B, and C in Case 2, but joint friendships that tended to be dispersed, comparable to D, E, and F in Case 2. Jones (1980) also identified an intermediate pattern that resembles Case 2, where network members shared some ties and maintained some separate ties.

The structure in Case 2 is likely to have cohesive and stabilizing effects on the target dyad, for many of the same reasons as in Case 1. Because of their greater degree of overlap, however, the networks in Case 2 may facilitate increased P-O interdependence even more.

The social structure in Case 2, minus the tie between P and O, is probably even more conducive to their meeting than in the previous case. If O has ties to virtually everyone that P knows, but no tie to P, P and O are very likely to encounter one another at some point. In many respects, networks such as P and O with intermediate interdependence and high overlap are in a variation of what Murstein (1970) called a "closed field," in which individuals are "forced to interact by reason of the environmental setting in which they find themselves" (p. 466). Although Murstein referred to occupational or classroom settings as closed fields, moderately cohesive networks are also closed fields in that they provide conditions in which two persons are likely to come together, regardless of whether they would independently choose to do so. Different variables presumably influence relationship initiation and change in different degrees, depending upon the degree of openness in the field. Attributes of the individual and the dyad (e.g., readiness for a romantic involvement; physical attractiveness, attitudinal similarity; liking) may play a larger role in attraction in an open field. The degree of network interdependence probably is a good predictor of progress in a closed field. In this way, freedom of personal choice operates within social constraints.

The structure in Case 2 not only is likely to bring P and O together in the first place, but it is likely to foster an increasing amount of interdependence between them. With increased P-O interdependence, the structure of both P's and O's networks is likely to shift toward even greater density and clustering and shorter distances separating network members (e.g., D., E, and F). The absorption of nonmembers into an existing clique will be affected by the strength of ties among network members, as well as by ceiling effects on the number of persons with whom it is possible to maintain contact (Friedkin, 1981).

Case 3. The network structure most apt to have binding and

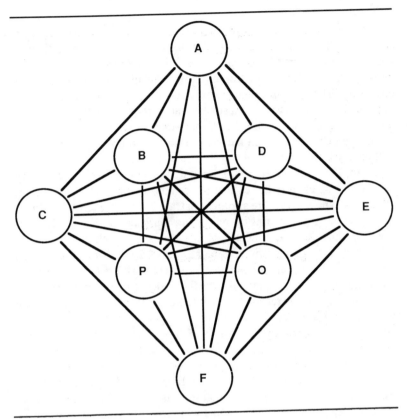

Figure 3.   Case 3

stabilizing effects on P and O is shown in Figure 3. In this pattern the P-O relationship is embedded in one large clique. The overlap of P's network with O's, and vice versa, is 100%, and the densities of their networks are equally high at 100%. Every member of P's network and O's is directly connected to one another.

This kind of structure may be an exaggeration of what might be found in real populations because individuals undoubtedly interact at times with people independently of their mates. However, if the definition of interactant is constrained to include only those with whom one spends large amounts of time or has frequent contact, this structure may be quite common. Jones (1980) identified a structure similar to this one in her study of newcomers. Eight out of 24 couples had networks in which spouses had completely shared ties and one or more common clusters, although not all of their joint ties were in a cluster, as in Case 3. Jones concluded that this structure inhibits change for both the individuals and couples within it. Individuals in these networks often interacted in groups, and engaged only in shared activities so that dyadic relationships tended to remain superficial. Although relationships were not always individually satisfying, they were a source of couple unity.

Highly dense individual networks that are completely overlapping will enhance the stability of the P-O relationship (see Hammer, 1980; Milardo, 1986; Salzinger, 1982). Because the condition of high overlap typically evolves over the course of romantic relationships (Milardo, 1982), the type of structure apparent in Case 3 is more likely to be found during later stages of dating or during marriage than initially. It is possible, however, to conceive of situations in which a relationship might begin with a very tight web of external associations that form a completely closed field, as in the case where partners have neighbors, friends, and family who are all actively involved with one another.

Regarding structural change within the network itself, networks that are fully saturated, as in Case 3, can be expected to remain in a stable state. As described above, networks with intermediate interdependence will move toward full saturation. Once the latter state is in place, changes in the network probably will be prompted by alterations in causal conditions internal to its members, their dyadic relations, or external to the network. For example, a tightly woven network of couple friends and of kin relations would be disrupted by the illness, death, or residential move of any of its constituents (see Fehr & Perlman, 1985) or by any sort of economic misfortune (e.g., the closure of a local factory) or natural disaster (e.g., Erikson, 1976). One common source of network change is the termination of pair relationships. Rands (this volume) found that the size and interdependence of people's networks declined after divorce.

Case 4. Comparing Figure 4 with Figure 3 highlights the importance of treating the "individual" as the unit of analysis and of using the property of overlap to describe the amount of consolidation between two networks, rather than use of the "couple" as the unit of analysis. Although both Cases 3 and 4 have been described as close knit (Bott, 1971), their impact on the target dyad is quite different due to differences in overlap. The structural interdependence of P's and O's networks is high in both Cases 3 and 4, with low distance, evidence of clustering, and

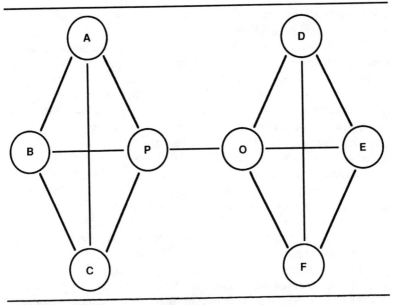

Figure 4.   Case 4

density at 100% for both networks in Case 3 and at 50% for both in Case 4. Yet overlap is 100% in Case 3 and 0% in Case 4.

Bott (1971) identified one family, the N's, who exhibited this pattern. Because Bott used the couple as the unit of analysis, the N's were categorized as having highly connected networks; nonetheless, Bott noted that "there was considerable segregation between Mr. and Mrs. N in their external relationships. In effect, Mrs. N had her network and Mr. N had his" (p. 70).

Just as the embedment of a dyad in a tight web of relationships promotes stability, the enclosure of members of a couple in separate cliques will interfere with it (Hammer, 1980; Milardo, 1986; Salzinger, 1982). Hammer found that within a network of church members, over 80% of the members who had conversational ties in common at Time 1 still had a direct connection one month later, but almost none of the members who lacked common ties at Time 1 were directly connected later. Furthermore, a lower number of common connections was associated with a much greater likelihood of completely severing ties a month hence. High levels of network interdependence in conjunction with low overlap also are likely to interfere with dyadic interdependence, as demonstrated by Bott's (1971) findings for the N's, who had a highly segregated division of labor.

The predictions just described will be mediated by the impact of other network influences. Jones's (1980) data on newcomers showed that, in cases where spouses were involved in clusters, the various clusters had divergent patterns of overlap. In some cases, the cluster to which one spouse belonged included the other spouse in activities while in other cases, the spouse was excluded. Jones concluded that the norms of existing clusters operated to influence the degree of overlap. In this way, expectations held by members of nonoverlapping networks, as well as the interactive pattern, will influence the character of the target dyad.

With regard to relationship initiation, if there were no tie between P and O to begin with, the pattern in Case 4 would work against the formation of an association due to the insulating effects of cluster membership. Salzinger (1982) found that the associates of cluster members were limited to bounded sets; 71% of the participants whose friendships were not limited to one cluster gained friends, but only 29% of cluster members gained friends over the study period. If, by chance, P and O do come in contact with one another, the growth of interdependence between them undoubtedly will be hampered by the structure of their networks. Preliminary support for the hypothesis comes from the work on the courtship types (Surra, 1985), which showed that partners who were more active with network members separate from their partners had low levels of dyadic interdependence.

There are several reasons why the structure in Case 4 might interfere with the development of dyadic interdependence. For one thing, networks of this sort are likely to resist any change in group membership. P's spending more time with O will mean less time with A, B, and C, thereby threatening group solidarity. Members of each network are likely to resist other changes that typically accompany increases in dyadic interdependence, such as the addition of P or O as new members and increased overlap.

For the sake of completeness, it should be noted that the structure in Case 4 does have benefits for network members. Granovetter's (1973, 1983) hypothesis on the strength of weak ties proposes that weak ties— presumably ties like the one between P and O—act as bridges between members of separate small groups more often than strong ties, which tend toward closure. Research has verified the hypothesis that bridges are more often composed of weak ties than strong, and has shown that weak ties are more often involved in the transmission of the information

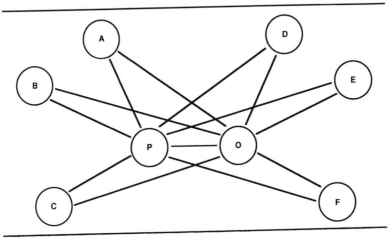

Figure 5.   Case 5

across subgroups (Friedkin, 1980; Weimann, 1983). Strong ties, in contrast, are more important in transmitting information within groups and in influencing group members (Weimann, 1983). The configuration in Case 4, then, may be especially efficient for keeping members of separate networks informed about each other's opinions and activities and for integrating subgroups within a larger collectivity.

Case 5 and Case 6. The last two patterns to be considered are less highly structured than the previous ones (see Figures 5 and 6). In Case 6, in particular, all indicators of network cohesion are low: density is 0% for both networks; overlap is 0%; there are no cliques in either network; and all network members, with the exception of P or O, are connected to each other through a distance of two steps. In Case 5, the networks are also loose knit, but because P and O know all of the same persons, overlap is high (100%), and density is somewhat higher than in Case 6, at 29% for P's network and O's. The members of each network do not know each other, however, except for P and O, who together form triads with every other member.

Both of these patterns have been identified in studies of network structure among married pairs. Bott (1971) found that 20% of the couples in the sample fit a pattern like that in Case 5. Typically these were couples whose relatives did not live nearby, who maintained joint friendships, but whose friends did not know one another or the spouses' kin. This case also might be found where spouses have single friends in common; for example, when many of the partners' friends are divorcing

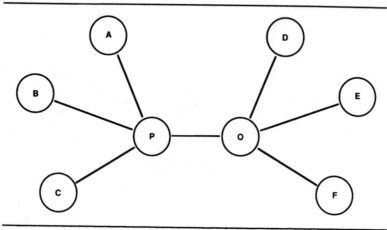

Figure 6.   Case 6

or when partners marry during high school. Regarding Case 6, Bott detected a pattern of "desocialized families," who were described as "transitional" (pp. 89-92), having moved from areas in which they had highly connected networks to one in which they had small, very loose networks. Jones (1980) also identified a pattern that was especially common among women who did not work outside the home, in which spouses had no common clusters or shared ties, although, unlike Case 6, one or both spouses sometimes had independent cluster memberships.

Although these two cases have similar low levels of structural interdependence, they will have variant effects on the target dyad because of the differences in overlap between the two. Generally speaking, the situation in Case 5 will reinforce the interdependence of the P-O relationship much more than that in Case 6, and the latter structure may have divisive effects on the dyad. In both cases, the structure of the networks is likely to change with changes in dyadic interdependence.

These observations are more easily understood when one considers how such structures might affect the target dyad over time. Both of these patterns are likely to enhance the probability of meeting others and making new friends. Individuals who are not members of clusters know more people and know more people who are more distant members of the network (Salzinger, 1982). One way in which Case 5 differs from Case 6 is that, because P and O know the same people in Case 5, the likelihood of them meeting each other, as compared with others, should be greater than in Case 6. Both cases are more open fields than structures discussed previously so that attraction between P and O is apt to be heavily influenced by nonnetwork variables (e.g., physical attractiveness).

It is ironic that network situations conducive to meeting new people may not promote the maintenance of relationships with them. In Case 6, the network will either be pulled together over time by a growing interdependence between P and O, or it will act to pull them apart, depending on the strength of the dyadic ties throughout the network. If individual and dyadic factors strongly promote a growing attraction between P and O, the increasing strength of their tie can be expected to draw in other members of their separate networks so that the typical movement toward transivity and overlap will appear (see Friedkin, 1980; Granovetter, 1973, 1983; Milardo, 1982, 1986; Weimann, 1983). If, however, the tie between P and O is weak or slow to develop, alternate attractions, which are readily available with this structure, may intervene to draw them apart. The latter eventuality is especially likely if either P or O has strong ties with other members of their networks.

The hypothesis that the structure in Case 6 weakens the target dyad is supported by Jones's (1980) data showing that, while overlapping spousal networks promoted continuity in self-definition and in defining the self in terms of the spouse, unshared networks were associated with greater change in self-definition and greater independence from the spouse. Bott (1971) reported that couples with a structure like that in Case 6 were moving toward greater sharing of tasks, the relationship was in a state of flux, and spouses reported dissatisfaction with their social relationships.

The developmental scenario in Case 5, like that in Case 6, depends heavily on nonnetwork influences and on the degree of dyadic interdependence between network members, especially early in the P-O relationship. Moreover, strong interdependence between P and alternate members of the network (e.g., competing dating relationships) may actually interfere with the growth of P-O interdependence. Assuming, however, that the initial attraction between P and O deepens, their increased involvement should move their networks toward greater density and clustering, which, in turn, should promote increased dyadic interdependence, progress, and stability.

COMMENTS AND CONCLUSIONS

This chapter surveyed the influences of interactive networks on the development of interdependence in close relationships. A review of the literature on social networks and on dyadic relationships demonstrated the power that networks can exert over the dyads within them. Defining the interactive network allows one to quantify one feature of the social context of close relationships.

One way that interactive networks hold sway over dyads is by means of the interactive events that transpire between network members and dating partners. Another mode of influence is through the patterning of the relationships within the network as a group. These interactive events and group properties affect any dyad within the network either directly, by shaping the content and character of dyadic interaction, or indirectly, by acting upon other forces that subsequently affect the dyad. In the latter case, networks play a part in determining such diverse causal conditions as the propinquity of the partners, their expectations for what is natural or proper in relationships, their feelings and beliefs about their partnership, and the availability of alternative associations.

In the process of discussing these topics, several themes kept reappearing. First, the influence of interactive networks is rooted in the structural bounds they place on individuals and dyads. This is only one type of network influence, however. At several points during the discussion, it became apparent that the impact of the interactive network is mediated by other psychological, subjective, and social factors that also have their origins in relations with network members. An example is seen in Case 4. Although analysis of the interactive network led to the prediction that the bond between P and O will weaken and eventually deteriorate entirely, the norms held by network members may intervene to support a parallel, but stable, relation between partners. Similarly, a distinction emerged between actual versus perceived support and interference.

More work is needed on the ideas that there are different kinds of networks with different constituencies and that each kind of network exerts unique influences. Although networks of interactants and of significant others have been distinguished on methodological grounds, it is time to explore the substantive implications of different networks.

Another theme that emerged was the interworking of multiple causes. The analysis of Cases 5 and 6 indicated, for example, that the nature of dyadic interdependence at some points in the development of a relationship may have stronger ramifications for the interdependence of the network itself than vice versa. The examination of various network structures underscored the notion that relationships develop as the result of a variety of causes that exert differential amounts of influence over the course of relationships.

One of the most promising features of social network analysis is its applicability to the study of the beginnings of relationships. Despite the assumption that relationship initiation usually occurs within open fields, most people probably meet friends and mates through their contacts with others in closed fields of networks of moderate interdependence. By quantifying the properties of the interactive network, it is possible to study such topics as the availability of alternative partners, the characteristics of pools of available partners, and the relationship between pools of availables and homogamy. Perhaps the single most important contribution of network analysis is that it allows one to formulate questions about the relative contribution of social structure and dyadic variables to relationship initiation and change.

Throughout the discussion, the close connection between theoretical and methodological concerns was reaffirmed. First, some procedures are more appropriate for studying interactive networks than others. Second, data should be gathered from third parties as well as members of dyads. Third, in order to study how interdependence in one dyad affects that in another, one must sample different kinds of network relationships. Studies of this sort would be informative about how interdependence between parents and children affects dating relationships or how alternative involvements affect dating and marital relationships. Fourth, adequate sampling across time and people is needed. With regard to the former, gathering data from several points in time is required to capture an adequate representation of developmental change in networks and dyads, especially because some network structures are unstable and difficult to sample. In the case of sampling from various populations, much of the power of interactive networks may be discernible only when investigators take their research off campus.

NOTES

1. In all cases, the density of P's network, or D_p, is calculated as:

$$D_p = \frac{100\,(Na)}{\frac{1}{2}\,N\,(N-1)}$$

where Na = number of actual ties, excluding those with P, and N = number of network members, excluding P. In Case 1:

$$D_p = \frac{100\,(6)}{\frac{1}{2}\,(4)(4-1)} = 100\%$$

P's network includes A, B, C, and O. The density of O's network, D_o, is figured as:

$$D_o = \frac{100\,(6)}{\frac{1}{2}\,(7)(7-1)} = 29\%$$

The members of O's network are A, B, C, D, E, F, and P.

2. It is difficult to compare Bott's (1971) intermediate pattern exactly to Case 1 because the level of analysis in that study was the couple rather than the individual. Likewise, the pattern identified by Jones (1980) that is closest to Case 1 was described as having some shared ties inside clusters, some shared ties outside clusters, and nonoverlapping ties maintained by at least one spouse. It appears that several of the structures discussed here were grouped to form the intermediate patterns in both investigations.

REFERENCES

Bateson, M. C. (1984). *With a daughter's eye: A memoir of Margaret Mead and Gregory Bateson.* New York: Morrow.

Bernard, J. (1964). The adjustments of married mates. In H. T. Christensen (Ed.), *Handbook of marriage and the family* (pp. 675-739). Chicago: Rand McNally.

Boissevain, J. (1974). *Friends of friends.* Oxford: Basil, Blackwell.

Bott, E. (1971). *Family and social network* (2nd ed.) New York: Free Press.

Davis-Brown, K., Salamon, S., & Surra, C. A. (1987). Economic and social factors in mate selection: An ethnographic analysis of an agricultural community. *Journal of Marriage and the Family, 49,* 41-55.

Driscoll, R., Davis, K. E., & Lipetz, M. E. (1972). Parental interference and romantic love: The Romeo and Juliet effect. *Journal of Personality and Social Psychology, 24,* 1-10.

Erikson, K. T. (1976). *Everything in its path: Destruction of community in the Buffalo Creek flood.* New York: Simon & Schuster.

Fehr, B., & Perlman, D. (1985). The family as a social network and support system. In L. L'Abate (Ed.), *Handbook of family psychology and therapy*: Vol. 1 (pp. 323-356) Homewood, IL: Dow-Jones Irwin.

Fischer, C. S., Jackson, R. M., Stueve, C. A., Gerson, K., Jones, L. M., & Baldassare, M. (1977). *Networks and places.* New York: Free Press.

Friedkin, N. (1980). A test of structural features of Granovetter's strength of weak ties theory. *Social Networks, 2,* 411-422.

Friedkin, N. (1981). The development of structure in random networks: An analysis of the effects of increasing density on five measures of structure. *Social Networks, 3,* 41-52.

Granovetter, M. (1973). The strength of weak ties. *American Journal of Sociology, 78,* 1360-1380.

Granovetter, M. (1983). The strength of weak ties: A network theory revisited. In R. Collins (Ed.), *Sociological theory* (pp. 201-233). San Francisco: Jossey-Bass.

Hammer, M. (1980). Predictability of social connections over time. *Social Networks, 2,* 165-180.

Hammer, M., & Schaffer, A. (1975). Interconnectedness and the duration of connections in small networks. *American Ethnologist, 2,* 297-308.

Hinde, R. A. (1979). *Towards understanding relationships.* London: Academic Press.

Huston, T. L. (1983). Power. In H. H. Kelley et al. (Eds.), *Close relationships* (pp. 169-219). New York: W. H. Freeman.

Huston, T. L., & Burgess, R. L. (1979). Social exchange in developing relationships: An overview. In R. L. Burgess & T. L. Huston (Eds.), *Social exchange in developing relationships* (pp. 3-28). New York: Academic Press.

Huston, T. L., & Robins, E. (1982). Conceptual and methodological issues in studying close relationships. *Journal of Marriage and the Family, 44,* 901-925.

Johnson, M. P., & Leslie, L. (1982). Couple involvement and network structure: A test of the dyadic withdrawal hypothesis. *Social Psychological Quarterly, 45,* 34-43.

Johnson, M. P., & Milardo, R. M. (1984). Network interference in pair relationships: A social psychological recasting of Slater's theory of social regression. *Journal of Marriage and the Family, 46,* 893-899.

Jones, W. L. (1980). Couple network patterns of newcomers in an Australian city. *Social Networks, 2,* 357-370.

Kelley, H. H., Berscheid, E., Christensen, A., Harvey, J., Huston, T., Levinger, G., McClintock, E., Peplau, L. A., & Peterson, D. (1983). *Close relationships.* New York: W. H. Freeman.

Kerckhoff, A. C. (1974). The social context of interpersonal attraction. In T. L. Huston (Ed.), *Foundations of interpersonal attraction* (pp. 61-78). New York: Academic Press.

Leslie, L. A., Johnson, M. P., & Huston, T. L. (1986). Parental reactions to dating relationships: Do they make a difference? *Journal of Marriage and the Family, 48,* 57-66.

Milardo, R. M. (1982). Friendship networks in developing relationships: Converging and diverging social environments. *Social Psychology Quarterly, 45,* 162-172.

Milardo, R. M. (1983). Social networks and pair relationships: A review of substantive and measurement issues. *Sociology and Social Research, 68,* 1-18.

Milardo, R. M. (1986). Personal choice and social constraint in close relationships: Applications of network analysis. In V. J. Derlega & B. A. Winstead (Eds.), *Friendship and social interaction* (pp. 145-166). New York: Springer-Verlag.

Milardo, R. M., Johnson, M. P., & Huston T. L. (1983). Developing close relationships: Changing patterns of interaction between pair members and social networks. *Journal of Personality and Social Psychology, 44,* 964-976.

Mitchell, J. C. (1969). The concept and use of social networks. In J. C. Mitchell (Ed.), *Social networks in urban situations* (pp. 1-50). Manchester, England: University Press.

Murstein, B. I. (1970). Stimulus-value-role: A theory of marital choice. *Journal of Marriage and the Family, 32,* 465-481.

Parks, M. R., & Adelman, M. B. (1983). Communication networks and the development of romantic relationships: An expansion of uncertainty reduction theory. *Human Communication Research, 10,* 55-79.

Parks, M. R., Stan, C. M., & Eggert, L. L. (1983). Romantic involvement and social network involvement. *Social Psychology Quarterly, 46,* 116-131.

Ridley, C. A., & Avery, A. W. (1979). Social network influence in the dyadic relationship. In R. L. Burgess & T. L. Huston (Eds.), *Social exchange in developing relationships* (pp. 223-246). New York: Academic Press.

Salzinger, L. L. (1982). The ties that bind: The effect of clustering on dyadic relationships. *Social Networks, 4,* 117-145.

Surra, C. A. (1980). Premarital origins of marital interaction: Toward a typology of premarital relationships, *Dissertation Abstracts International, 42,* 4183A. (University Microfilms No. 8105811).

Surra, C. A. (1985). Courtship types: Variations in interdependence between partners and social networks. *Journal of Personality and Social Psychology, 49,* 357-375.

Surra, C. A., & Huston T. L. (1987). Mate selection as a social transition. In D. Perlman & S. Duck (Eds.), *Intimate relationships: Development, dynamics, and deterioration* (pp. 88-120). Newbury Park, CA: Sage.

Sussman, M. B. (1953). Parental participation in mate selection and its effect upon family continuity. *Social Forces, 32,* 76-81.

Weimann, G. (1983). The strength of weak conversational ties in the flow of information and influence. *Social Networks, 5,* 245-267.

3

Social Networks and the Transition to Motherhood

Kathryn McCannell

The transition to motherhood is an event central to women's experience, setting in motion a complex process of change in both inner and outer worlds. Arrival of a first child leads to shifts in identity, in intimate relationships, and in roles and responsibilities. It is a passage that can be seen as foundational in the life cycle of many families. As such, it has been subject to scrutiny from psychoanalytic viewpoints (e.g. Benedek, 1960; Pines, 1972) as well as social science investigations of the degree of crisis experienced (Dyer, 1963; Hobbs, 1965, 1968; Hobbs and Cole, 1976; Jacoby, 1969; LeMasters, 1957; Miller and Sollie, 1980). Few researchers, however, have examined the interplay between this life cycle transition and social network dimensions. The purpose of this chapter is to systematically address this gap, by examining both the shifts in social relationships that occur during this passage and the role networks play in easing postpartum adjustment. The chapter is divided into three parts. First, the existing literature pertaining to social networks and the transition to motherhood is reviewed, with a critique on conceptual and methodological grounds. Next, a recent longitudinal research project investigating social networks and motherhood is described. The data are both descriptive and explanatory, adding insights to our understanding of the social processes surrounding this transition. Finally, therapeutic and preventive implications of a network understanding of motherhood are discussed.

OVERVIEW OF RESEARCH

Increasingly social scientists are acknowledging that the shape and character of family life are affected by social networks. Recent reviews document the role of the extended family as a support system (Fehr & Perlman, 1985), and the impact of network support on various life events (Blieszner, this volume; Gottlieb, 1980; Saulnier, 1982). The relationship between transitions and social networks is seen as reciprocal and interactive; the network can be conceptualized as either an independent variable, affecting the outcome of the transition, or as a dependent variable, subject to change due to movement through the family life cycle.

The Social Network as a Dependent Variable

What impact does arrival of a baby have on the mother's social world? As needs and circumstances change are size and composition of the network affected? Do relationships with family members change? These questions will be addressed through a review of existing studies.

Duvall (1967) believes transition to parenthood is a time when peers who no longer provide an appropriate reference group drop out of one's social circle. There is little empirical evidence to either support or refute this assertion for either men or women. In a study of friendships among Detroit men, Stueve & Gerson (1977) reported that frequency of contact dropped with arrival of children, although there was no decline in felt intimacy with best friends. They also found that family life brought social interaction into the home, as opposed to public places such as bars or restaurants. As the role shift required of new mothers tends to be more extreme in our society compared to that required of new fathers, arrival of the first child might be expected to exert greatest impact on the woman's network. With this in mind, Richardson & Kagan (1979) asked 40 first-time mothers to rate the direction of change (positive or negative) in various relationships since arrival of their baby. Quality of change ratings indicated an average shift in a negative direction for old friends and for husbands. The finding regarding husbands is consistent with a recent report by Belsky, Spanier & Rovine (1983) who conclude that there is a small but significant decline in self-reported marital adjustment across the transition to parenthood. They also note that a wife's marital adjustment appears to be more sensitive to the effects of a new baby, a finding in agreement with Waldron & Routh (1981),

Harriman (1983) and Miller & Sollie (1980). Thus, if the marriage is construed as constituting one sector, or "content" of a network, it appears that the transition to motherhood will modestly decrease adjustment in this area.

In the Richardson & Kagan study mentioned earlier, some women reported turbulent breaks with old network ties, some a gradual drifting apart, and some reported increased contact and greater closeness, particularly when old friends were also parents. This latter finding points to the importance of the availability of similar others, and suggests the value of social networks in providing for social comparisons. For example, in discussing the role of social support during pregnancy, Grossman and colleagues (1980) speculate that there is a unique kind of confirmation and helpful communication that can come only from other women who are currently pregnant or who have been through the experience. A similar assertion could be made for the value of having a close friend who is also a mother. Thus the "constituency" of a network can be seen as a relevant dimension in the provision of social support.

A more direct test of changes in network composition was investigated by Belsky & Rovine (1984), who interviewed 72 couples, 41 of whom were first-time parents, during the last trimester of pregnancy, and at three and nine months postpartum. Each couple was asked to rate their frequency of contact with their own parents, and to evaluate on 5-point scales the quantity of assistance they were receiving in regards to material support (money and household items), emotional support, and help with babysitting. Each spouse was asked individually to list up to eight significant others, and to provide information on the frequency of contact, nature of the relationship, and whether the network member had children under the age of five years. As expected, contact with parents of young children increased significantly over time. In addition, emotional support from family members was greater in the case of first-time parents than for couples bearing laterborns, and it was perceived as greatest at three months postpartum (compare Sussman & Burchinal, 1962).

With regard to relationships with extended kin, Belsky & Rovine found that overall family contact increased over time, noting that wives in their study reported more contact with relatives than husbands. Many couples report feeling closer to kin, and for some the onset of parenting presents an opportunity to rekindle family relationships (Richardson & Kagan, 1979).

Changes in provision of social support and in network composition may be moderated by a variety of variables. For example, Belsky & Rovine (1984) attempted to explore how proximity was related to contact with network members. Couples who lived in the same area as their parents tended to have more frequent contact than those living at a distance, but did not receive any more material or emotional support. Thus it appears that quantity of provisions is not dependent on physical proximity. While frequency of contact with the grandparents may be greater for those who live nearby, the value of aid received from afar is still significant. The increased contact afforded by proximity may also increase potential for network interference and resultant conflict, a possibility not examined by the investigators.

The Belsky & Rovine study is noteworthy in its use of a dual developmental focus upon both individual and group change. The authors correlated each network measure with itself across the three units of measurement to assess the stability of network measures. This approach revealed that across periods of six months, couples who tended to have frequent contact with family and friends before the birth of their child tended to continue their high level of contact even after the child's birth. Belsky et al. suggest that a "pattern of constancy in the face of change characterizes the development of social network contact across the transition to parenthood" (1983, p. 461).

The review of research relating to network shifts accompanying the transition to motherhood provides a tentative picture of the changes that occur. It appears that contact with parents increases, and that ties to friends who are also parents become more salient. The available portrait is certainly sketchy, and numerous questions remain unaddressed. Information is unavailable on the temporal shifts that occur in network size, although such changes tend to occur with other major life transitions such as divorce (Wilcox, 1981) and engagement (Milardo, 1982). Regardless of changes in overall size, it may be that some sectors within the network decrease (e.g., nonparents) while others increase (e.g., parents).

Very little is known about moderators of network shifts. For example, how do work status or one's feelings regarding employment affect network changes? Pistrang (1984) notes that paid employment has psychological significance for many mothers of infants, and found that when work status was congruent with interest in working the experience of motherhood was more positive. She argues that a woman's "work involvement" must be considered as an individual difference variable in future research on new motherhood.

Issues relating to measurement strategies are central to further investigation of the transition to motherhood. For example, in the Belsky et al. study cited earlier, use of a couple's rating of quantity of support serves to mask any differences in the mother's and father's perceptions of support. This is an important shortcoming, as there is reason to expect that both women's experience of parenthood and their involvement in networks differ from that of men. Huston, Surra, Fitzgerald, and Cate (1981), in studying courtship development, found that changes in activities with the network that accompany the transition to marriage are more severe for women than men. They conclude that women may adjust associations with the network to a greater extent than men as they move toward marriage. Steffensmeier (1982) states that there is "clear and overwhelming empirical evidence that a statistically significant difference exists in the degree of transition (to parenthood) difficulty experienced by males and females" (p. 322), with women experiencing greater difficulty. Thus, future investigations need to examine network processes for new mothers and fathers separately. Such inquiry may reveal that the sex difference in difficulty experienced is partially related to differences in network change experienced by men and women as they become parents.

Investigators interested in refining our knowledge of network shifts are confronted with a variety of measurement strategies. Milardo (1983; this volume) discusses the relative advantages and limitations of the various methods of identifying networks currently available, concluding that the degree of overlap between networks generated by divergent methods is open to question. He recommends researchers select a methodology after clearly identifying the network constituency of interest. Problematic measurement issues relating to study of networks and the transition to motherhood will be highlighted in the next section, where research relating to the impact of network variables on postpartum adjustment is reviewed.

The Social Network as an Independent Variable

With regard to the general issue of network support during life transitions, Mueller (1980) has proposed that the stressfulness of various life events could best be measured by examining the degree of disruption caused in network relationships. Gottlieb (1980) has suggested that social support is particularly important during passages that require a reorientation to or rearrangement of the social network. He cites first-time parenthood, college entrance, and divorce as examples of life transitions requiring such a reorientation. Carveth & Gottlieb (1979) investigated the relationship between three measures of social support and objective and subjective indices of stress by distributing questionnaires to 99 mothers eight weeks following delivery. Results indicated low to moderate positive correlations between measures of support and the existence of stress. Carveth & Gottlieb interpret this seemingly unexpected finding as reflecting increased use of social supports as stresses mount, and state that longitudinal measures would be necessary to determine if prior use of support related to a decrease in later indices of stress.

Several limitations in this study are worth noting. First because of missing data, all "social support" analyses were based upon a core of only five network members for whom all respondents provided valid responses. Second, the operationalization of support included amount of contact, a rating of the importance of the relationship, and a rating of the frequency of problem-centered discussions with each of the network members. Aspects of social support dealing with concrete assistance (e.g., help with babysitting, household tasks), reinforcement-related activities (e.g., socializing) or satisfaction with one's network were not included. As well, because approximately one-half of the mothers had more than one child, this study does not deal with the relationship between network support and stress unique to first-time mothers.

Several authors have utilized a longitudinal approach in investigating social support and various dimensions of the early motherhood experience. Crockenberg (1981) measured infant irritability and maternal social support at three months, and rated security of infant-mother attachment at one year. She found that the best predictor of secure attachment was social support, and that it was particularly important for mothers with irritable babies. Cutrona (1981) studied 85 first-time mothers from the third trimester of pregnancy to the second month after childbirth. While the primary purpose of her research was to test the reformulated learned helplessness model of depression in the context of postpartum adjustment, she also examined "non-cognitive vulnerability factors," including inadequate social support, stressful life events, hormonal sensitivity, and psychiatric history. Results indicated that social and environmental factors were the best predictors of postpartum depression, more so than attributional style. More specifically, it was found that perceived inadequacy of social support was a strong predictor of depression at every time point.

Crnic, Greenberg, Robinson, & Ragozin (1984) examined the impact of stress (life events) and social support on high-risk and normal mother-infant pairs across an 18-month period, beginning at birth. The mothers were asked four questions regarding availability of and satisfaction with support from intimate relationships (spouse/partner), and two questions regarding neighborhood or community support. Both stress and support were significant predictors of maternal attitudes and the quality of interaction with infants. Mothers' perceived satisfaction with intimate and community support related positively to life satisfaction, satisfaction with parenting, and the quality of behavioral interactions with infants. These results were strongest when the variables were measured concurrently; the long-term predictability of the support and stress measures was generally low. The authors assessed the stability of the stress and support measures by calculating Pearson correlations of each measure with its counterpart at each measurement interval. The variables showed only moderate stability, as one might expect if indeed transitions do exert change in support systems.

In the above study, intimate social support was the most stable variable across the 18-month time span of the study. Intimate support also showed the most positive relationship with both attitudinal and behavioral measures at all measurement points. This finding supports the notion that spousal support plays a very important role in the postpartum period, a premise with substantial empirical backing. Investigators have consistently found a significant correlation between a high level of marital adjustment and experiencing a lesser degree of difficulty in the transition to parenthood (Cowan and Cowan, 1983; Dyer, 1963; Hobbs, 1968; Hobbs & Cole, 1976; Russell, 1974). Grossman and colleagues (1980) found that the quality of the marriage was one of the strongest predictors of women's psychological adaptation to pregnancy and parenthood, although it predicted maternal adaptation (relationship with the child) only slightly.

The majority of the studies cited above were not designed to study social network variables. Rather, they tend to address the overall value of social support during the transition to motherhood. Thus basic structural network concepts that may determine level of support, such as size, density, or the presence of multiplex ties, have not been examined. It is generally assumed that network size is positively related to mental health, as several studies have found small networks among those experiencing problems in living (Erickson, 1975; Pattison, Defrancisco, Wood, Frazier & Crowder, 1975), and it appears to be an important factor in determining the availability of social support (McCannell Saulnier & Rowland, 1985).

While size is clearly an important structural dimension of networks, recent research suggests subjective, or qualitative, dimensions may be equally if not more important. In a study of the psychological adjustment of 86 pregnant adolescents, Barrera (1981) found that total network size was not significantly related to any of the measures of symptomatology. Rather, satisfaction with support and the need for support proved to be the strongest predictors of symptomatology. The relevance of satisfaction with one's network support was also documented by Colletta (1979), who found both amount of support received and satisfaction with this assistance had an impact on the child-rearing practices of 72 single-parent mothers. Divorced mothers who were unsatisfied with the amount of support they received tended to interact with their children in a harsher, more authoritarian manner than those who were more satisfied (compare Crnic et al, 1984; Cutrona, 1981).

There appears to be confusion between the concepts of "social support" and "social network," with some authors using the terms interchangeably. As Fehr and Perlman (1985) note, it is important that the concepts be kept distinct, with "network" referring to a set of people and "support" to the provisions supplied. Networks can serve a variety of different purposes and meet important needs. However, their deleterious consequences must not be overlooked. The negative impact of networks lies in their potential to undermine self-esteem, to reinforce problem behavior, and to restrict access to new opportunities. Milardo (1983) observes that measurement strategies that ask for a list of significant others typically omit individuals with whom interaction is negative. As well, it may be that a single network member is the source of both rewarding and negative interchange. Such was the case in an investigation of the networks of families with a child at risk of out-of-home placement (McCannell Saulnier & Rowland, 1985). Mothers reported network members who were perceived as "blocking change," having a negative influence, or creating discomfort.

The foregoing review has identified some of the methodological problems and conceptual issues in the current literature on social networks and the transition to motherhood. It is apparent that a multifaceted conceptualization of social network variables is necessary, one that includes both quantitative and qualitative measures. The importance of longitudinal designs in unravelling the interrelationship of networks and transitions is evident; only then will it be possible to assess phases within a passage and their dynamic interplay with interpersonal systems. In the next section results of a recent research project, which attempted to answer some of the questions outlined above, are presented.

A LONGITUDINAL ANALYSIS OF SOCIAL NETWORKS AND THE TRANSITION TO MOTHERHOOD

The purpose of the investigation described below was to study both process and outcome—what actually happens to the social network during the transition to motherhood, and what impact do network variables have on the degree of difficulty experienced by first-time mothers? The network variables examined in relation to difficulty were size, constituency of the network, satisfaction with help received, degree of disruption experienced in social ties, and quantity of infant care provided by the spouse. Changes in overall network size over time and in the "professional" sector were assessed. Perceptions of network members' attitudes regarding maternal employment were also examined. The data reported here are part of a larger investigation of various dimensions of the transition to motherhood (McCannell Saulnier, 1984).

METHOD

Participants were selected on a volunteer basis from prepared childbirth groups in a central Canadian city. Instructors were asked to provide names of couples who had signed up for "early-bird" sessions and were less than five months pregnant. Only primiparous women, married or living with a mate, were contacted. A letter was sent describing the study, then a follow-up phone call was placed to determine if the woman wished to be interviewed. Interviews took place in participants' homes. The response rate was very high, with over 90% of those contacted agreeing to participate. Fifty-five pregnant women were interviewed, 45 mothers recontacted two months after birth, and 39 of these women followed up one year later. Attrition was due to 13 moves, 2 refusals to continue, and 1 stillbirth. All results refer to the group of 39 women who were present at all measurement times. The mean age of the mothers was 25.2 years, with a range from 20 to 31 years. With regard to joint income, approximately 60% of the sample earned more than $25,000 per year. Three-quarters of the women in the sample indicated that their pregnancy was planned.

The three interview times were chosen to provide information on supports and adjustments at key points in this life transition. By the fifth month of pregnancy the fetus is a moving, tangible reality. The two-month postpartum contact point was chosen to gain information at a time when the demands of the new role would be very salient, and the fourteen-month follow up was chosen to provide a picture of network shifts and adjustments after some degree of equilibrium had been established.

Social Network Assessment

Using the technique developed by McCallister & Fischer (1978), each respondent's "core" network—the network that is felt to most influence attitudes, behavior and well-being—was tapped. This approach defines the core network as the set of people who are most likely to be the sources of a variety of rewarding interactions with the respondent, such as discussing a personal problem, loaning money, or socializing. The method is based on exchange theory (Thibaut & Kelley, 1959) and implies that people who are sources of rewarding interactions will be particularly important in shaping attitudes and behavior. A master list of names was drawn up based on a set of five name-eliciting questions (e.g., "With whom do you engage in social activities?"), and the respondent was then asked to add any people who were important to her but whose names had not appeared in response to the name-eliciting questions. The women were asked if each member of their networks was a friend, relative, or other role relation (such as minister), whether he or she had children, and how many lived within a 10-minute drive. Questions regarding the number of close women friends who were also mothers, the number of network members who were recent additions, the frequency of contact with network members, and the existence of a "professional" network (doctor, lawyer, insurance agent, banker, minister, dentist) were also included. Satisfaction with help received from network members and disruption in network relationships since arrival of the baby were assessed on 7-point scales. Each woman was asked to rate on a four-point scale ranging from "most favorable" to "most unfavorable" what she perceived the attitude of her husband, parents and in-laws to be toward her working while her child was a preschooler. Questions relating to quantity of child care provided by the spouse were also administered. The network questions were administered at all three times of measurement.

Assessment of Difficulty in the Transition to Motherhood

A modified version of the Hobbs' Difficulty Checklist (1965) was presented, which asks respondents to indicate the degree to which they have been "bothered"—not at all, somewhat or very much—by a variety of difficulties other new parents have experienced. The items tap potential problem areas such as finances and sexuality as well as emotions, for instance, feeling "edgy" or disturbed about feelings toward the baby. The scale measures reactions to events, rather than the frequency of these events. Five items designed to tap the personal crisis aspects of new parenthood were added for the present research, such as feeling tied down or burdened, concerned about slipping behind in a career, and feeling "out of touch" with old friends. Cronbach alpha for the 27-item checklist was found to be .76 at Time 2 and .57 at Time 3. The correlation between scores on the checklist and a subjective question asking the women to rate the overall degree of difficulty they had experienced was .40, $p < .05$, at both interview times, suggesting that the scale has a moderate degree of validity.

RESULTS AND DISCUSSION

Network Size

In order to explore the changes in network dimensions that occurred during pregnancy and the first year of motherhood, several repeated measures analyses of variance were performed, with no between-subject factors, and with time serving as the sole within subject factor. Total size of network, the number of kin members, the number of network members with children, the proportion of network members with children, and the size of professional network were used as dependent variables.

With regard to total network size, significant changes were found over time ($F(2, 74) = 5.63, p < .005$). The mean network size decreased from 16.6 (s.d. = 6.5) during pregnancy, to 14.6 (s.d = 5.7) shortly after birth, to 13.5 (s.d. = 4.8) at the one year follow up.

With regard to the number of kin within the network, results also indicated a significant decrease over time ($F(2, 74) = 12.1, p < .001$). During pregnancy the women's networks had an average of 8.5 kin (s.d. = 4.8), at the two-months postpartum interview the mean number was 6.9 (s.d. = 3.3), and one year later an average number of 5.0 (s.d. = 3.7) kin were reported.

The majority of the women in the sample (58% at Time 2; 53% at Time 3) felt that frequency of contact with their kin had increased since arrival of the baby. This means that although fewer kin were included in the network, as noted previously, those who remained were seen more frequently. This trend was not as marked with regard to contact with in-laws; at Time 2, 51% reported an increase and at Time 3, 48% reported an increase. A small percentage of women at both times reported a decrease in contact with kin and in-laws following the birth of their child (own kin, 4% and 7% at Times 2 and 3; in-laws, 2% and 8%). With regard to contact with friends, at Time 1 26% of the sample reported an increase, 33% a decrease, and 41% perceived contact to have remained the same. The corresponding figures at Time 3 were as follows: increase in contact (31%); decrease in contact (31%); remained the same (38%).

The repeated measures analysis of variance for number of network members with children showed no significant changes over time. However, the means were increasing in the expected direction; the pregnant women reported an average of 3.8 network members with children, (s.d. = 2.7), this increased to a mean of 4 members (s.d. = 2.4) shortly after birth, and further increased to an average of 4.7 members (s.d. = 2.3) at the one-year follow-up. As well, the proportion of other parenting adults within the network (ratio of parents to total network size) significantly increased over time, from 24% at Time 1 to 28% after birth to 36% at Time 3 ($F(2, 72) = 11.70, p < .001$).

The number of professionals in the network also increased over time, at least marginally, ($F(2, 76) = 3.30, p < .04$), with mothers of one-year-olds reporting larger professional networks than during pregnancy.

Very little data is available to describe the characteristics and functions of ties within an individual's system of social relationships. Thus several descriptive parameters found in this investigation will be presented. The number of network members who provided specific supports is noted in Table 1.

The finding that network size does, as predicted, decrease over the span of this life transition provides empirical support for a phenomenon about which family theorists have previously speculated. The fact that network size decreased by an average of three members, did not, however, result in smaller sectors of people providing various functions. This is noteworthy in that it implies that the remaining network members were "used" more extensively by the new mothers. This suggests that network members may have experienced more demands,

TABLE 1
Network Characteristics: Mean Number of Members
Providing Various Functions

	Time 1	Time 2	Time 3
Total network size*	16.6	14.6	13.5
$\overline{X}$ providing each function:			
Help with household tasks	1.6	1.8	1.5
Socializing	10.2	8.8	11.0
Discuss personal worries	4.8	3.8	4.6
Advice in important decisions	1.6	1.6	2.3
Could lend money	3.3	3.3	3.7

*NOTE: These figures do not include spouse.

and the possibility for overload and tensions in relations may increase.

The increase over time found in the proportion of network members with children suggests that the shifts in commitments and priorities brought about by becoming a mother were mirrored in the composition of her social circle. The finding that contact with kin tends to increase was replicated. It is interesting to note, however, that for a small proportion of women in the sample, kin contact decreased. This suggests that for some, arrival of a child triggers conflicts with the family of origin, leading to distance and perhaps alienation from the older generation.

Employment Status and Network Attitudes

With the sample divided into two groups—those who were in the home full-time, and those who were employed outside the home—comparisons were made on an "attitudes to work" scale. This consisted of a composite of three items rating the attitude of husband, family, and in-laws toward maternal employment while the child was a preschooler. Overall, women in the home perceived the attitudes of important others in their network to be significantly less favorable toward employment than women who were working outside the home.

This finding suggests the importance of perceived attitudes toward maternal employment, and illustrates the power of our networks in shaping beliefs and actions. It may also reflect the power of individuals to shape the beliefs of network members. Either way, given that guilt over engaging in employment outside the home is experienced by some new mothers, it seems clear that this could be exacerbated or alleviated by the attitudes of significant others in the network.

Relationship of Network Variables to Difficulty

In examining the impact of various network dimensions on difficulty experienced in adjusting to motherhood, a stepwise multiple regression approach was used. This approach is designed to yield the maximum $R2$ with the minimum number of independent variables for the sample at hand (Cohen & Cohen, 1975). Times 1, 2, and 3 refer to measurement occasions during pregnancy, shortly after birth, and approximately one year following birth.

Several factors that qualify interpretation must be noted; for example, the size of the sample places limits on the generalizability of the findings, particularly with regard to the multiple regression analyses. The subject-to-variable ratio in the initial multiple regression was approximately seven subjects per variable. A ratio of 10 subjects per variable would be more acceptable. As Cohen and Cohen (1975) note, the smaller the sample size, and the more independent variables used, the more opportunity for the sample $R2$ to be larger than the true population $R2$. Two steps were taken to minimize this danger. First, the adjusted, or "shrunken" $R2$ (Cohen & Cohen, 1975, p. 106) which is smaller than the sample $R2$ but is thought to provide a more realistic estimate, was reported. Second, histograms were examined to ensure there were no bimodal distributions or extreme outliers.

The type of sample employed also places limits on the findings. Whether or not the results are generalizable to other populations—for example, those from different socioeconomic backgrounds, teen mothers, or women who do not have the support of a trained partner during childbirth—remains a question to be answered by future research. Inclusion of a control group of married childless women would help to rule out the possibility that the network changes observed were unconnected to childbearing. With these caveats in mind, the results of the research will be presented and theoretical consequences discussed.

Predicting Time-2 difficulty from Time-2 network variables. Stepwise multiple regression was performed using network variables at Time 2 as predictors of Time-2 difficulty. Size of network, content of network, satisfaction with network, help received from husband, and degree of disruption felt in network relationships were entered as predictors. Content of network was examined by entering total number of network members who were also parents, and the number of close female friends with whom the subject discussed child-rearing concerns. The satisfaction variable consisted of a composite of four items referring to satisfaction with help received from family, in-laws, friends and husband. The "help-from-husband" variable consisted of a composite of three items regarding husband's involvement in diaper changing, bathing the baby, and time spent as primary caretaker.

Results indicated a significant overall multiple r of .54, $p < .01$. Of the six variables entered, three were chosen and together accounted for approximately one-third of the variance in difficulty scores at Time 2. The degree of disruption experienced in social relationships entered first, accounting for 14% of the variance. The number of other parents in one's network added an increase of 9% to the equation, and satisfaction with help received from network members added a further 7% of explained variance. The amount of help received from husband, the number of female friends, and total size of network did not enter the equation, as they did not result in a significant increase in R2. In order to examine the impact of the quality of marital adjustment on difficulty experienced, scores on the Spanier Dyadic Adjustment Scale (Spanier, 1976) were added to the regression equation. With marital adjustment included, the multiple r increased to .61, $p < .01$. The marital relationship can be considered to constitute a "content" within one's network. Thus when the above-mentioned network variables are entered into a multiple regression equation on difficulty scores, nearly 40% of the variance is accounted for. Shortly after arrival of a child, mothers who experienced difficulty tended to report disrupted network ties, few other parents in their network, dissatisfaction with help received from network members, and poorer quality of marital adjustment.

Predicting Time-3 difficulty from Time-3 network variables. Stepwise multiple regression paralleling that done to examine Time-2 relationships was done using Time-3 variables. At this period as well, a large proportion of the variance can be accounted for given knowledge of particular network dimensions (multiple $r = .57$, $p < .025$). While the overall pattern is similar to that found at Time 2 (content, satisfaction, and disruption variables entered), there are several noteworthy differences. Satisfaction with one's network is entered into the equation first, accounting for 50% of the explained variance. Women who were dissatisfied with the amount of help they were receiving from network sources tended to report high difficulty scores. A second difference is the inclusion of the number of female friends, as opposed to total number of parents. An unexpected finding was the existence of a positive coefficient for this relationship, suggesting that women with more

TABLE 2
Zero-order Correlations for Social Network and
Difficulty Scale Measures, Time 2, (N = 39)

	2	3	4	5	6	7	8
1. Total network size	.47*	−.11	−.19	−.00	−.02	.01	−.30*
2. Members with children		.09	−.18	−.09	−.21	.07	−.37*
3. Female friends			−.13	.07	−.29	.03	−.20
4. Disruption				−.19	.00	.10	.05	.36*
5. Help from husband					−.11	−.09	−.12
6. Satisfaction with network						.15	.33*
7. Marital adjustment							.32*
8. Difficulty scale							

*$p < .05$.

TABLE 3
Zero-order Correlations for Social Network and
Difficulty Scale Measures, Time 3, (N = 39)

	2	3	4	5	6	7	8
1. Total network size	.50*	.36*	−.21	−.14	.20	−.14	.21
2. Members with children		.61*	−.21	−.33*	−.09	−.05	.10
3. Female friends			−.19	−.23	−.18	−.02	.13
4. Disruption				.36*	.22	.23	.36*
5. Help from husband					.23	.04	.11
6. Satisfaction with network						.55*	.42*
7. Marital adjustment							.26
8. Difficulty scale							

*$p < .05$.

female friends with whom they discussed child-rearing concerns tended to report higher difficulty scores. At neither Time 2 or 3 did variables relating to actual quantity of help received from husband, or total network size enter into the question.

To examine the impact of quality of marital adjustment on difficulty experienced at Time 3, scores on the Spanier were added to the regression equation. Results indicated that at Time 3, knowledge of marital adjustment did not lead to a significant increase in overall R^2.

To assess the possibility of multicollinearity, zero-order correlations describing the relationships among the predictor variables were examined (see Tables 2 and 3).

The independent variables do not appear to be substantially correlated to each other, with the exception of network size and number of members with children. The finding that size of network did not enter the multiple regression equation may be accounted for by its correlation with presence of peers. Thus, size of network would appear to have an indirect effect on difficulty experienced in the transition to motherhood.

Further examination of network satisfaction. As satisfaction with network proved to be an important predictor of difficulty scores at both time points, further regression analyses were performed to explore which sources were influential in accounting for its impact. Satisfaction with help from husband, family, in-laws and friends were regressed on difficulty scores at Time 2 and Time 3. Results indicated that at Time 2, satisfaction with help received from husband was the most important predictor, accounting for 13% of the variance ($r = .36, p < .05$). Once it was entered in the equation, no other satisfaction variables added a significant increase in overall R2. However, at Time 3 the picture had changed. A significant overall multiple r of .49, $p < .025$ was found. Satisfaction with help received from family and from in-laws was entered into the equation, together accounting for 24% of the variance in difficulty scores. Thus it appeared that in the early stages of adjusting to new motherhood, satisfaction with help received from husband was important, while one year later satisfaction with help provided by family and in-laws became a more salient factor.

The relationship between the network variables investigated in this research and difficulty experienced in adjusting to motherhood is summarized in Figure 1. Differences in the pattern found at Time 2 and Time 3, and in the components of satisfaction that were found to be significant, are illustrated in the figure.

At both measurement times following arrival of the baby, network dimensions proved to be potent predictors of difficulty experienced. However, the pattern found at each time point differed slightly, illustrating the value and richness of a longitudinal design in under-standing a life transition.

In the first postpartum contact, degree of disruption felt in social ties, quality of marital adjustment, the presence of other parents in the network, and satisfaction with help received from husband were the most significant contributors. All relationships were in the predicted direction. Conceptually, it appeared that content (other parents), disruption, and quality (satisfaction) were the most relevant network dimensions. The value of being part of a circle of other parenting adults, with whom concerns and anxieties regarding the new role may be shared, is confirmed by these results. Actual quantity of help received

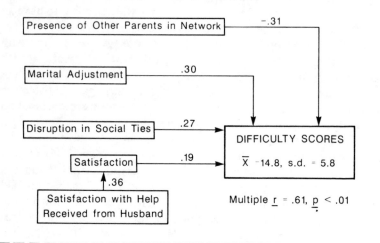

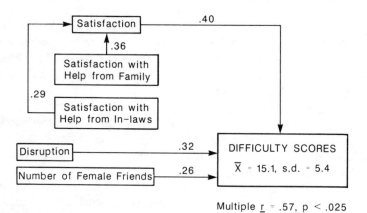

Note: The standardized regression coefficient (beta) is used to indicate the strength of each variable in the overall regression equation.

Figure 1.   Summary of the relationship of network variables to degree of difficulty experienced in the transition to first-time motherhood, concurrent correlates.

from spouse was not as significant as the reported satisfaction with that help. Also, the prediction that size of network (quantity) would relate inversely to difficulty was not confirmed when tested in the multiple-regression equation. This may be explained by the restricted range of network size found in the sample (none of the women had particularly small networks) or by the redundancy between the measures of size and presence of peers.

When the women were contacted one year later, network variables continued to play an important role. At Time 3, satisfaction with help received from family and in-laws, degree of disruption felt, and number of female friends available to discuss child-rearing concerns were the best predictors of difficulty. A major change from Time 2 was the absence of any variables pertaining particularly to the husband; neither marital adjustment or satisfaction with help from husband added significantly to the equation. At one year postpartum, satisfaction with provisions from family and in-laws took precedence over satisfaction with that provided by spouse. The finding that satisfaction with help received was the best sole predictor at Time 3 suggests that increased child-rearing demands may be felt by mothers of one-year-olds, thus increasing the importance of perceived quality of assistance.

Mueller's (1980) assertion that disruption in ties may be a key factor in the stressfulness of life cycle events received empirical support in this investigation of the transition to first-time motherhood. Future research examining the relevance of disruption in other life-cycle transitions is needed.

An unexpected finding was the positive association between number of female friends and degree of difficulty. It was expected that contact with other women would provide reassurance and thus ease the transition. However, it may be that when the child reaches one year of age, and discipline issues emerge, the existence of many points of view adds confusion and doubt. A related explanation is that having many female friends with whom to discuss child-rearing concerns leads to a sense of competition. This notion received support in the open-ended responses of the mothers at one year, a common theme being "don't compare your child with others." Alternatively, it may be that people with difficulties search out friends, although they may not actually solve the problems.

Do network variables at one point in time predict future difficulty? Further analyses were designed to examine whether network dimensions at one point in time predicted future difficulty. Generally, the results of several multiple regressions were nonsignificant. While the present study found evidence of concurrent links between social support and difficulty experienced in adjusting to first-time motherhood, network variables at one point in time were not found to be significantly related to difficulty at a future point. At first glance this discrepancy may seem surprising; however, from a systems theory standpoint such a finding is plausible. For example, one would not necessarily expect satisfaction with help provided by network sources at two months postpartum to lessen parenting stress at the one-year follow-up. Satisfaction with the current level of assistance provided would seem to be a stronger influence. This is consistent with Crnic et al.'s (1984) finding that the long-term predictability of support and stress measures was generally low, although concurrent relationships were strong. The predictive power of network variables needs to be more closely scrutinized in future studies of life cycle transitions that utilize prospective designs.

Maternal Employment and Difficulty

The impact of maternal employment status on difficulty experienced was examined using a one-way analysis of variance. The sample was divided into two groups; those who were in the home full time, and those who were involved outside the home, on either a part-time or full-time basis. At both time points the trend indicated that women at home experienced greater difficulty; this difference was statistically significant at Time 3 only. It may be that the rewards experienced through gainful employment offset the difficulties associated with parenting. A selection factor may also be operating, such that women with difficult babies choose to stay home. Another possibility relates to the time factor involved; women who are at work are not exposed to the child care stress as extensively, and thus may rate difficulties lower.

CONCLUSIONS AND IMPLICATIONS

The studies reviewed here provide clear evidence for the importance of network variables in understanding the transition to first-time motherhood. Arrival of the first child is a time fraught with ambiguity and joy, a time when attitudes toward the task of parenting are developing. It is a very important life event, during which a maternal identity is incorporated into one's self-concept. Network variables play a central part in mediating these processes.

The necessity of utilizing a multidimensional assessment of the social network has been illustrated. Quality, quantity, and content are each important aspects of the network, yet each may play a different role in relation to adjustment. Further, as illustrated in the research project described, this association may change throughout the course of a transition.

This chapter has focused on network variables and the experience of women as they become parents. It is quite likely that men's experience differs, and that different network variables exert influence on adjustment. One can only speculate about such relationships. For example, do "working fathers" experience conflict about their dual roles? Is this eased by network support? Do the networks of "househusbands" bear similarity to those of women at home? Is quantity of network support more important to men than quality? The utility of a network perspective in enriching our understanding of the transition to motherhood has been demonstrated. The task for the future is to refine this understanding and to explore sex differences in network variables.

The issue of negative interchange within the network in relation to the transition to motherhood has not been adequately addressed. While some social ties strengthen, it seems plausible that strain occurs in others. Conflict over "correct" parenting, ambivalence over being a "working mother," and resentment regarding perceived inadequacy of help offered are but a few possible sources and consequences of tension within the network.

The contextual understanding of the transition to motherhood provided by social network concepts yields several preventive and therapeutic implications. First, prenatal education classes need to incorporate information on the social and marital changes accompanying new parenthood, as well as providing information on physiological changes. Second, parent education and support groups are needed in the community. Half of the women in the study described earlier indicated a desire to associate more with other new parents in a formal, structured way. Currently, most parent education programs are aimed at parents of school-age children, yet the need for information and support during the preschool years is also present. A continuation of prenatal classes throughout the first year of infant development would seem to be a logical extension and present an opportunity to build family strengths. Third, a network orientation to understanding this transition helps to identify people who may be at "high risk"—women who may be more vulnerable to isolation than others. Teenage parents and those who undergo the transition to motherhood later in life, what LaRossa (1983) would term "off-time" events, are unlikely to have peers experiencing a similar life event, and may be even more susceptible to a "shrinking" social network at this time of increased need.

A final implication pertains to clinicians working with a woman experiencing difficulty at this point in her life cycle. It may be more fruitful to examine the context of her life and her support systems and to intervene in these areas, rather than to delve into personality dynamics alone. Indeed, the feminist interpretation of postpartum depression as "on-the-job stress" (Rosenberg, in press) takes into consideration the assistance a woman is receiving as a very important part of her "working conditions." Noting that any front line person at the beck and call of needy individuals is prone to burnout, Rosenberg identifies lack of feedback as one of the job characteristics creating stress. She cites evidence that day-care workers feel the support and feedback they receive from coworkers is one of the key features distinguishing their work from motherwork. The greater difficulty experienced by full-time mothers, a finding in the research described, may partially reflect a deficit in some features of the network. Loss and isolation are definite themes in depression, and clinicians must be alert to the role the social network can play in undermining a new mother's confidence or in creating ambivalence. The resources available within the woman's "personal community" need to be assessed.

The process of becoming a mother is an unfolding drama, with exits and entrances from old and new characters as the scenes shift. Social network processes are extremely relevant in understanding this transition. Being a mother is clearly a role that needs a supporting cast, and perhaps, at times, applause.

REFERENCES

Barrera, M. (1981). Social support in the adjustment of pregnant adolescents: Assessment issues. In B. Gottlieb (Ed.), *Social networks and social support* (pp. 69-97). Newbury Park, CA: Sage.

Belsky, J., and Rovine, M. (1984). Social-network contact, family support, and the transition to parenthood. *Journal of Marriage and the Family, 46,* 455-463.

Belsky, J., Spanier, G., and Rovine, M. (1983). Stability and change in marriage across the transition to parenthood. *Journal of Marriage and the Family, 45,* 567-579.

Benedek, T. (1960). The organization of the reproductive drive. *International Journal of Psychoanalysis, 61,* 1-15.

Carveth, W. B., and Gottlieb, B. H. (1979). The measurement of social support and its relations to stress. *Canadian Journal of Behavioral Science, 11,* 179-188.

Cohen, J., and Cohen, P. (1975). *Applied multiple regression/correlation analysis for the behavioral sciences.* Hillsdale, NJ: Lawrence Erlbaum.

Colletta, N. (1979) Support systems after divorce: Incidence and impact. *Journal of Marriage and the Family, 41,* 837-846.

Cowan, P. A., and Cowan, C. P. (1983). *Quality of couple relationships and parenting stress in beginning families.* Paper presented at the meeting of the Society for Research in Child Development, Detroit, MI.

Crnic, K., Greenberg, M., Robinson, N., and Ragozin, A. (1984). Maternal stress and social support: Effects of the mother-infant relationship from birth to eighteen months. *American Journal of Orthopsychiatry, 54,* 224-236.

Crockenberg, S. B. (1981). Infant irritability, mother responsiveness, and social support influences on the security of infant-mother attachment. *Child Development, 52,* 857-865.

Cutrona, C. (1981). *Depressive attributional style and nonpsychotic postpartum depression.* Unpublished doctoral dissertation, University of California, Los Angeles.

Duvall, E. M. (1967). *Family development* (3rd ed.). Philadelphia: J. B. Lippincott.

Dyer, E. D. (1963). Parenthood as crisis: A restudy. *Marriage and Family Living, 25,* 196-201.

Erickson, G. (1975). The concept of personal network in clinical practice. *Family Process, 11,* 487-497.

Fehr, B., and Perlman, D. (1985). The family as a social network and support system. In L'Abate, L. (Ed.), *Handbook of family psychology and therapy, Vol. 2* (pp. 323-356). Homewood, IL: Dow Jones-Irwin.

Gottlieb, B. H. (May, 1980). *Social networks and social support in the design of preventive interventions.* Paper presented at a Symposium on Helping Networks and the Welfare State, University of Toronto, Ontario.

Grossman, F. K., Eichler, L., Winnickoff, S., with Anzalone, M., Gofseyeff, M., and Sargent, S. (1980). *Pregnancy, birth and parenthood.* San Francisco: Jossey-Bass.

Harriman, L. C. (1983). Personal and marital changes accompanying parenthood. *Family Relations, 32,* 387-395.

Hobbs, D. F. (1965). Parenthood as crisis: A third study. *Journal of Marriage and the Family, 27,* 367-372.

Hobbs, D. F. (1968). Transition to parenthood: A replication and an extension. *Journal of Marriage and the Family, 30,* 413-417.

Hobbs, D. F. and Cole, S. P. (1976). Transition to parenthood: A decade replication. *Journal of Marriage and the Family, 38,* 723-731.

Huston, T., Surra, C., Fitzgerald, N., and Cate, R. (1981). From courtship to marriage: Mate selection as an interpersonal process. In Duck, S. and Gilmour, R. (Eds.), *Personal Relationships 2: Developing Personal Relationships* (pp. 53-88). London: Academic Press.

Jacoby, A. P. (1969). Transition to parenthood: A reassessment. *Journal of Marriage and the Family, 31,* 720-727.

LaRossa, R. (1983). The transition to parenthood and the social reality of time. *Journal of Marriage and the Family, 45,* 579-591.

LeMasters, E. E. (1957). Parenthood as crisis. *Marriage and Family Living, 19,* 352-355.

McCallister, L., and Fischer, C. (1978). A procedure for surveying personal networks. *Sociological Methods and Research, 7,* 131-149.

McCannell Saulnier, K. and Rowland, C. (1985). Missing links: An empirical investigation of network variables in high-risk families. *Family Relations, 34*, 557-561.

McCannell Saulnier, K. (1984). Social networks and the transition to motherhood: A longitudinal analysis (Doctoral dissertation, University of Manitoba, 1983). *Dissertation Abstracts International, 45*, 1590B.

Milardo, R. M. (1982). Friendship networks in developing relationships: Converging and diverging social environments. *Social Psychology Quarterly, 45*, 162-172.

Milardo, R. M. (1983). Social networks and pair relationships: A review of substantive and measurement issues. *Sociology and Social Research, 68*, 1-18.

Miller, B., and Sollie, D. (1980). Normal stresses during the transition to parenthood. *Family Relations, 29*, 459-465.

Mueller, D. P. (1980). Social networks: A promising direction for research on the relationship of the social environment to psychiatric disorder. *Social Science and Medicine, 14A*, 147-161.

Pattison, E., Defrancisco, D., Wood, P., Frazier, H., and Crowder, J. (1975). A psychosocial kinship model for family therapy. *American Journal of Psychiatry, 132*, 1246-2150.

Pines, D. (1972). Pregnancy and motherhood: Interaction between fantasy and reality. *British Journal of Medical Psychology, 45*, 333-343.

Pistrang, N. (1984). Women's work involvement and experience of new motherhood. *Journal of Marriage and the Family, 46*, 433-449.

Richardson, M. S., and Kagan, L. (1979). *Social support and the transition to parenthood.* Paper presented at the meeting of the American Psychological Association, New York.

Rosenberg, H. (in press). Motherwork, stress, and depression: The cost of privatized social reproduction. In Maroney, H. J. and Luxton, M. (Eds.). *Women in Canada: Political Economy and Political Struggle.*

Russell, C. S. (1974). Transition to parenthood: Problems and gratifications. *Journal of Marriage and the Family, 36*, 294-302.

Saulnier, K. (1982). Networks, change and crisis: The web of informal support. *Canadian Journal of Community Mental Health, 1*, 5-23.

Spanier, G. B. (1976). Measuring dyadic adjustment: New scale for assessing the quality of marriage and similar dyads. *Journal of Marriage and the Family, 38*, 15-28.

Steffensmeier, R. H. (1982). A role model of the transition to parenthood. *Journal of Marriage and the Family, 44*, 319-335.

Stueve, C. A., and Gerson, K. (1977). Personal relations across the life cycle. In C. Fischer, (Ed.), *Networks and places: Social relations in the urban setting* (pp. 79-98). New York: Free Press.

Sussman, M., and Burchinal, L. (1962). Parental aid to married children: Implications for family functioning. *Marriage and Family Living, 24*, 320-332.

Thibaut, J., and Kelley, H. H. (1959). *The social psychology of groups.* New York: John Wiley.

Waldron, H., and Routh, D. (1981). The effect of the first child on the marital relationship. *Journal of Marriage and the Family, 43*, 785-788.

Wilcox, B. (1981). Social support in adjusting to marital disruption: A network analysis. In B. Gottlieb, (Ed.), *Social networks and social support* (pp. 97-117). Newbury Park, CA: Sage.

4

Precious Moments with Family Members and Friends

Reed W. Larson
Nancy Bradney

There are the times we will always remember: occasions in youth when we discovered a spiritual kinship or moments when we shared a feeling of incredible freedom; times in midlife when someone close reawakened deep feelings, or occasions when people laughed until their sides split; and moments in old age when time stood still, or when through spoken or unspoken language we suddenly felt as though we had known someone since birth. There are many other moments like these. Some are unnotable in the larger scheme of our lives, but they nevertheless make a significant difference in our daily experience: walking home together, talking over events at school, sharing warm feelings around the dinner table. There are coffee breaks when we laugh off frustrations, late night phone calls when we feel finally comforted, shared pranks, weekly tennis matches, regular bridge games.

It is these shared moments, the individually forgettable as well as the never-forgotten, that make friends and family dear. The special nature of these moments may often be the very reason we choose to maintain relationships. They are distinguished, first, by a unique *quality*, one that makes these moments stand out from others in our lives. Second, there is the potent fact that this quality is *shared*. When two or more people take part in experiencing a common event, their individual experiences are channeled together and heightened as they respond to each other in a reciprocal chain. Third, these shared experiences leave behind *memories*, which become symbols of an enduring relationship, serving as touch-stones to evoke the past and shape future interactions.

In this article we are seeking to understand the dynamics of these special, rewarding and transient experiences, from youth to old age. When do they occur? What kinds of situations make them happen? The investigation deals with moment-to-moment interactions (McClintock, 1983) and with the emotional side of relationships (Berscheid, 1983). Our basic approach will be to compare experience during time spent with family and friends at several different junctures in the life span. By contrasting what occurs with kin and with friends we hope to discover something about the unique qualities underlying these special occasions.

Of course, who fits in the categories of "family" and "friends" shifts at different points in the life span. The question is, do these changes alter the opportunities for special and enjoyable interactions? Or do the enduring exigencies of family life, the requirements of sharing a home and the responsibilities of kinship, dictate a constancy in the kinds of experiences that can be expected with family members?

Similarly, there are shifts across the life-span in friendships as well as constancy, in that friends are nearly always companions with whom we have chosen to spend time. We will restrict our definition here to non-kin friends. We question whether these shifts in relationships and the shifting circumstances of relationships make special moments with these significant others more or less likely. Or are there qualities of friendship per se that make enjoyable occasions with friends equally accessible across the life-span?

A METHOD FOR STUDYING
DAILY EXPERIENCE

In our research we have examined the frequency of different subjective states in people's daily lives, including their interactions with others. When do enjoyment and absorption occur? When do people experience boredom, pain and anxiety? We have been concerned with identifying the activities and circumstances of everyday life that lead to these different subjective experiences. For this article our focus will be on the occurrence of positive feelings in interpersonal relationships. This focus undoubtedly excludes some very exceptional and intimate moments with others, for example when two people are sharing an acutely painful event. However, we suspect that even in many instances of shared pain people will report a state of happiness and strength derived from the presence of someone with whom they are close.

Investigation of the emotional experiences within a relationship poses an important but difficult task for research, one that has generally been neglected (Berscheid, 1983; Reis, 1984). Because emotions are so readily subject to fluctuation, change, and reinterpretation, they are not easily documented. Studies that rely on retrospective reports of experience—via interviews or questionnaires—are vulnerable to significant distortion because moments of happiness may be forgotten and bouts of anger patched up. The inability of people to accurately recollect the details of their subjective experience is well documented (Bernard, Killworth, Kronenfeld & Sailer, 1984; Milardo, this volume; Mischel, 1968).

The challenge posed by this topic might be seen in terms of Hinde's (1979) distinction between interactions and relationships. Interactions are the specific exchanges that take place between people; they occur in the present moment. Relationships, on the other hand, are made up of the shared understandings and feelings that endure and evolve over time; relationships may be derivative from interactions, but exist in a time plane that transcends the present moment. The methodological problem in documenting the emotional experience of daily interactions is that our recollections of them are heavily colored by our concept of the enduring relationship. By asking for reports on experience retrospectively, the researcher is likely to learn more about relationships than interactions.

Therefore, in order to study the emotional side of interactions it is necessary to have a research method that documents experience as it happens. The procedure we have used is called the Experience Sampling Method (ESM) (Larson & Csikszentmihalyi, 1983). Research participants carry electronic pagers for one week and are sent signals at random times across the waking hours of the day. Their instructions are to fill out a report on their activity and subjective state each time they receive a signal. In the studies reported here the signals were received seven times daily, one within every two-hour block of time, hence giving us 40 to 50 reports per person. The rest of our discussion will be based on data collected in this way from samples of respondents representing three different age groups.

Adolescents. This sample was composed of 75 high school students, ages 13 to 18, randomly selected from the population of a large, suburban Chicago school. The sample was stratified to include equal numbers of boys and girls, equal numbers from all four grades, and equal numbers from lower- and upper-middle class neighborhoods (Csikszentmihalyi and Larson, 1984).

Adults. This sample was composed of 104 volunteer participants from five Chicago-area businesses. They included secretaries, assembly line workers, railroad workers, managers and engineers. Ranging from ages 19 to 65, 67 women and 40 men participated. Most, 55%, had at least some college education.[1]

Older adults. This sample was composed of 92 retired Canadians drawn from the Kitchner-Waterloo metropolitan area of southwestern Ontario. It included 40 men and 52 women between ages 55 and 85. The sample was very well educated for their birth cohort, with 42% having received some college education. Close to two-thirds had held white collar or professional jobs.[2]

EXPERIENCE WITH FAMILY AND FRIENDS IN ADOLESCENCE

Adolescence is a useful place to begin examining the emotional dynamics of shared experience. Because of maturational and associated developmental changes, this is a time of life when youth first have the prerequisites for deep personal exchange with another person. They gain the capacity to think about emotions abstractly and understand them as separate from the situations that induce them (Kagan, 1984; Weiner and Graham, 1984), and they are able to analyze the effect of other people on their state. In addition they become able to put themselves in the position of others (Harris, Olthoff, and Terwogt, 1981; Hoffman, 1984) and to communicate more effectively and intimately (Berndt, 1982). This joint development of emotional cognizance and interpersonal insight provides the tools for learning to share and influence another's emotional states, and it sets the stage for learning to control and manage relationships. Together these developmental achievements enable adolescents to participate in interactions for the first time with mutuality.

**Mutual Relationships and Positive Interactions:
Teenagers' Experiences with Friends**

There is good reason to believe that the capacity for mutuality is first realized with friends. Relationships with friends, in contrast to those with family members, are more equal in status. Friends, as distinguished from parents, do not routinely pull rank and assert authority, hence interactions with them can be more reciprocal (Youniss, 1980). Friends are also like oneself—they have the same problems, the same worries and triumphs. Thus, while the world of one's parents may be unfathomable, the feelings, desires and impulses of friends can be understood, at least in part, simply through self-understanding.

Perhaps for these reasons, when the adolescents in our study were signalled at random times, they reported feeling significantly more open and free when they were with friends than with their families (see Table 1). As one girl said, with her friends, "You don't have to talk, you can say *anything*; if it's too crazy they'll tell you." They experienced a level of empathy and mutual understanding, combined with a trust in sharing, that simply did not exist with their parents or siblings.

The reciprocity that characterizes teenage friendships is also reflected in the greater commonality of goals adolescents feel they have with friends as opposed to family members (Table 1). Whether gossiping

TABLE 1
The Experience of Adolescents with Friends and Family
(N = 73)

	With Friends (mean mean[1])	With Family (mean mean)	t
Perceptions of situation			
Openness (1 to 7)	5.13	4.58	4.56***
Freedom (1 to 7)	5.14	4.70	3.87***
Common goals (1 to 6)	4.50	3.89	3.25**
Positive feedback (1 to 6)	4.94	4.42	3.57***
Joking (1 to 6)	4.04	3.34	5.35***
Subjective state			
Affect (−12 to 12)	5.64	3.75	5.57***
Arousal (−15 to 15)	4.45	2.83	4.16***

SOURCE: Adopted from Larson, 1983.
1. Average scores were computed for each individual and these were used to compute the t-statistics. The table presents the mean of these means.
*p < .05; **p < .01; ***p < .001.

about peers or doing homework together, they subsequently described one another as "on the same wave length." When goals did diverge, it appeared to us as though teenagers' own norms ultimately brought them into line, almost always without need for harsh words. The mechanism of this self-regulation among friends was suggested in a small study in which we found adolescents reporting more frequent feelings of guilt with their friends than at other times (Larson and Bradney, 1985). It would appear that when teenagers are with their friends they are especially sensitive to their peers' expectations, with the result that they keep their behavior more closely attuned to them.

The spontaneous modifications of teenagers' behavior to conform with the requirements of friendships may contribute to our seeing fewer occasions of hostile exchange among friends than family members. The daily interactions among friends appear to be sustained largely without explicit sanctions. The teenagers in the study reported receiving more positive than negative feedback from their friends (Table 1). In contrast to parents or siblings, friends are more likely to respond favorably to anything other friends say or do. They are more openly supportive. Friends also were more often rated as joking rather than serious. In other words, friends' exchanges of thoughts, acts, and feelings were more affirmative than their interactions with all others with whom they had less mutual relationships.

This affirmative exchange, characterized by freedom, openness and positive feedback, has clear implications for the quality of subjective experience. All of these properties are related to deep enjoyment (Csikszentmihalyi, 1975). Indeed, the adolescents in our study were very articulate in describing how they manipulate situations with friends in order to create a shared state of positive feeling (Csikszentmihalyi & Larson, 1984).

The ESM data include numerous occasions when the random signals found these adolescents in the mildest of unusually enjoyable experiences with their friends. Our subjects described moments of rapture with friends at a rock concert, relaxation and hilarity as they sat around telling jokes, oceanic feelings of harmony as they moved in and out of a crowd at a party, profound exhilaration when alone with a new-found lover. They reported great times even in an activity as aimless as throwing beer cans on lawns. On the average their emotional states with their friends were extremely high, much higher than their typical states with their families (Table 1). Clearly, for adolescents it is with friends that precious moments with others are most likely to occur.

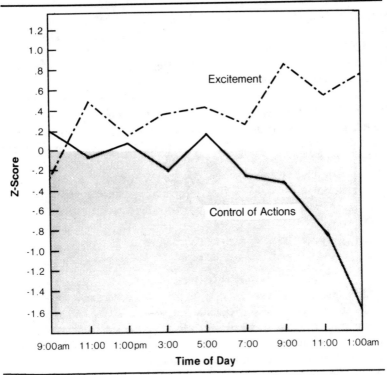

Figure 1.   The Path of Experience with Friends on the Weekend.

The Dynamics of Adolescent Interactions with Friends: Careening Enjoyment

The properties of give and take that make friends so enjoyable also have a bearing on the course of specific interactions with them. Freedom, openness, and mutual supportiveness provide the structure of a positive feedback system, a system in which "go" messages prescribe the flow of the exchange (Larson, 1983).

The consequences are demonstrated by the sequence of states our adolescents reported on Friday and Saturday nights. Figure 1 shows increasing excitement as the night progresses, but it is coupled with the increasing loss of any feeling of control. As an uninterrupted positive feedback system, interactions with friends face the inevitable hazard—a tendency to run out of control (sometimes called a "runaway positive feedback"). Continual positive exchange fuels enjoyment, and without moderating feedback the group careers without limits. Thus it is not surprising that delinquency, unanticipated sexual intercourse and other spontaneous actions evolve out of interactions among adolescent friends. As we all have occasion to reflect when we have stayed out too late the night before, shared positive experience with others is intoxicating and easily dulls even the adult's best judgment.

One could, of course, explain this pattern of experiences in many familiar ways, for example by reference to young people's use of friendships to explore new definitions of the self. And yet, it is not necessary to reach outside the dynamics of the experiences themselves to understand their potency. Irrespective of any specific functional roles friends might serve, they provide an optimal situation for positive experience. In old age we will witness this same enjoyment unique to friendship, except without some of the hazards of adolescent interactions.

A Contrasting Context: Teenagers' Experience with Family Members

The adolescent's self-reports during interactions with their families demonstrate a system of both positive and negative exchanges. Conflictual interactions with parents are more common, and fights with siblings appear to be a staple of family life. The data in Table 1 show that the overall properties of the interaction system are less favorable, and that adolescents' moods with their families are less positive than with friends.

One difference between family and friends is the type of activities carried out with each. Whereas the majority (58%) of time with friends is spent in leisure, maintenance and leisure activities take up large amounts of teenagers' time with family members (47% and 48% respectively). Even if we compare only the times when teenagers aim to have enjoyment with their families in shared leisure activities, friends are still experienced as more enjoyable (see Table 2).

An underlying structural difference between relationships with family members and friends is that the family does not function on the principle of mutuality. Because it falls to parents to socialize their children, their assertion of authority and administration of negative feedback are a necessary part of family interactions, even though they may occasionally be misunderstood. As one 14-year-old boy from a well-educated, upper middle class family said of his mother, "She just tries to gain control of the whole situation over you, and just puts you

TABLE 2
Adolescent Experience with Friends and Family
in Leisure Activities (N = 69)

	With Friends (mean mean)	With Family (mean mean)	
Perception of situation			
Openness	5.11	4.68	2.91**
Freedom	5.19	5.02	1.22
Common goals	4.90	4.23	3.23**
Positive feedback	4.92	4.59	2.45*
Joking	4.04	3.30	4.16***
Subjective state			
Affect	5.75	4.18	2.99**
Arousal	4.79	3.28	2.69**

SOURCE: Adopted from Larson, 1983.
*p < .05; **p < .01; ***p < .001.

down—'I'm older than you are and your elder, so do what I say.'"
Understandably, family interactions, whether focused on leisure or household labor, are usually less immediately gratifying to adolescents than interactions with their friends.

The contrasting possibilities of exchange with family and friends are summarized in the characterizations of a best friend and a mother by the same 14-year-old. Asked what makes his friend happy, he says:

> When he accomplishes something, when he's got things off his chest, and he feels very secure about himself, which he at times doesn't. He feels very insecure about himself, although when he doesn't he gets very happy.

Compare this sensitive and empathic portrayal of his friend with what he is able to say of the occasions for his mother's happiness:

> When I give into her easily. When I do my chores and don't cause her much . . . Not when I just do my chores, but when I do them and I'm so happy all the time. When I feed into her little reality world she feels happy.

With his friend there exists the groundwork for true mutuality. With his mother there is simply a tug of war.

Our data include many instances of close and sensitive interactions among adolescents and their families. They include long, intimate talks between mothers and daughters and basement projects shared by fathers and sons. In general, however, these warm times are counterbalanced by frequent squabbles with parents or siblings. The lack of reciprocity based on equal status in relationships, as well as the inevitable constraints of any smooth-functioning living unit appear to militate against adolescent's having consistently high quality experiences with their families.

FROM ADOLESCENCE TO MARRIED LIFE

Same-Sex to Opposite-Sex Friends

Across the years of high school the contrast between adolescents' experience with their friends and families is relatively stable: friends generate mainly positive experiences, and family generates experiences which are on the average neutral. Within the context of friends, however, a notable shift occurs in the identity of these friends. This change reflects a preparation for adulthood.

Between the freshman and senior year of high school, our students demonstrated a surprisingly consistent pattern in their changing preferences for various kinds of companions. Ninth graders in the study spent the most time with individuals of their own gender; tenth graders with *groups* of same-sex friends; eleventh graders with mixed sex groups; and twelfth graders with one person of the opposite sex (Csikszentmihalyi and Larson, 1984). Not unexpectedly, along with this shift in the time spent with these different companions, we witnessed a substantial shift in the occasions of their most positive experiences (Table 3). The freshmen had higher moods when they were with friends of their own sex. But within a period of four years it is the opposite sex that makes them feel on top of the world. There is little doubt that puberty has endowed freshmen with the impulses and inclinations that make "girls" or "boys" an object of extreme interest, but it would appear that they are not yet able to engage in satisfying exchanges with the opposite sex. Only with age and the maturation of understanding is it possible for adolescents to experience mutuality and stable enjoyment in heterosexual interactions. In the advanced years of high school the good times with same-sex buddies are replaced by enthrallment in reciprocal exchange with someone who is a little different from themselves.

This transition in preferred companions foreshadows the change in attachments that will shape adulthood for most of us. It is not much later that a girl- or boyfriend becomes a spouse and the mutuality

TABLE 3
The Shift from Same- to Opposite-Sex Friends

	Average Affect[1] (z-score)		Amount of Time Spent with:[2] (percent)	
	Same-Sex Friends	Opposite-Sex Friends	Same-Sex Friends	Opposite-Sex Friends
9th grade	.47	.18	81	19
10th grade	.41	.61	61	39
11th grade	.09	.51	45	55
12th grade	.25	.54	56	44

SOURCE: Adopted from Csikszentmihalyi and Larson, 1984.
1. A higher score indicates more positive affect.
2. Values add across to 100%.

originally exchanged between lovers is transformed into the common ground of a new family. Through marriage, young adults attempt to appropriate the reciprocity and enjoyment discovered in adolescent friendships. The family built around that relationship will usually be a primary context of interpersonal experience for the rest of an individual's life. But does the newly constituted family provide adults with comparable opportunities as rewarding in quality as the times spent earlier with friends?

THE EXPERIENCE OF ADULTS

Constancies of Family Life: Adults' Experience with Their Families

By combining the adolescent data with those from our samples of adult workers and older adults, we can construct a picture of the path of interpersonal experience that spans much of the lifetime. Figure 2 shows the percentage of time our respondents reported being with family members and friends at different age periods.[3] One can see that with marriage and entry into adulthood the amount of time with family members—now one's spouse and children—increases dramatically. Indeed, within the adult sample, there is a large difference between the married and unmarried in the amount of time reported with family (32% vs. 16%). During the years of heavy family responsibility, which extend to middle and late adulthood, the amount of time spent with friends decreases correspondingly (see Figure 2).

The tables now are turned within the family situation: The former

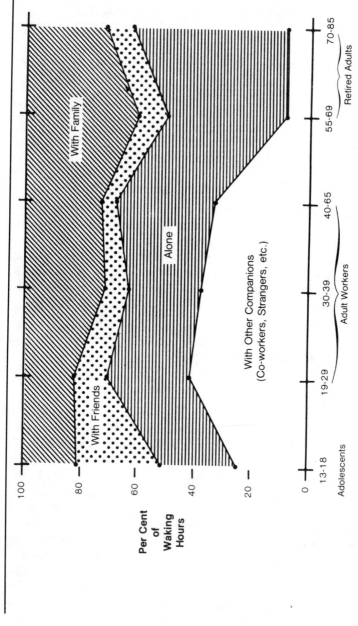

Figure 2. Amount of Time Spent with Different Companions Across the Life Span.

adolescent is now the parent. He or she is now the authority responsible for setting limits and providing sanctions for children's behavior. And yet our data suggest that, for adults, the times spent with the family are experienced in much the same way as when the parent was an adolescent. Adults report approximately the same neutral to low levels of happiness and excitement with their families as do members of our adolescent sample (Figures 3 and 4).[4] Unfortunately the data from this sample do not allow us to separate times when respondents were with different members of the family. However, analyses of these and similar data from another study suggest that the time parents spend with their children elicits states that are as low if not lower than those experienced with the spouse or the family as a whole (Graef, Csikszentmihalyi and Gianinno, 1983; Wells, 1985).

The parent may now be in a more powerful position, but parents appear to be as restricted as their children by the family's limited potential for enjoyable interactions. The quality of experience connected with limiting children's behavior and administering sanctions apparently is not that much different from that connected with being limited and receiving sanctions. And, apparently, any added cognitive powers that come with age also make little net difference in the capacity of adults to find enjoyment within the family. Neither parent nor child can feel toward one another the kind of openness, freedom, or reciprocity that they feel with their friends (Youniss, 1980). There are undoubtedly long-term satisfactions in being a parent, but they are not visibly manifest in the immediate moment. Occasions of extreme warmth and enjoyment are no more frequent in the home than occasions of discord and disharmony.

The potential for enjoyment with the family is limited not only by asymmetry, but also by the daily realities associated with living together and sharing a home: the inevitable conflicts over use of the bathroom or automobile, the shared concerns about money and bills, and the requirement that some of the time spent together must involve repetitive and uninteresting maintenance tasks. The daily experience of adults, like that of their children, is subject to repeated encroachment by the routine. This is not to say that family interactions may not be meaningful. The neutral and low-intensity emotional tone of the family may serve as a valued refuge. But it must be recognized that the basic qualities of family interactions arise from the humdrum and the mundane.

One's spouse, originally a person with whom one could have fun and

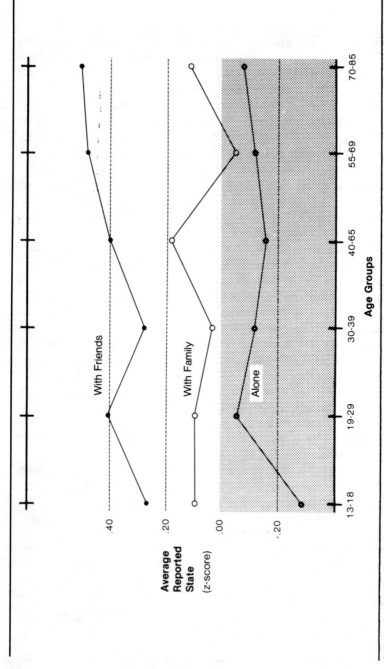

Figure 3.   Happiness with Different Companions Across the Life Span.

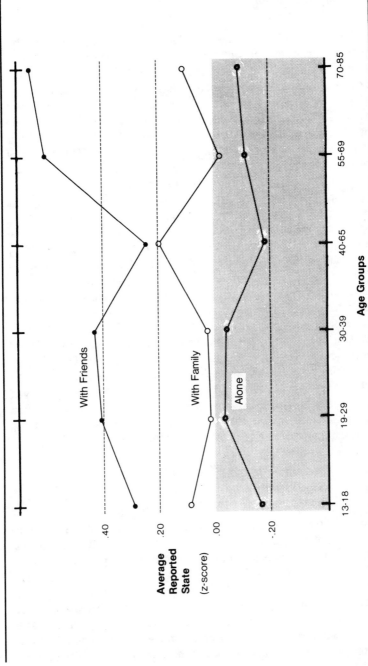

Figure 4. Excitement with Different Companions Across the Life Span.

good times, may still represent opportunities for the kinds of enjoyable exchanges that were a part of courtship. Yet data from our sample of older adults suggest that this potential for positive experience is not evident, at least not in the latter half of the life. The average state of these older adults when they are alone with their spouses is remarkably low; it is not that much different than what they report when they are completely alone (Larson, Mannell, & Zuzanek, 1986). Clearly, by this age the husband or wife is no longer a frequent and reliable source of immediate enjoyment.

At what point in the life-span does the spouse cease to be an enjoyable companion? Unfortunately, our data on young and middle-aged adults do not allow us to separate time with spouses from time with children. Judging from the aggregate findings, however, it would appear that the majority of time spent with one's spouse after marriage is not very exceptionally enjoyable (Figures 3 and 4). The large increase in amount of time together or in each other's vicinity, along with the constant and chronic concerns of everyday life, would appear to have dulled spouses' capacity for shared enjoyment.

A husband and wife may be obligated to escape from the family context in order to enjoy each others' company. This conclusion is suggested by the findings from the older adults. The very best times of aged married couples occur when one's spouse and friends are gathered together (Larson et al., 1986). The context provided by the company of friends *together with* one's spouse was more positive for the adults than any other. Throughout adulthood and into old age it appears that it is still friends that generate the best times with others.

Adults' Experience with Friends: The Transformation of Attention

Our data reveal a striking continuity across the life-span in the power of friends to generate enjoyment. With marriage and family the amount of time adults spend with friends declines dramatically (from 12% to 4% within our data). And in old age, in spite of the freeing up of time when children leave home and retirement takes place, the amount of time adults spend with friends remains quite small (Figure 2). Yet throughout adulthood and old age, friends continue to play the role they did in adolescence as a reliable source of positive experience. Data from our samples of adults offer a remarkable illustration of the similarities at disparate age periods in the special quality of experience people have when they are with friends as distinguished from other companions. Across all age groups, reported levels of happiness and excitement with friends are consistently high, and they appear to become even higher in old age (Figures 3 and 4).

Brown (1981) provides a valuable narrative of the structural changes in friendships that underlie this continuity of experience. In young adulthood, the decline in the prominence of friends after marriage is accompanied by a conversion of friendships into joint marital acquaintanceships. The intimacy of adolescence may wane and friendships may become more "compartmentalized," often associated with specific activities, such as a weekly golf game or periodic joint family gatherings. In middle age, a point at which our data show a dip in excitement with friends, others have also found a decrease in interest toward friends. In old age, however, as people are released from the demands of family and job, friendships regain some of their breadth and intimacy (compare Blieszner and Johnson, this volume).

Friends appear to retain a unique power to help create positive experience throughout these changes, except, possibly, during middle age. Adult friendships may not be as uncontrolled and rowdy as those of adolescents, but they are as enjoyable. Research by others confirms the relationship between friendship and positive affect (Bradburn, 1969; Diener, Emmons, & Sandvik, 1985; Wessman & Ricks, 1966) and suggests that adults' interactions with friends draw on the same elements of openness, reciprocity, and positive feedback that we documented in adolescence (Adams, 1967; Blau, 1973; Hess, 1972).

One of the most interesting findings in our analysis of adult interactions with friends concerns their influence upon immediate thoughts. We tend to think of emotional experience solely in terms of its affective qualities, yet its most profound effect is often the one it can have upon our attention. In fact, in his research on enjoyment, Csikszentmihalyi (1975) portrays the attentional elements of the experience as much more central than the affective.

When with friends, our older adults reported thoughts that were categorically different from those at other times. They reported many more thoughts that transcended the usual preoccupations of their everyday lives (Larson et al., 1986). Their attention was more often directed to ideas, to play, and to other people. Concern with the trivialities of day-to-day existence appeared to recede from their consciousness.

No matter what our age, the special moments we enjoy with others can turn our world inside out, temporarily reversing the usual relations of figure and ground. With friends our attention becomes focused, distractions lessen, awareness of time disappears: We emerge into a world in which the intimacy and joy shared with others is the fundamental reality, and for a time the world becomes a different place. Adults as well as adolescents seek out friends to get away from daily concerns, to transcend pragmatic preoccupations, and to experience the all-absorbing enjoyment they find in friendships.

CONCLUSION: EXPERIENTIAL RESOURCES WITHIN THE SOCIAL NETWORK

The thesis of this article has been that signficant others have great importance, at least in part because of the unique kinds of experiences they offer. The data have illustrated the power of family members, and especially friends, to affect moods and transform attention. Friends can make us happy, changing our thoughts from preoccupation with the trivial, mundane, or wearying routines of daily life to attention centered on more meaningful personal exchanges. Irrespective of whether these significant others serve a supportive function, we value them simply as companions. They are partners in the pursuit of liberating experience.

The social network of friends and family members might be thought of as a web of opportunities for different kinds of experience. It may include people we seek out to cheer us when we are down, people with whom we share a feeling of great trust and closeness. And it may include people we go to when we want to forget, people with whom we can share enthrallment in some new pursuit, or raucous joking, or vigorous exercise. This article provides only a cursory view of these experiential resources, considering them all in terms of the single dimension of enjoyment.

The data we have reviewed suggest striking consistency across the life span in the experiential opportunities that family members and friends characteristically provide. On the average, the family is experienced as a neutral context. For adolescents this may mean that it provides a sort of time out from the emotional intensity of friendships. For adults, in midlife and old age, the family is a more comprehensive context where the bulk of adult attention outside of work is centered, and where the business of living is carried out. Family experience is not distinguished by great times, but the family may provide a stable emotional backdrop for the rest of life. In general, it appears that the family is a context in which the long-term, not the immediate, rewards of interactions are most salient.

Friends, in contrast to family members, are a reliable resource for positive experience. Adolescents share experiences with friends ranging from mutual understanding to uninhibited, free-flowing good times. In adulthood, interactions with friends also appear to transform affect and attention by offering adults a reprieve from the demands of work and family. Friends enhance one's enjoyment and interest, affording pleasurable experience that times with family members alone cannot provide. From adolescence to old age, friends are partners in enjoyment. We value them just because of the special times, the precious moments, that we have with them time and again.

NOTES

1. The authors are grateful to Mihaly Csikszentmihaly and Ronald Graef for use of the data from the adult sample. A full description of this data set may be found in Csikszentmihalyi and Graef (1980).

2. The authors are grateful to Jiri Zuzanek and Roger Mannell from the University of Waterloo for use of the data from the older adult sample. A full description of this data set may be found in Larson, Zuzanek, and Mannell (1985).

3. No significant gender differences were found in the amount of time respondents within each age category spent with family as compared to friends. Gender differences might well have been expected in the adult sample had it contained a more representative selection of women, including those with no employment or part-time employment.

4. No significant gender differences were found in the average happiness or excitement that respondents in each age category reported with family as opposed to friends.

REFERENCES

Adams, B. (1967). Interaction theory and the social network. *Sociometry, 30*, 64-78.
Bernard, H. R., Killworth, P., Kronenfeld, D. & Sailer, L. (1984). On the validity of retrospective data: The problem of informant accuracy. *Annual Review of Anthropology, 13*, 495-517.
Berndt, T. (1982). The features and effects of friendship in early adolescence. *Child Development, 53*, 1447-1460.
Berscheid, E. (1983). Emotion. In H. Kelley et al. (Eds.), *Close relationships* (pp. 110-168). New York: W. H. Freeman.
Blau, Z. (1973). *Old age in a changing society*. New York: New Viewpoints.
Bradburn, N. (1969). *The structure of psychological well being*. Chicago: Aldine.
Brown, B. (1981). A life-span approach to friendship: Age-related dimensions of an ageless relationship. In H. Lopata & D. Maines (Eds.), *Research on the interweave of social roles, Vol. 2: Friendship* (pp. 23-50). Greenwich, CT: J.A.I.
Csikszentmihalyi, M. (1975). *Beyond boredom and anxiety*. San Francisco: Jossey-Bass.

Csikszentmihalyi, M. & Graef, R. (1980). The experience of freedom in daily life. *American Journal of Community Psychology, 8,* 401-414.

Csikszentmihalyi, M. & Larson, R. (1984). *Being adolescent.* New York: Basic Books.

Diener, E., Emmons, R. & Sandvik, E. (1985). *The dual nature of happiness: Independence of positive and negative moods.* Unpublished manuscript.

Graef, R., Giannino, S. & Csikszentmihalyi, M. (1979, August). *Positive and negative measures of well-being in everyday life.* Paper presented at the 87th Annual Covention of the American Psychological Association, New York.

Harris, P., Olthoff, T. & Terwogt, M. (1981). Children's knowledge of emotion. *Journal of Child Psychology and Psychiatry, 22,* 247-261.

Hess, B. (1972). Friendship. In M. Riley, M. Johnson & A. Foner (Eds.), *Aging and Society. Vol. III: A sociology of age stratification* (pp. 357-393). Russell Sage, New York.

Hinde, R. (1979). *Towards understanding relationships,* New York: Academic Press.

Hoffman, M. (1984). Interaction of affect and cognition in empathy. In C. Izard, J. Kagan & R Zajonc (Eds.), *Emotions, cognition, and behavior* (pp. 103-131). Cambridge: Cambridge University Press.

Kagan, J. (1984). The idea of emotion in human development. In C. Izard, J. Kagan & R. Zajone (Eds.), *Emotions, cognition, and behavior* (pp. 38-72). Cambridge: Cambridge University Press.

Larson, R. (1983). Adolescents' daily experience with family and friends: Contrasting opportunity systems. *Journal of Marital and Family Therapy 9(4).* Tables 1 and 2 reprinted from Volume 9 Number 4 of Journal of Marital and Family Therapy. Copyright 1983 American Association of Marriage and Family Therapy. Reprinted by permission.

Larson, R. & Bradney, N. (1985, April). *Mutual emotions among friends.* Paper presented at the biannual meeting of the Society for Research on Child Development, Toronto.

Larson, R. & Csikszentmihalyi, M. (1983). The Experience Sampling Method. In H. Reis (Ed.), *New directions for naturalistic methods in the behavioral sciences* (pp. 41-56). San Francisco: Jossey-Bass.

Larson, R., Mannell, R. & Zuzanek, J. (1986). The daily experience of older adults with family and friends. *Psychology and Aging, 1,* 117-126.

Larson, R., Zuzanek, J. & Mannell, R. (1985). Being alone versus being with people: Disengagement in the daily experience of older adults. *Journal of Gerontology, 40,* 375-381.

McClintock, E. (1983). Interaction. In H. Kelley et al. (Eds.), *Close relationships* (pp. 68-109). New York: W. H. Freeman.

Mischel, W. (1968). *Personality and assessment.* New York: John Wiley.

Reis, H. (1984). Social interaction and well-being. In S. Duck (Ed.), *Personal relationships 5: Repairing relationships* (pp. 21-45). New York: Academic Press.

Sullivan, H. (1953). *The interpersonal theory of psychiatry,* New York: Norton.

Weiner, B. & Graham, S. (1984). An attributional approach to emotional development. In C. Izard, J. Kagan & R. Zajonc (Eds.), *Emotions, cognition, and behavior* (pp. 167-191) Cambridge: Cambridge University Press.

Wells, A. (1985). *Variations in self-esteem in the daily life of mothers.* Unpublished Ph.D. dissertation, University of Chicago.

Wessman, A. & Ricks, D. (1966). *Mood and personality.* New York: Holt, Rinehart & Winston.

Youniss, J. (1980). *Parents and peers in social development.* Chicago: University of Chicago Press.

5

Changes in Social Networks Following Marital Separation and Divorce

Marylyn Rands

The breakup of a marriage dramatically affects other aspects of one's life. Among those changes are fluctuations in the former partners' relationships with their family and friends. Following separation, some relationships are likely to diminish or to end completely, while others may become more satisfying. Often new ties will be formed that are more adaptive to the altered lifestyle. Although individuals differ in how much their network is affected by marital separation, almost everyone experiences some degree of change.

This chapter provides a framework for examining network change during the process of separation, divorce, and adaptation to singlehood or remarriage. It will look at some unpublished data assessing such changes and will show how a network approach can be used to compare subgroups—males and females, for instance. Issues such as the implications of network stability versus turnover, the impact of supportive

AUTHOR'S NOTE: The research described here was supported by a grant to George Levinger at the University of Massachusetts, Amherst, and was part of my doctoral dissertation. I extend my appreciation to R. Steven Schiavo and George Levinger for their helpful comments on an earlier draft, and to Elise Beatrice for her assistance with various tasks in the preparation of this manuscript.

versus interfering or rejecting networks, and the problem of developing new attachments will be explored.

THE SOCIAL CONTEXT OF MARRIAGE

Network change following divorce is in some ways a reversal of the changes that occurred with marriage. Individuals are each initially connected to their own kin, friends, and other associates. During courtship and marriage, they gradually loosen some of their individual ties and develop a shared network (Boissevain, 1974; Farrell & Rosenberg, 1977; Johnson & Leslie, 1982; Lowenthal & Chiriboga, 1975; Milardo, 1982; Milardo, Johnson, & Huston, 1983; Shulman, 1975).

The characteristics of the marital network differ, however, from networks before marriage. Marrieds, especially if they have children, interact more frequently with kin than do nonmarrieds. (Belsky & Rovine, 1984; Brandwein, Brown, & Fox, 1974; Spicer & Hampe, 1975). After marriage, socializing tends to occur more often in a couple context (Farrell & Rosenberg, 1977), and interaction with network members becomes more stable and less exchange-oriented (Shulman, 1975). When a marriage dissolves, the shared network is likely to be pulled apart to some extent (Huston & Levinger, 1978), sometimes by choice, sometimes not. The individual's network is likely to resume its premarital characteristics.

ASSESSING SOCIAL NETWORK CHANGE

A social network can be conceived as a cluster of persons, with the focal person (P) at the center connected through affective and behavioral interdependence to others (O's) who are kin, friends, or associates. These others may themselves be interconnected (see Barnes, 1972; Fischer, Jackson, Stueve, Gerson, Jones, & Baldassare, 1977; chapters by Milardo and Surra, this volume), and each network member is a potential center for his or her own network. The network itself is embedded in a social context where structural constraints affect personal choice for interaction (Milardo, 1986; Milardo, in press). This conception allows us to map social networks in systematic ways, to focus our analysis, and to generate hypotheses within a theoretical framework. Although here we concentrate on the social networks of the maritally separated or divorced, this technique is suitable for studying any social network.

Social Network Mapping

Network mapping allows us to distinguish three distinct attributes of networks: (a) their *structure*—What does the map look like? (b) their *composition*—Who are its members? and (c) their *interaction patterns*— What is the nature of the interpersonal interconnections? Network structure and composition are macrolevel variables; they describe relatively long-lasting, general conditions. Interaction patterns can be described at either the macrolevel or microlevel of analysis; that is, they can refer either to ongoing patterns of interaction or to temporary events. Let us look at these categories more closely.

1. *Networks vary in their structure.* Networks are typically described on the basis of their size, density, and segmentation. *Size* refers to number of members, *density* refers to the degree of association among members, and *segmentation* refers to the number and connectedness of subgroups of members. Regarding segmentation, networks can be integrated (most of the members interact with each other), dispersed (few of the members interact with each other), or segmented (clusters of members interact, but there is little connection among clusters). We can raise several questions related to network structure: Do individuals reduce or increase the number of their social contacts after marital separation? Do more network members know each other during marriage than after separation? How much contact occurs between associates chosen from different settings, such as work or home?

2. *Networks vary in their composition.* Composition refers to the characteristics of the network members. They can be described, for example, as kin or nonkin, male or female, married or nonmarried. Questions can be raised regarding network composition: Do the maritally separated associate more with nonmarried than with married individuals? Are friends or relatives more likely to satisfy affiliative needs?

3. *Networks vary in their interaction patterns.* Interaction can be described in terms of its patterns of frequency or duration, its intensity, its symmetry, the diversity of interchanges, and the degree of partner goal facilitation (Kelley, Berscheid, Christensen, Harvey, Huston, Levinger, McClintock, Peplau, & Peterson, 1983). Focus on interaction can range from the microlevel (e.g., verbal interchanges in two partners' recent conflict) to the macrolevel (e.g., the global nature of their mutual self-disclosure). Relations among interaction variables, structural variables, and member composition can be tested: Are members of large social networks more, or less, likely to know each other? Are spouses in dense networks more likely to assume traditional gender roles (Bott, 1957)?

3a. *P-O interaction.* It is useful to distinguish the interaction between the central person and other network members (P-O), and that among the network members themselves (O-O). Information about P and O is usually obtained from P, either through self-report or through direct observation, and therefore, tends to receive the major emphasis in network studies. For example, we could ask or observe P to answer the following: With whom does P spend leisure time? What is the nature of P's self-disclosure?

3b. *O-O interaction.* Information about O-O interaction is more difficult to obtain. Indirect reports, obtained from P, are likely to be biased, whereas direct observation of all network members is impractical. Intermediate strategies have been used. One approach, for example, has been to interview a subset of network members regarding their interaction with each other (e.g., Laumann, 1969).

The way that network members interact is likely to be affected by their relationship with P. Whether one member gossips about P or invites a certain person to a party may depend on the nature of the P-O bond. Network interaction will also influence P; if network members support the separation or P's new associates, P is more likely to maintain the relationship with O. O-O interaction may differ from marriage to separation as network members adapt to changes in their relationship with each of the former spouses.

Other Research Questions

The network map, revealing structure, composition, and interaction patterns, provides an organizing scheme for systematically exploring a variety of research questions. Using these three attributes of networks, we can examine network variation across time or between subgroups. A social network approach also provides a basis for examining the complex associations between relationship and psychological variables. It is assumed, for example, that social support affects psychological well-being (e.g., Gottlieb, 1981; McCannell, this volume). While it is true that social support may promote well-being, interfering or rejecting networks are likely to create distress (Shumaker & Brownell, 1984). Further, while social interaction may promote well-being, a feeling of well-being in itself is likely to increase one's capacity for social interaction.

THE SOCIAL NETWORKS OF
THE RECENTLY DIVORCED

The results of a 1979 study of divorced persons (Rands, 1980) will be presented here, along with other findings that illustrate the nature and effects of network change. This study is one of the few to apply a systematic social network analysis to the study of divorce.

On the basis of structured interviews, the networks of 40 recently divorced persons, 20 male and 20 female, were compared from one time period during their marriage to another period following their separation. Names of respondents were obtained using public records of the Hampshire County Probate Court in Northampton, Massachusetts. Respondents had been married from 2 to 24 years and separated an average of 23.4 months. This was the first divorce for all but one female. Out of 16 mothers, 15 had child custody, and out of 12 fathers, 6 had child custody. Out of the 40 respondents, 5 males and 5 females had been married to each other.

Networks were compared from marriage to separation on their structure, member composition, and P-O interaction, and these variables were compared for males and females. Psychological well-being was also assessed. (Comparisons of parents and nonparents and comparisons according to respondent's age are not reported here.)

Descriptions of the network were obtained for two time points: Marriage (Time 1) and separation (Time 2). Several strategies were used to maximize respondents' recall of past events. Time 1 was determined by having each respondent graph, on a time line representing the length of marriage, anchor points of important events and his or her "confidence during each of these years that your marriage would go on indefinitely into the future." Time 1 was then chosen to be the most recent period before separation (a) when the respondents still felt reasonably confident of staying married to their partner, and (b) when the respondent's social relationships were still typical of those held during the marriage (i.e., they had not begun to change due to the impending marital separation). Time 2 was chosen to be that period of time after separation when a respondent "really began to feel like a single person again." Time 1 was an average of 23.3 months before separation, while Time 2 was an average of 8 months after separation. Each time period was roughly three months (i.e., summer, 1975).

The network was defined as those persons with whom there had been actual exchanges during the specified time period. Names were elicited by asking six questions about the targets of interaction at each time point: sharing activities, getting together for spare time interests, sharing feelings, seeking advice, giving or receiving favors, and making a special effort to stay in touch (see Fischer et al., 1977; Fischer, 1982; Milardo, this volume).

Information describing network composition was collected on all network members—the "Total Network" (e.g., sex, age, emotional closeness). Information about composition, P-O interaction, and density was obtained for a subset of the eight "most important" members—the "Top Eight" (e.g., how they first met, frequency and duration of contact). Other measures of P-O interaction were made for the "Top Four" (e.g., self-disclosure, physical contact). This reductive strategy was taken to minimize respondent fatigue, while at the same time to gain information at various levels of analysis. Questions about psychological well-being (e.g., life-satisfaction, happiness, loneliness) were asked for three timepoints, Times 1 and 2, and at the time of the interview (Time 3).

Selected findings are presented here to give a general picture of the networks at each time point. We first look at network stability—that is, the turnover of associates from marriage to separation. We'll then provide a general picture of network structure, composition, and P-O interaction at each time point. As an example of how network analysis can be used to compare individuals' social experiences, we'll then focus on the social networks of males and females. We'll also look at findings regarding the psychological correlates of network participation. After these results are presented, several other issues relevant to the social experience of the divorced are discussed, and a critique of network analysis is provided.

Network Stability

As might be expected, network membership changed considerably following marital separation. At Time 2, an average of 8 months after separation, only about 60 percent of the original members remained (an average loss of .27 members per month). By Time 3, an average of 23.4 months after separation, 51% of the initial associates remained (an average loss of .12 members per month since Time 2). Note that network turnover is highest immediately following divorce, then tapers off.

Stability varied for different types of relationships. Relatives were more stable than friends (62% versus 56%), and one's own relatives were more stable than one's spouse's (92% versus 33%). Stability was higher for same-sex than cross-sex associates (64% versus 52%), higher for unmarried than for married ones (68% versus 60%), and higher for one's own first acquaintances than for one's spouse's (76% versus 30%).

Network Structure

Networks changed in size, density, and segmentation following marital separation, becoming smaller, less dense, and more segmented. Total size decreased significantly from an average of 20.75 members during marriage to 17.95 following separation, a 14% shrinkage ($p < .01$).

Density, based on how many members knew each other, was calculated by dividing the number of actual linkages by the number of potential linkages. Acquaintance among members decreased significantly from 83% to 65% after separation ($p < .01$).

Members of the Top Eight were drawn from more contexts after separation (5.70 versus 4.98; $p < .06$). Segmentation was calculated by counting clusters of network members as indicated in respondents' own representations of their Top Eight.

Composition of the Social Network

Network change was also assessed by comparing member characteristics across time (see Table 1). After separation, respondents interacted with significantly fewer relatives, especially in-laws, both in their total network and in the Top Eight. The absolute number of friends remained stable (thus showing no change from Time 1 to Time 2), although a significant number were dropped and new ones added.

Respondents reported more same-sex than cross-sex associates at either time point. The absolute number of both same-sex and cross-sex members in the total network decreased from marriage to separation, but analysis of the Top Eight showed that same-sex persons became significantly more important and cross-sex persons less important after separation. During marriage, respondents were twice as likely to associate with married persons than nonmarried ones; after separation, they were about equally likely to associate with either group.

There were significantly more married persons than nonmarried ones at either time point. However, following separation the number of married associates dropped significantly and the number of nonmarried ones rose.

There were changes in the origin of initial acquaintance for the Top Eight. During marriage, members were most likely to be kin (39%), and second most likely to be persons met through the spouse (16%). After separation, kin were still most common (41%), but persons met through a friend (18%) or at work (14%) were next most likely, and persons met

TABLE 1
Network Composition at Two Time Points

	Marriage Time 1	Separation Time 2
Relationship to respondent		
Total network		
relatives	9.90	7.00*
nonrelatives	10.85	10.95
Top eight		
relatives	4.20	2.43**
friends	2.75	3.33
Sex composition		
Total network		
same sex	11.12	10.28**
cross sex	9.62	7.68**
Top eight		
same sex	4.27	4.53**
cross sex	3.71	3.39**
Marital status		
Total network		
married	13.45	9.50**
nonmarried	6.38	7.93*
Top eight		
married	4.38	3.48
nonmarried	3.62	4.42

NOTE: The significance level is based on the results of t-tests (2-tailed) comparing respondents' ratings at the two time points.
*p .003; **p .001.

through the spouse were now only a minor part of the network (1%). During marriage, one's own acquaintances were more than three times as likely to appear as members of the Top Eight as were the spouse's acquaintances (53% versus 16%), whereas at Time 2, one's own acquaintances were almost nine times as likely to be chosen (44% versus 5%). (Mutual acquaintances are excluded here.)

In summary, the postseparation network comes to resemble the premarital network, becoming less kin-centered, less heterosexual, and less couple-oriented. Relations with one's own relatives are maintained, but not one's spouse's, nor are connections with the spouse's acquaintances. The merging process that occurred with marriage is reversed.

Interaction with Network Members

Interaction was assessed using four measures: (1) The respondent's feeling of closeness to each network member, (2) frequency,

(3) duration of contact with the Top Eight, and (4) feelings and activities shared with the Top Four.

Emotional intensity. Average feelings of closeness to network members was equal from Time 1 to Time 2 (2.4-2.6 on a 4-point scale). Closeness, however, did change for one-half the continuing members, decreasing for one-third, and increasing for one-sixth.

Frequency and duration of contact. Respondents were asked how often they got together with each of the Top Eight, and how much time they spent together. Average frequency and duration of contact with the Top Eight did not change following marital separation. However, interaction with kin was significantly more frequent and long-lasting than with friends during marriage, whereas interaction with friends was more frequent and long-lasting than with kin during separation.

Social exchange. Five categories of items assessed self-disclosure, physical contact, positive affect, negative affect, and joint activities with the Top Four (modified from Rands & Levinger, 1979). Following separation, average self-disclosure increased, whereas physical contact decreased. Both sexes tended to show less negative affect (males significantly so) and to spend less time in joint activities. There was no change in expression of positive affect.

Interaction with specific individuals shifts in predictable ways. Interaction was highest with the spouse, second highest with the average of the Top Four at separation, and lowest with the three adults other than the spouse during marriage. These findings illustrate the high behavioral and affective interdependence in the marital relationship (Rands & Levinger, 1979), and a shift to other members when the spouse is no longer available, probably in an effort to fulfill needs that were once met with the spouse. This finding supports the "fund of sociability notion" (see Weiss, 1974).

GENDER DIFFERENCES
IN SOCIAL NETWORKS

One's social experience following marital separation depends on many factors: whether one is male or female, a parent or childless, younger or older, and so on. This section will compare males and females as an example of how network analysis can illuminate differences in social experience.

There were surprisingly few gender differences found in the present study. Males and females named approximately the same number of network members, from approximately the same contexts, and with about equal degrees of participation. Females named more kin than did males, both before and after marital separation, though not significantly more. Both sexes reported significantly fewer kin after separation (p < .05), and although their frequency and duration of time spent with kin in the Top Eight decreased, there were no gender differences. This finding is contrary to Anspach (1976) and Spicer and Hampe (1975), who found that females' involvement with kin increased after divorce, and it conflicts with other findings that show females to be more involved with kin than males (Booth, 1972; Weiss, 1974). However, 19 of the 20 females in the present study were working at least part time, which might account for the absence of this common gender difference. Both sexes reported greater frequency and duration of time spent with friends after separation.

Overall, both males and females reported an approximately equal number of same-sex and cross-sex ties during marriage; after separation, however, females (but not males) reported significantly fewer cross-sex ties and more same-sex ones (p < .01), in part because there was a drop in the number of male associates for women (p < .05), while males continued to have about an equal number of ties with either sex. In addition, after separation males identified significantly more cross-sex relationships (3.45) than did females (2.80) in their respective Top Eight networks (p < .01). Booth and Hess (1974) have also noted that males tend to have more cross-sex friendships than do females.

For separated females, physical contact—although less than during marriage—was as high as for married males. It is traditionally more acceptable for females than for males to express physical affection, such as hugging, with friends or kin. Such norms probably account for females' higher level of physical contact with network members (Rands & Levinger, 1979).

Other gender differences. On the average, females' confidence in their marriage's durability waned before that of the males. Time 1, which was defined as "that time most closely preceding separation when confidence was still relatively high," was earlier in the marriage for females—an average of 28.15 months before separation, compared to 18.45 months for males. This suggests that females are quicker to detect problems in their marriage. These differences, combined with the finding that more females than males initiated separation, indicate that females are more attuned to relationship problems. Hill, Rubin, and Peplau (1979) reached a similar conclusion in their study of the breakup of affairs.

SOCIAL NETWORKS AND
PSYCHOLOGICAL WELL-BEING

One's physical and psychological well-being is assumed to vary with social participation (e.g., Brownell & Shumaker, 1984; Shumaker & Brownell, 1984; Gottlieb, 1981; Perlman, this volume). For the recently separated or divorced, networks are expected to provide emotional and instrumental support, to alleviate the stress of single life, to provide integration into social groups and the wider community, and to ease the transition to a new close relationship (Weiss, 1974; Weiss, 1975).

This study examined associations between social network variables and psychological well-being by measuring patterns of self-esteem, life satisfaction, and loneliness across the three time points. Because these findings showed different patterns for males and females, we will look closely at these gender differences. For males, well-being was positively associated with network turnover: To the extent that a male dropped his relationships with kin, married associates, and females, and established relationships with friends, especially unmarried male friends, his reports of well-being increased. Males with high network turnover also rated themselves as more physically attractive than males with a low turnover. For females, well-being after separation appeared to have little to do with the degree of turnover of associates.

The proportion of friends versus relatives was associated with well-being, but differently for females and males. Females with a high proportion of friends during marriage expressed greater self esteem, life satisfaction, and happiness; after separation, the ratio did not seem to matter. On the other hand, males with a high proportion of friends after separation reported greater well-being. Again, during marriage the ratio did not seem to matter. A network predominantly consisting of friends, then, appears beneficial at different times for males and females. The reasons for these varying patterns need to be explored.

Although there was no correlation between an individual's well-being during marriage and separation, both males and females reported themselves significantly more satisfied with life after separation. This improvement came earlier for males than for females; males' satisfaction showed a significant increase by Time 2 (on the average within 7.5 months after actual separation), whereas females' did not show improvement until the time of the interview (an average of 28.5 months after separation (cf. Hetherington, Cox, and Cox, 1977). Considering that females also experienced doubts earlier in the marriage than did males, the period of stress for marital breakup appears longer for women than for men.

As is commonly found, initiators of the separation tended to be female more often than male (Hill, et al., 1979; Kressel, Lopez-Morillas, Weinglass, & Deutsch, 1979; Peplau, 1978). Being the initiator had positive effects on respondents' well-being at separation, especially for males. Men whose wife made the decision to separate reported the least happiness, lowest self-esteem, and most loneliness; men who themselves chose to separate rated most positively on these variables. Female noninitiators and initiators were intermediate to these two groups, with initiators reporting slightly more life-satisfaction than noninitiators.

IMPLICATIONS OF NETWORK STABILITY

It is not entirely clear when network stability is helpful and when it is not. This study found high psychological well-being for men with high turnover, but no connection for women. Wilcox (1981), however, found that women also benefited from less stable networks: Change in associates appeared to facilitate adjustment by providing a looser, more flexible network that allowed women to explore new roles and to make new acquaintances, features that would also seem important for the recently separated.

But why did turnover relate differently to well-being for females and males? One explanation is that males' friendships are relatively inter-changeable, more sociable than intimate (Parsons & Bales, 1955; Pleck, 1975). Change of associates could provide stimulation, variety, and reinforcement of one's desirability. Females, on the other hand, are believed to prefer intimacy with one or a few confidants more than simple sociability (see also Brown, Brohlchain, & Harris, 1975). Information about the turnover of female friendships may reveal little, then, unless we know how close the friendships were. The loss of merely sociable friends may be insignificant, whereas the loss or gain of close ones may be vital.

Another problem with assessing the effects of network change is that we do not know how much change is typical. Networks are likely to be less stable during any sort of transition. A longitudinal study of women returning to school found, for example, that only 40% of their social network remained the same eight months after entering school compared to the month prior to entry (Rands & Schiavo, 1984). For these women, however, such changes may not be permanent. A woman returning to college may temporarily curtail her interaction to meet other demands on her time, but may reactivate dormant relationships when she has more leisure. The divorced are more likely to permanently lose a proportion of their ties, such as the opportunity to associate with relatives or friends of the former spouse. The implications of temporary versus permanent loss remain to be explored.

SUPPORTIVE VERSUS INTERFERING NETWORKS

When a couple divorces, there are few rules to guide family and friends through the inevitable changes. Relationships must be reinterpreted or they will fade (Weiss, 1975). Changes in the separating person's needs or preferences may cause one or the other to withdraw when interaction becomes difficult or ambiguous (Spanier & Thompson, 1984).

One area of change to be negotiated is likely to be the nature of social support. Once conceived in exclusively positive terms, researchers are beginning to realize that help during times of stress is often received with mixed feelings (Shinn, Lehmann, & Wong, 1984). Family members are the primary ones to offer assistance, generally providing emotional support to females and financial support to males (Spanier & Thompson, 1984). Such support, however, may promote feelings of dependence, and in a culture that strongly encourages independence, especially from parents, the divorced may suffer a loss of self-esteem, causing them to withdraw from the relationship if they cannot in some way reciprocate the help they receive.

Further, some types of concern may be unwanted. Friends and relatives sometimes interfere, offering undesired attention or criticism (Johnson & Milardo, 1984), particularly when their anxiety over the individual's well-being or behavior is highest. If one's associates are not able to adapt to the changing requirements of the relationship—to help facilitate new goals (Levinger & Rands, 1985)—then termination or emotional withdrawal by one or both parties, although painful, may be seen as the best solution.

DEVELOPING NEW ATTACHMENTS

The divorced tend to remarry. Spanier and Thompson (1984) report that one-fourth of divorced persons remarry within the first year following divorce and one-half remarry within three years (p. 14), and there is evidence that those who do remarry are psychologically better off than those who do not. Studies have shown that the formerly married are more lonely than either the married or the never-married (Weiss, 1982), and that being unattached is a critical factor affecting loneliness (Perlman, this volume; Rubenstein & Shaver, 1982; Russell, 1982).

Other studies suggest that psychological well-being following divorce makes remarriage more likely (Spanier & Furstenberg, 1982). Beginning to date again is one way to gain psychological benefits, including being distracted from daily problems, having something to anticipate, averting loneliness, and gaining a chance to reaffirm one's self-worth (Spanier & Thompson, 1984).

Being unattached, however, may itself affect an individual's willingness to socialize. The divorced, like the widowed, are likely to feel uncomfortable in formerly routine social situations in which the absence of a partner creates asymmetry or awkwardness (Lopata, Heinemann, & Baum, 1982). When situations for socializing are difficult to arrange, the divorced may feel they have too little control over the amount of time spent alone or with others (Larson, Csikszentmihalyi, & Graef, 1982). Difficulties in achieving desired levels of social interaction can start a cycle of self-blame, where the isolated individual attributes reasons for social isolation to the self, in turn reducing self-esteem and the willingness to take risks to form new relationships (Peplau, Miceli, & Morasch, 1982).

Gender differences emerged in the dating patterns of the present sample. Males were more likely than females to be involved in a close heterosexual relationship at the time of the interview (70% versus 40%). This difference is more striking when we consider that females had been separated an average of 10.5 months longer than males; females had had more time to get involved with a new partner, yet fewer had done so (cf. Hetherington, Cox, & Cox, 1977).

These findings suggest that divorced women either are more cautious about entering new relationships or that they have fewer opportunities for finding suitable partners. About a third of the women in the present study did indicate that the postdivorce period is a time for thinking things through before beginning a new relationship. Spanier and Thompson (1984) also found that women were more reluctant than men to begin dating. Similarly, females in Weiss' (1975) study reported themselves more cautious than males about becoming sexually involved with others, preferring to wait until an emotional bond had been established.

A sizeable number of women, though, considered the lack of male partners to be a problem. Divorced women appear to be at several disadvantages in meeting eligible partners: Many are single parents, tied to the home (Kohen, Brown, & Feldberg, 1979); most wait for men to initiate encounters; and the age range of eligible partners is generally smaller for women than for men (Spanier & Thompson, 1984). These factors combine to make it more difficult for women than men to remarry. Indeed, a 1975 census found that 12% of divorced or separated women ages 25-54 had not remarried, compared to only 8% of such men (U.S. Bureau of the Census, 1975).

Although few females were involved in a new attachment relationship, those who were so involved reported higher psychological well-being in direct correlation to their degree of commitment. To the extent they were dating, closely involved with, or living with a close partner, females reported themselves higher in self-esteem, happier, and more satisfied with their life. Males' present involvement was not associated with their ratings of well-being.

Women with new partners also remembered themselves less content during their marriage than females who had no present involvement. Perhaps when the divorced compare their present lifestyle to the former married one, any discrepancy between actual and desired patterns of social interaction becomes salient (Perlman, this volume; Peplau & Perlman, 1982). For women, at least, having a new close relationship was accompanied by recollections of earlier unhappiness.

CONCLUSION

This chapter attempted to show how social network mapping can guide inquiries of life experience. It shows how network structure and content can be assessed, and how these variables provide a structure for analyzing complex questions, such as network change or the links between structure or composition and other variables.

This social network analysis contributed to our understanding of the social experiences of the recently divorced. First, we see that there is relatively high turnover in associates. Not surprisingly, most of the change was in relationship with in-laws. However, a large number of friends tended to be replaced, usually with unmarried same-sex ones. The changes in network composition demonstrate a reversal of the changes that occurred at marriage, supporting Huston and Levinger's (1978) prediction that the postseparation network will come to resemble the premarital one.

Friendships contributed to well-being, but differently for males and females. For women, having friends was important during marriage; for men, having friends was important after separation. These findings accord with Fischer and Phillips' (1982) conclusion that it is isolation from nonkin that is most strongly associated with personal unhappiness (cf. Larson & Bradney, this volume). Marriage tends to isolate women, more than men, from nonkin; however, marriage tends to isolate men, more than women, from confidants other than the wife.

This study showed changes in social exchange with the four closest adults. It confirmed the high behavioral and affective interdependence of the marital relationship compared to other close relationships (Rands & Levinger, 1979) and showed that interaction with close associates increases following marital breakup, suggesting that individuals have a need for levels of intimacy that, if not met in a single close relationship, will be met through a combination of other relationships (Weiss, 1974). Further analyses could explore how relationships alter their functions in response to life changes.

At the macrolevel of analysis, then, we get a picture of changes in social involvement from marriage to separation. It is unlikely that respondents would have been able to directly verbalize these patterns.

Macrolevel analyses, however, are not as accurate at predicting individual behavior as microlevel ones (Ajzen & Fishbein, 1980). The special appeal of network analysis has been its comprehensive approach for mapping a set of complex relationships. As measurement strategies progress, important questions will require convergence of macrolevel and microlevel approaches.The links among members need to be described not only as simple connections (i.e., kinship versus friendship), but in terms of partners' mutual thoughts, feelings, and behaviors. Network analysis potentially enables this combination of macrolevel and microlevel approaches.

The present study touched only briefly on microlevel variables. It found that emotional closeness, while staying the same on the average, changed for half of the network members. It showed that certain behaviors (e.g., self-disclosure) are likely to increase, whereas others are likely to decrease (e.g., physical contact). This preliminary foray into the potentially rich microlevel interaction—the thoughts, feelings, and behaviors shared by P and O—needs to be extended. Network analysis, combined with microlevel analyses of relationship processes, can deepen our understanding of the subtle shifts that occur in social relationships following events such as marital separation.

REFERENCES

Ajzen, I., & Fishbein, M. (1980). *Understanding attitudes and predicting behavior.* Englewood-Cliffs, NJ: Prentice-Hall.

Anspach, D. F. (1976). Kinship and divorce. *Journal of Marriage and the Family, 38,* 323-330.

Barnes, J. A. (1972). Social networks. *Addison-Wesley Module in Anthropology, 26,* 1-29.

Belsky, J., & Rovine, M. (1984). Social-network contact, family support, and the transition to parenthood. *Journal of Marriage and the Family, 46,* 455-462.

Boissevain, J. (1974). *Friends of friends: Networks, manipulators and coalitions.* Oxford: Basil Blackwell.

Booth, A. (1972). *Sex and social participation.* American Sociological Review, 37, 183-193.

Booth, A., & Hess, B. (1974). Cross-sex friendship. *Journal of Marriage and the Family, 36,* 38-47.

Bott, E. (1957). *Family and social network: Roles, norms, and external relationships in ordinary urban families.* New York: Macmillan.

Brandwein, R. A., Brown, C., & Fox, E. M. (1974). Women and children last: The social situation of divorced mothers and their families. *Journal of Marriage and the Family, 36,* 498-514.

Brown, C. A., Brohlchain, N. N., & Harris, T. (1975). Social class and psychiatric disturbance among women in an urban population. *Sociology, 9,* 225-254.

Brownell, A., & Shumaker, S. A. (1984). Social support: An introduction to a complex phenomenon. In A. Brownell and S. A. Shumaker (Eds.). Social support: New perspectives in theory, research and intervention. Part I. Theory and research. *Journal of Social Issues, 40,* 1-10.

Farrell., M. P., & Rosenberg, S. (Sept. 1977). *Male friendship and the life cycle.* Paper presented at the Annual Meeting of the American Sociological Association.

Fischer, C. S., Jackson, R. M., Stueve, C. A., Gerson, K., Jones, L. M. & Baldassare, M. (Eds.) (1977). *Networks and places: Social relations in the urban setting.* New York: Free Press.

Fischer, C. S. (1982). *To dwell among friends: Personal networks in town and city.* Chicago: University of Chicago Press.

Fischer, C. S., & Phillips, S. L. (1982). Who is alone? Social characteristics of people with small networks. In L. A. Peplau and D. Perlman (Eds.), *Loneliness: A sourcebook of current theory, research and therapy* (pp. 21-39). New York: John Wiley.

Gottlieb, B. J. (Ed.). (1981). *Social networks and social support.* Sage Studies in Community Mental Health (Vol. 4). Newbury Park, CA: Sage.

Hetherington, Cox, & Cox (1977). The aftermath of divorce. In J. H. Stevens & M. Matthew (Eds.). *Mother-child, father-child relations.* Washington, DC: National Association for the Education of Young Children.

Hill, C. T., Rubin, & Peplau, L. A. (1979). Breakups before marriage: The end of 103 affairs. In G. Levinger and O. C. Moles (Eds.). *Divorce and separation: Context, causes, and consequences* (pp. 64-82). New York: Basic Books.

Huston, T. L., & Levinger, G. (1978). Interpersonal attraction and relationships. In M. R. Rosenzweig and L. W. Porter (Eds.), *Annual review of psychology* (pp. 115-156). Palo Alto, CA: Annual Reviews.

Johnson, M. P., & Leslie, L. (1982). Couple involvement and network structure: A test of the dyadic withdrawal hypothesis. *Social Psychology Quarterly, 45,* 34-43.

Johnson, M. P., & Milardo, R. M. (1984). Network interference in pair relationships: A social psychological recasting of Slater's theory of social regression. *Journal of Marriage and the Family, 46,* 893-899.

Kelley, H. H., Berscheid, E., Christensen, A., Harvey, J. H., Huston, T. L., Levinger, G., McClintock, E., Peplau, L. A., & Peterson, D. R. (1983). *Close relationships.* New York: W. H. Freeman.

Kohen, J. A., Brown, C. A., & Feldberg, R. (1979). Divorced mothers: The costs and benefits of female family control. In G. Levinger and O. C. Moles (Eds.). *Divorce and separation: Context, causes, and consequences.* New York: Basic Books.

Kressel, K., Lopez-Morillas, M., Weinglass, J., & Deutsch, M. (1979). Professional intervention in divorce: The views of lawyers, psychotherapists, and clergy. In G. Levinger and O. C. Moles (Eds.), *Divorce and separation: Context, causes, and consequences* (pp. 246-272). New York: Basic Books.

Larson, R., Csikszentmihalyi, M., & Graef, R. (1982). In L. A. Peplau & D. Perlman (Eds.), *Loneliness: A sourcebook of current theory, research and therapy* (pp. 40-53). New York: John Wiley.

Laumann, E. O. (1969). Friends of urban men: An assessment of accuracy in reporting their socioeconomic attributes, mutual choice, and attitude agreement. *Sociometry, 32,* 54-69.

Levinger, G., & Rands, M. (1985). Compatibility in marriage and other close relationships. In W. Ickes (Ed.), *Compatible and incompatible relationships* (pp. 309-331). New York: Springer-Verlag.

Lopata, H. Z., Heinemann, G. D., & Baum, J. (1982). In L. A. Peplau and D. Perlman (Eds.), *Loneliness: A sourcebook of current theory, research and therapy* (pp. 310-326). New York: John Wiley.

Lowenthal, M. F., & Chiriboga, D. (1975). *Four stages of life: A comparative study of women and men facing transitions.* San Francisco: Jossey-Bass.

Milardo, R. M. (in press). Changes in social networks of women and men following divorce: A review. *Journal of Family Issues.*

Milardo, R. M. (1982). Friendship networks in developing relationships: Converging and diverging social environments. *Social Psychology Quarterly, 45,* 162-172.

Milardo, R. M. (1986). Personal choice and social constraint in close relationships: Applications of network analysis. In V. J. Derlega and B. A. Winstead (Eds.), *Friendship and social interaction* (pp. 145-165). New York: Springer-Verlag.

Milardo, R. M., Johnson, M. P., & Huston, T. L. (1983). Developing close relationships: Changing patterns of interaction between pair members and social network. *Journal of Personality and Social Psychology, 44,* 964-976.

Parsons, T., & Bales, R. (Eds.). (1955). Family, socialization and interaction process. Glencoe, IL: Free Press.

Peplau, L. A. (1978). Women and men in love. *Society for the Advancement of Social Psychology Newsletter, 4,* 9-10.

Peplau, L. A., Miceli, M., & Morasch, B. (1982). In L. A. Peplau & D. Perlman (Eds.), *Loneliness: A sourcebook of current theory, research and therapy* (pp. 135-151). New York: John Wiley.

Peplau, L. A., & Perlman, D. (Eds.). (1982). *Loneliness: A sourcebook of current theory, research and therapy.* New York: John Wiley.

Pleck, J. H. (1975). Man to man: Is brotherhood possible? In N. Glazer-Malbin (Ed.), *Old family/new family: Interpersonal relationships* (pp. 229-244). New York: D. Van Nostrand.

Rands, M. (1980). Social networks before and after marital separation: A study of recently divorced persons. *Dissertation Abstracts International, 44,* 2828b. (University Microfilms No. 4988)

Rands, M., & Levinger, G. (1979). Implicit theories of relationship: An intergenerational study. *Journal of Personality and Social Psychology, 37,* 645-661.

Rands, M., & Schiavo, R. S. (May, 1984). *Family and personal issues for women returning to college.* Paper presented at the seventh annual Nebraska Symposium on Building Family Strengths, Lincoln, NE.

Rubenstein, C., & Shaver, P. (1982). The experience of loneliness. In L. A. Peplau and D. Perlman (Eds.), *Loneliness: A sourcebook of current theory, research and therapy* (pp. 206-223). New York: John Wiley.

Russell, D. (1982). The measurement of loneliness. In L. A. Peplau and D. Perlman (Eds.), Loneliness: A sourcebook of current theory, research and therapy (pp. 81-104). New York: John Wiley.

Shinn, M., Lehmann, S., & Wong, N. W. (1984). Social interaction and social support. In A. Brownell and S. A. Shumaker (Eds.). Social support: New perspectives in theory, research and intervention. Part I, theory and research. *Journal of Social Issues, 40,* 1-10.

Shulman, N. (1975). Life cycle variation in patterns of close relationships. *Journal of Marriage and the Family, 37,* 813-821.

Shumaker, S. A., & Brownell, A. (1984). Toward a theory of social support: Closing conceptual gaps. In A. Brownell and S. A. Shumaker (Eds.). Social support: New perspectives in theory, research and intervention. Part I, Theory and research. *Journal of Social Issues, 40,* 1-10.

Spanier, G. B., & Furstenberg, F. F. Jr. (1982). Remarriage after divorce: A longitudinal analysis of well-being. *Journal of Marriage and the Family, 44,* 709-720.

Spanier, G. B., & Thompson, L. (1984). Parting: The aftermath of separation and divorce. Newbury Park, CA: Sage.

Spicer, J. W., & Hampe, G. D. (1975). Kinship interaction after divorce. *Journal of Marriage and the Family, 37,* 113-119.

United States Bureau of the Census. Marital status and living arrangements: March, 1975. (Current population reports, Series P-20, No. 287). Washington, DC: U.S. Government Printing Office.

Weiss, R. S. (1982). Issues in the study of loneliness. In L. A. Peplau & D. Perlman (Eds.), *Loneliness: A sourcebook of current theory, research and therapy* (pp. 71-80).

Weiss, R. S. (1974). The provisions of social relationships. In Z. Rubin (Ed.). *Doing unto others* (pp. 17-26). Englewood Cliffs, NJ: Prentice-Hall.

Weiss, R. S. (1975). *Marital separation.* New York: Basic Books.

Wilcox, B. L. (1981). Social support in adjusting to marital disruption. In B. H. Gottlieb (Ed.), *Social networks and social support* (pp. 97-115). Sage Studies in Community Mental Health (Vol. 4). Newbury Park, CA: Sage.

6

Individual Development and Intimate Relationships in Middle and Late Adulthood

Rosemary Blieszner

Individuals grow and change physically, psychologically, and socially throughout life. This development takes place in a context of personal relationships which themselves change over time. A person's level of development influences the nature of relationships, and social interactions affect the individual's evolution, in an ongoing reciprocal process.

Although a number of recent essays compared and contrasted friendship at different life stages (e.g., Dickens & Perlman, 1981; Reisman, 1981; Tesch, 1983), only one of these (Brown, 1981) acknowledged the conjoint development of individuals and close relationships over the life course. Similarly, in the family relationship literature there has been little explicit recognition of the enduring nature of family influences on a person's development. Comparisons of kin and nonkin relationships across the life cycle have tended to focus mainly on structural aspects of relationships (e.g., Shulman, 1975; Stueve &

Gerson, 1977), with only minor attention given to their functions and meanings in the lives of the respondents (cf. Larson & Bradney, this volume). Yet complex interactions among members of the entire social network can and do influence the course of development, and changes within a given person can change interaction within the network (Milardo, this volume; Plath, 1984).

The present chapter examines this interface of individual development and relationship systems for the middle and late adulthood years. The discussion begins with a review of major developmental issues that have potential effect on the person's intimate relationships with the spouse and close friends. Then the focus turns to examining marriage and friendship in each of the middle and late adulthood stages.

Individuals in the middle years are defined here as those who have established a primary family setting and selected an occupation—they are between the late 30's and early 60's. People in late adulthood typically are retired from their formal occupational roles, but have many more years left to live. Thus in the second half of life a lengthy shared history of social interaction has already had extensive influence on relationship partners, and the influence of enduring relationships will continue indefinitely, although perhaps in new forms. In addition, the years of middle and late adulthood offer many opportunities to acquire new family members and friends; these new relationships are likely to affect the development and well-being of participants, as well.

MIDLIFE CRISIS
OR THE PRIME OF LIFE?

During the middle years, complex changes in appearance and physiological functioning become increasingly noticeable (Finch & Hayflick, 1977). These changes can have a profound effect on a middle-aged person's sense of becoming and feeling older and less attractive (Troll, 1975). The middle years are often a time of questioning the rules that have guided earlier decisions and relationships (Gould, 1978), reawakening the "adolescent" search for a personal identity and future direction in life (Rubin, 1979), and expressing concern about accomplishing a satisfactory level of work success (Levinson, Darrow, Klein, Levinson, & McKee, 1978). Many persons in midlife mention an increased awareness that life is finite and time for accomplishing goals is limited (Neugarten, 1968). Should someone at this stage become seriously ill, or experience the life-threatening illness or the death of a close relative or friend, concern about mortality is likely to be emphasized further (Cytrynbaum, Blum, Patrick, Stein, Wadner, & Wilk, 1980).

For some, these changes and redefinitions bring dismay at failure to attain the personal or career goals that had been planned. But for others, the middle years signal a heightened awareness of one's power and competence and influence in many realms of life. The "executive processes of personality" (Neugarten, 1968) attain central importance. Increased self-awareness and selectivity, greater ability to manipulate and control the environment, a stronger sense of mastery, and a more diverse array of cognitive and social strategies are characteristics of midlife adults at their prime.

Classical theorists in the study of human development underscored the connection between developmental progress and human relationships. Erik Erikson (1963) postulated a series of challenges for each major segment of life. He suggested that successful psychosocial development is associated with a favorable outcome of each conflict as one proceeds through life. For middle-aged adults, the primary dilemma is between "generativity" and "stagnation." Generativity is a concern for the welfare of individuals and society in the future. Middle-aged adults involved in the launching of children are expressing generativity, as are others engaged in productive or creative activities at work or in the community (See Gruen, 1964; Ryff & Heincke, 1983; Vaillant & Milofsky, 1980). In contrast, those who are caught in stagnation are absorbed in excessive self-concern and self-indulgence.

Robert Havighurst (1972) identified "developmental tasks" to be accomplished during each period of the life course. Like Erikson, he asserted that completion of each set of tasks provides a firm foundation for meeting the challenges of the next stage, and he similarly focused on midlife missions involving interpersonal relations. He listed the launching of children toward responsible and satisfying adulthood, attending to the relationship with one's spouse, assuming filial responsibility toward one's aging parents, and contributing to social and civic organizations among the major goals of the middle years.

THE GOLDEN YEARS
OR THE FINAL DECLINE?

As individuals age beyond the middle years, additional changes occur in physiological and psychological processes. The older adult's body gradually loses its capacity for peak performance in various functions (see Shock, 1977). Although age-related physical changes can have a direct impact on social behavior if they are extensive and severe, in actuality the vast majority of older adults lead independent lives as residents of the community. Only a small proportion of seniors, dominated by those who are very old (85 and above) or very frail, are sufficiently impaired by physical or mental deterioration to depend upon long-term care from other people.

With the passing of middle age, the focus on mastery of "executive" aspects of personality shifts to increased introspection and review of one's life experiences. Neugarten (1977) described a change from a very active to a more passive mode of dealing with the environment, and an increased interiority characterized by an orientation to one's inner world. In Erikson's (1963) scheme, the process of life review can yield a sense of "ego integrity" which signifies general satisfaction with one's choices and behavior over the span of life. On the other hand, increased introspection could lead to a feeling of deep regret about the way life was lived, and the belief that it is too late to choose another course of action. Erikson held that it is such "despair" that causes some older people to be angry and bitter and to have a strong fear of death. The developmental tasks that Havighurst (1972) ascribed to the final stage of life acknowledge the inevitable changes of aging. He cited the need for older adults to adjust satisfactorily to poorer health, less strength, reduced income, different living arrangements, and even the deaths of loved ones. Elderly persons who have achieved a degree of ego integrity with reference to past events in life are likely to adapt to these changes with graceful acceptance. Those who are dissatisfied with their past lives find it more difficult to cope with the current situation.

Besides the tendency to focus more on interior aspects of personality and less on the external world, the later years may also be characterized by shifts in sex role orientation. Gutmann (1977) suggested that older adults become more tolerant of aspects of their personalities that they were unable to express fully in their earlier years. Members of both genders appear to become more androgynous as they grow older. (Gutmann, 1977; Neugarten & Gutmann, 1968). Although efforts to replicate these findings with current cohorts of adults have not been successful (Sorell, Smyer, & Hooker, 1984), corroborative evidence of late life personality shifts and gender differences in personality is available from other lines of research (e.g., Gambria, 1979-80; Lowenthal, Thurnher, Chiriboga, & Associates, 1975).

More precise verification of personality trends in the middle and later years awaits longitudinal research, but there is no doubt that personality patterns and sex role orientation affect the reactions of individuals to changes in themselves and their life circumstances. In addition, a number of other variables are involved in the determination of why some people adapt to mid- and late-life transitions and challenges better than others. Genetic characteristics and level of health, factors associated with socioeconomic status, and previous experiences all contribute to one's ability to cope. But by far one of the most important elements is the amount and kind of social support available to a person experiencing change or stress (Cobb, 1976; L. Weiss, 1977; Rands, this volume; McCannell, this volume). The next section defines the nature and functions of social support in adulthood.

SOCIAL SUPPORT
AND LIFE STAGE TRANSITIONS

Social support provides one with the knowledge that he or she belongs to a group and is loved and valued, information which strengthens the individual's ability to solve problems and adjust to change (Cobb, 1976). Families, friends, and other network members provide support in a variety of ways ranging from concrete and relatively impersonal events to emotional and deeply personal events (Fischer, 1982; Kahn & Antonucci, 1981).

Another view of support emerges from R. Weiss's (1974) description of the "provisions" of social relationships. People gain feelings of attachment, social integration, opportunities to be nurturant, reassurance of their worth, a sense of reliable alliance, and guidance from their social interactions. Weiss maintained that all of these must be provided by the network in order for a person to have a sense of well-being. Because relationships tend to be specialized, and different relationships are typically associated with each provision, Weiss concluded that a variety of relationships is necessary to avoid the distress that accompanies lack of one or another provision. For example, if a sense of attachment, or peace and security, is missing, a person experiences emotional isolation; lack of integration—the sharing of common concerns and interests—leads to social isolation.

The attachment and social integration provisions, and the types of distress associated with them, are of particular interest in our consideration of the close relationships of middle-aged and older adults.

Attachment is gained from relationships with relatives and very close friends with whom the individual feels comfortable (R. Weiss, 1974). Divorce or widowhood are two mid- or late-life events which often precipitate emotional isolation (Lopata, 1973; Rands, this volume; R. Weiss, 1975). Emotional isolation, resulting from lack of truly intimate ties, leads to a generalized sense of anxiety and apprehension (R. Weiss, 1973). The social integration provision is obtained from a network of relationships which offer companionship, opportunities for exchanging favors, and occasions for sharing information, ideas, and interpretations of experiences (R. Weiss, 1974). Social isolation is the consequence of a deficient network of peers, and it results in boredom and restlessness (R. Weiss, 1973).

For middle-aged adults, social support is helpful as the person experiences normative transitions such as launching children into the adult world (McCannell, this volume) or confronting the beginning of physical declines (Johnson, this volume). Middle-aged people also depend on family and friends for support as they think through and resolve issues related to occupational satisfaction, financial planning, community involvement, meeting the needs of elderly parents, or clarifying their personal identities. Both emotional and social integration are essential to their ability to proceed through the middle years successfully.

In contrast to middle agers, older adults are likely to seek social support for assistance in adjusting to retirement, identifying meaningful and enjoyable activities, and coping with physical changes. Supportive close relationships are particularly crucial to the elderly who experience death of their spouse or other close persons—a major life event more likely to happen at this stage than at any other time of life. The emotional isolation brought on by widowhood might lead to social isolation as well if the widowed person is excluded from couples-oriented activities. Retirement may remove older people from social contacts with others. Residential change, such as moving from a familiar community to a new geographic area or a nursing home, or physical disability, which may limit possibilities of driving, walking, traveling, or otherwise maintaining social activity, can also lead to social isolation.

As an individual moves through the stages of adulthood and needs for social support change (Bengtson & Kuypers, 1985), some sources of social support may remain constant. For instance, spouses and close friends are usually age peers, and thus can understand the concerns and needs of a person as they all grow older together. On the other hand, certain experiences may evoke new needs and new support resources. The widow who seeks the advice and company of other widows for the first time, or persons who move to a new residence in retirement and make new friends therein, are examples. An unexpected event such as serious illness or divorce may motivate the traumatized individual to seek new friends or counselors.

In our society, older people in particular may find themselves caught in a social dilemma. Just at the age when intimates could contribute to maintaining their morale and help them cope with major life adjustments, the availability of close persons often decreases. Widowhood, retirement, residential change, or physical decline may limit the person's ability to maintain social contacts. A second factor contributing to the problematic social circumstances of older adults is the concurrent decrease in availability of close friends due to their change of residence, physical disability, or death. Thus older people may need to seek new sources of social support to substitute for lost personal relationships. Because of age stratification in our society, the source of new relationships is generally limited to other old people (Hochschild, 1973). However, the extent of substitutability of relationships in the social networks of elderly adults has been examined only recently (Johnson, this volume).

Relationships with marital partners and very close friends tend to endure for many years, and adults typically name spouses and/or close friends as their most important confidants. Thus the following sections of this chapter explore interactions with such significant others in greater detail, and compare these relationships during middle and old age.

MARITAL INTIMACY
IN THE SECOND HALF OF LIFE

Because marital partners in the United States are usually age peers, it is likely that both partners will experience middle age and old age at the same time, and either partner's questions and concerns related to development in the middle or later years are likely to affect both spouses (Kelley, 1981).

The impact of individual developmental transitions on marital quality and stability depends, of course, on factors such as each partner's ability to satisfy the other person's needs for emotional support and assistance in clarifying goals or solving problems. Amount of love for the partner and commitment to the relationship, and the ability to tolerate stress, ambiguity, or change are crucial characteristics of each partner in the second half of life, just as at any other period of transition. Couples whose marriages have endured to middle age or later may grow closer as a result of sharing and supporting each other's concerns. Or the stress of conflicting developmental trajectories could lead couples to grow apart and tolerate an unhappy marriage which no longer seems to meet their needs, or seek divorce (compare Skolnick, 1981).

In order to ascertain how marital partners jointly negotiate changes in midlife and old age, and the impact of their actions on their marital quality and stability, researchers must question both spouses and ask directly about the ways they cope with their individual developmental changes in the context of marriage. Although such couple data are not yet available, several scholars have examined marriages of mid-life and older men and women. We turn now to considering their findings.

Middle Years

How do the aforementioned developmental issues of middle-aged adults impact on their marriages? The answer must be explored separately for husbands and wives, as the different socialization experiences of men and women result in divergent developmental concerns and perceptions of marriage.

Experiences of husbands. Descriptions of the marriage relationship of middle-aged men can be found in several recent studies of the middle years. Farrell and Rosenberg (1981) interviewed a stratified random sample of 200 younger men (ages 25 to 30) and 300 middle-aged men (ages 38 to 48), then conducted two follow-up, in-depth interviews at home and at work with 20 families from the middle-aged group. The results supported previous research, which found that marital satisfaction is typically high among newlyweds, low during the child rearing years, and high in the launching and later years (Spanier & Lewis, 1980). The decline in marital satisfaction evidenced in the comparison of the young and middle-aged groups was greatest for the lower-class respondents, particularly those who had been in a state of upheaval and unhappiness for most of their lives. These men were not experiencing problems in middle age as sudden crises. Rather, they had suffered a chronic lack of social, psychological, and economic resources throughout their lives, and these deficits continued to interfere with their personal development and their marital relationship as they proceeded through the middle years. In contrast, another subgroup of respondents reported that their marriages were rewarding and they felt very close to their wives. These were men who were able to find appropriate solutions to major life problems, based on a history of adequate personal and social resources and previous successes.

The qualitative analyses from the follow-up interviews suggested several major alterations in the marital relationship in middle age as compared to younger adulthood. First, the wives were perceived to have more resources—money, competence, and information derived from employment outside the home—compared to younger wives. This resulted in the wives also having more power and autonomy in the marriage, but it produced strain within the husband-wife relationship for men who resented what they perceived to be challenges to their authority. The initial stages of renegotiating the nature of the marital relationship resulted in increased conflict and decreased marital satisfaction. But for the couples who were able to resolve the conflicts and transform the earlier relationship to a more egalitarian one, both marital satisfaction and personal contentment were higher than ever.

The researchers noted another interesting difference between the younger respondents' marriages and those of the middle aged men. The husbands and wives seemed to have grown from the similarities of personality and interests found among dating partners and newlyweds, to a state of psychological complementarity in the middle years. Each partner used the other spouse's characteristics to "complete, balance, or bolster" his or her own (Farrell & Rosenberg, 1981, p. 130).

For many couples, conflicts involve child rearing issues. But as children leave home in the middle-age period, the emotional balance of the family must be restructured. Couples who successfully transform their marital relationship at this time are apt to report increased marital satisfaction as a result.

Tamir (1982) analyzed data from a representative national sample of adults. She compared responses of 128 middle-aged men (ages 40 to 49) to those of 230 younger men (ages 25 to 39) and 193 older men (ages 50 to 69). As found in the studies discussed previously, the middle-aged men in Tamir's analysis were involved in extensive self-assessment and review of personal goals and accomplishments. More than the younger or older men, the middle-agers relied on their wives for support during times of inner conflict or stress. They appeared to be in the process of reestablishing a genuine, person-to-person relationship with their wives, especially if they were college educated. College graduates derived more self-esteem from marriage than those with less education, and unhappy marriages were more threatening to the psychological well-being of college-educated middle-aged men than either younger or older men. Tamir concluded that marriage has become a more crucial component of middle-aged men's lives than ever before.

Lowenthal et al. (1975) interviewed 216 blue-collar, white-collar, and middle-range professional adults in four age groups: high school seniors, newlyweds, middle-aged adults facing the empty-nest transition, and older adults preparing for retirement. The college-educated middle-aged men in this study, as in Tamir's (1982) research, were willing to scrutinize their marital relationships and accept at least some of the responsibility for any perceived inadequacies in the marriage. Men with less education were either less introspective or less willing to admit any negative personal characteristics. Lowenthal et al. (1975) reported that the middle-aged men seemed to be aware that they did not meet their wives' expectations for companionship or attention, but they did not appear to be motivated to change. However, these men were confident of their adequacy as family providers, and their wives concurred.

Experiences of wives. In the past, family scholars wondered whether traditional women who did not work outside the home would be devastated in middle age by the "emptying of the nest." Research has shown that such a reaction to the launching of children is not typical. On the contrary, middle-aged noncareer women tend to be concerned about finding a suitable personal identity and occupational activity in the dual contexts of an increased amount of free time and an emergent review of life goals and accomplishments.

Rubin (1979) conducted intensive interviews with 160 women aged 35 to 54. All of these women had focused on marriage and parenthood as their primary tasks in earlier years. At the time of the interviews, they were in the process of identifying other interests and opportunities for personal fulfillment. They expressed eagerness to relinquish parental responsibilities and pursue new directions. They reported increased feelings of intimacy and more pleasurable sexual activity with their husbands since the distractions of children were removed. However, the assertiveness that often emerged as these women sought new life directions brought major changes in their marital relationships. Many reported that their husbands were threatened by such assertiveness and independence. Some women abandoned their newfound goals because they felt their marriages would end if they continued their pursuits.

In the Lowenthal et al. (1975) interviews, the middle-aged women were the most critical of their spouses, compared to all the other groups of women and men. Three-fifths of them gave neutral or negative evaluations of their husbands, whereas only one-fifth of people in the other groups attributed mainly negative characteristics to their spouses. The middle-aged women's negative views of marriage were based on histories of conflicts over and with teenage children, and they looked forward to the departure of children from the home so that marital relations might improve.

Another view of marriage for women in the middle years is available in the Baruch, Barnett, and Rivers (1983) study of a random sample of 238 women aged 35 to 55, with an average of 14 years of education. Themes of achievement and work, reflecting the mid-life developmental concerns described earlier, dominated the interviews. These women were not focused exclusively on husbands and children as may have been the case in previous generations. Married women stated that marriage provided intimacy, sharing, richness, and warmth in their lives. In contrast to Lowenthal et al. (1975) or Rubin (1979), these women seemed to have constructed a pattern of marriage that suited their personal lifestyles and goals. Thus they were less troubled by conflicts between their mid-life aspirations and constraints imposed by traditional definitions of marital roles. Social class differences may account for these findings, as the Baruch et al. (1983) sample was less heterogeneous in education and occupational status than the other two.

Later Years

The following sections present a discussion of the connection between the developmental concerns of older adults and their marital relationships. Several developmental issues are prominent at this stage: the chance of becoming widowed is greater than at any previous time of life, retirement typically signals dramatic shifts in daily activities and relationships, any major physical declines or limitations which emerge in late life will affect significant relationships, and any personality shift in the focus of gender roles holds implications for spousal interactions. Furthermore, there is more diversity of abilities and life styles among members of this age group, and thus between genders, than at any other period of the life span (Maas & Kuypers, 1974). At the same time, few studies have analyzed gender differences in late-life marriage at the level of detail indicated in the previous sections on the middle years.

Personality changes in the later years may be one of the strongest influences on the marital relationship. As older men become more reflective and older women grow more assertive and dominant, spouses must adapt to each other's new interaction style. For many couples, these shifts signal more equality, sharing, and couple-oriented activities than ever before (Zube, 1982). Within this context, older couples rely on each other increasingly for companionship and love, particularly as their interactions with others in the social network decrease (Stinnet, Carter, & Montgomery, 1972). Huyck (1982) emphasized that the late life move toward androgyny is illustrated more by husbands' expressions of satisfaction with increased companionship (and by wives' complaints about overly dependent husbands) than by any major reallocation of household tasks (which does not usually take place; Keating & Cole, 1980).

Kelley (1981) provided a useful framework for analyzing the effects of late-life development on marriage. Interdependence refers to the ways in which and the extent to which partners influence each other's actions and well-being. The interdependence that has developed over the years of a marriage is based both on the spouses' personal characteristics (personality, values, and so forth) and on their patterns of interaction. The high level of marital satisfaction often expressed by older couples is probably due to the understanding, acceptance, and communication that have evolved during their years together (Stinnet et al., 1972).

The degree of interdependence, the equality of dependence between spouses, the number of shared interests, and the amount of coordination of activities are properties of interdependence that can explain a couple's reactions to late life events. For instance, the consequences of retirement are likely to depend on the number of leisure activities that the couple shared in the past. If they pursued few interests or activities together, by retirement their leisure preferences may be so divergent that they obtain little satisfaction from each other's company. In contrast, couples who shared leisure interests earlier in life probably enjoy having more time to be together in the later years.

In one study of the effects of the husband's retirement on marriage (Keating & Cole, 1980), there were no major changes in marital communication and no differences between husbands and wives in morale. The men, however, who felt less productive and useful, were significantly less happy with retirement than the women. Despite some loss of privacy and independence, the wives enjoyed having an increased sense of purpose as they assisted their husbands in adjusting to retirement and coordinated both their separate and joint activities. Interestingly, the husbands were not aware of their wives' supportiveness.

In one of the few studies of the effects of the wife's retirement on marriage, Szinovacz (1980) reported that marital relations improve if the wife's retirement reduces work-related stress and increases mutually satisfactory joint activities. On the other hand, if the wife is unable to find suitable activities to substitute for the prestige and fulfillment derived from employment, her retirement can lead to her personal unhappiness and to strain in the marriage. Contrary to a common assumption, such women are unlikely to derive satisfaction from increased involvement in household tasks.

The implications of interdependence extend to the domain of physical well-being. If one mate becomes seriously ill, there are several ramifications for the marriage. The sick person is likely to become increasingly dependent on the healthier partner, which may disturb the balance of equality and power in the relationship. The healthier partner is likely to retain interest in previously enjoyed activities, but if the ill mate cannot participate in them, conflicts of interest may result. Despite these potential negative effects of illness on marriage, Johnson (1985, this volume) suggests that older spouses are quite supportive of their disabled partners, and that illness does not adversely affect the quality of the marriage. Interdependence as expressed in a history of sharing and caring is one of the reasons that marriage remains satisfactory despite one partner's health problems.

An interesting aspect of the connection between aging and long-term marital interdependence which requires investigation is Kelley's (1981) hypothesis about the effects of increased interiority on marriage. As very old adults become more preoccupied with reviewing their lives and dwelling on their own thoughts and needs, do they become less sensitive to the needs and interests of their spouses? Or, is it more the case that aging partners change their expectations of marriage in conformance with their psychological and physical development?

FRIENDSHIP IN THE SECOND HALF OF LIFE

Middle Years

There is relatively little information in the literature about the nature and meaning of friendship in the middle years. Whereas it would be too simplistic to assert that middle-agers have little need for friends, the dearth of empirical evidence may actually reflect the interpersonal priorities of those in the middle years. It may be that the demands and competition at work, along with family and civic responsibilities, take most of the middle-aged person's time and energy, with little remaining for friends (Brown, 1981). Another explanation may be that the middle-aged person's needs for intimacy are met by family members. Shulman (1975) found that the middle-aged respondents were more likely to confide in relatives than in friends. Also, both Shulman (1975) and Lowenthal et al. (1975) reported that middle-aged people claimed fewer friends than either younger or older adults. Lowenthal et al. (1975) found that, of the four age groups studied, the middle-aged women and men attributed the least complex set of characteristics to their friends. This may signify that middle-aged adults are more selective about their friendships (Brown, 1981), choosing to maintain a few relationships with people who are quite similar to themselves (Reisman, 1981). On the other hand, friends may serve important functions for the middle-aged adult by focusing attention away from the routine aspects of daily life toward the spontaneity of recreation, although the demands of work and family may severely limit opportunities for nurturing friendships (Larson & Bradney, this volume).

It is not clear whether mid-life friendships are as intimate as those of earlier or later stages. The men in Farrell and Rosenberg's (1981) study stated that their friendships were less intense with less self disclosure than in earlier periods, but this was due to a gradual diminishing of involvement with friends that started at the time of marriage, rather than a sudden development in middle age. On the other hand, Stueve and Gerson (1977) found no age-related differences in intimacy, although the frequency of contact with friends was lower for middle-aged men than for younger ones.

One factor which might make a difference in the quality of middle age friendships is the extent to which a person experiences this stage as a crisis. Farrell and Rosenberg (1981) found that feelings of unhappiness and depression in men in crisis strained their friendships; these were the most socially isolated respondents.

Later Years

A great deal of research on late-life friendships has been conducted, possibly in recognition of the fact that social support needs may be more intense at this time than at any other stage of life. With regard to the special developmental concerns of old people, we find that friends serve several important functions in their lives. First, friendship relations maintain role continuity (Blau, 1973). While the roles of spouse and worker often cease in old age, the role of friend can endure throughout life and help the elderly person to retain social status and integration, which enhances the quality of life (Mancini, 1980). Second, friendships contribute to self-esteem and morale, especially in the face of major late-life changes. Friends are companions who prevent loneliness and offer emotional support and advice in coping with retirement and widowhood (Lowenthal & Haven, 1968). Third, friendships involve the sharing of activities and the reciprocal exchange of assistance. Friends enjoy spending time with each other, and they are available to help in times of emergency as well as in routine situations (Rosow, 1970; Shulman, 1975; Wood & Robertson, 1978). Because they usually are peers with similar needs and resources, it is relatively easy for old people to reciprocate assistance from their friends. In this way, they can maintain self-respect and avoid feelings of dependence that may result from receiving help from younger people but being unable to return favors in kind (Arling, 1976).

On the other hand, having a circle of friends made up mostly of age peers can present problems for the elderly person. The friends are vulnerable to infirmity or death, and may not be available to provide support when it is needed. Also, a person who is among the first in the group to retire or become widowed may find that the others, lacking common experience, are unable to give the needed assistance.

After the family- and work-focused period of the middle years, there is often an increase in the amount of contact with friends in the young-old stage (Brown, 1981; Lowenthal et al., 1975). Retirement brings additional leisure time that can be spent in socializing, for those with the health and financial resources to do so. As the years pass, though, friend interaction tends to diminish, and old-old people are more likely to rely on family members for assistance than on anyone else (Brown, 1981).

CONCLUSION

Social support needs endure throughout the life cycle, but the particular requirements for sources and types of social support vary with a person's stage in life and associated cognitive and personality development, and with the particular contemporary life transitions or events. Individuals in the middle stage of adulthood need affirmation of their achievements and emotional bolstering as they become aware of both their failure to reach certain goals and a limited amount of time left to accomplish them. They may also need encouragement to pursue a new path in education or occupation, and support as they reassess their marriages, their values, and their lifestyles. Individuals in the latest stage of adulthood are more likely to need some direct instrumental aid along with comfort as they become increasingly aware of physical and social losses. Thus it is likely that at least some existing relationships take on new forms and functions as the years pass. Others may be discontinued if they no longer meet a person's needs or if the effort required to maintain them is too great for the person to expend. It is also possible that new relationships will be developed in the context of alterations in a person's needs or circumstances. Physical, social, psychological, or environmental changes may lead to new close friendships or even marriage in the later years.

One of the fundamental tenets of gerontology is that members of a given birth cohort become increasingly heterogeneous as they age. Because there are numerous pathways in family life and work that adults in our society may take, it is inaccurate to portray "the middle aged" or "the elderly" as single easily characterized groups of people. Yet the greater part of research on adult social relationships has used samples of white middle-class persons. Our understanding of the interaction between adult developmental processes and marriage or friendship would be enhanced greatly by studies conducted with members of diverse socio-economic, racial, and ethnic groups.

Moreover, gerontologists now recognize numerous age-related differences in adults 65 years of age and older. The "oldest old," those past 80 or 85 years, are much more likely to be frail and dependent on others for daily care than are the "young old" in their late 60's and early 70's. It is reasonable, then, to assume that there are relationship differences or changes within the group of adults aged 65 and above. The middle stage of adulthood spans several decades, and it is also reasonable to assume that relationships are not static through these years. However, it is difficult if not impossible to draw conclusions about age-related changes in relationships by comparing the results of various studies. Divergent sampling procedures and/or characteristics of respondents (other than age) and/or operationalization of key relationship constructs limit the generalizability of results across studies. Comparisons of subcohorts of middle-aged and older adults within the same study represent a more valid means of tracking relationship processes.

The marital satisfaction literature provides an illustration of this point. Spanier and Lewis (1980) reviewed research from the 1970s on marital quality across the family life cycle. They concluded that these studies provide convincing evidence of a curvilinear trend in marital satisfaction, with a high level among newlyweds, a low level during the child-rearing years, and a high level in the launching and later stages of marriage. However, when Gilford (1984) assessed marital quality among 318 persons aged 55 to 90 years, and analyzed the data for three age groups instead of just one, she found significant age group differences. Marital satisfaction was highest for those between 63 and 69, as compared to those 55 to 62 or 70 to 90. Furthermore, in Guilford's multiple regression analyses fewer predictors of marital satisfaction and a smaller amount of explained variance emerged for the two older groups of respondents as compared to the youngest group. These findings may be explained by the increased introspection and poorer health of very old people as discussed earlier, and they demonstrate the importance of investigating dimensions of close relationships for multiple age groups of elderly persons. Although data concerning interactions of older adults with friends and others in the social network have not been reported for subgroups of the over-65 cohort, it is likely that age-related differences would be found for these relationships as well.

It is important to note that analyses based on multiple age groups of participants in a given study yield average age differences in relationship characteristics. Cross-sectional studies may approximate developmental trends in relationships, but do not directly assess change over time. Longitudinal investigations of the same relationships at several points in time are required to determine the extent of actual change within relationships.

Another set of methodological issues concerns the type of data which are gathered about adult relationships, and the analyses which are conducted. The usual approach has been to ask questions of just one relationship partner. Additional insights could be generated if both spouses or members of friend pairs provided information from their respective viewpoints. Questions which elicit data on the psychological significance of relationships themselves and perceived changes in relationships would broaden the scope of social network data. Measurement and data analysis techniques geared to dyadic concepts, that is, patterns of interaction (Huston & Robins, 1982; Thompson & Walker, 1982), would provide a more complete picture of intimate relationships.

New research questions present many opportunities for students of adult close relationships. For instance, in attempting to debunk the myth that most older adults are socially alienated and lonely, researchers (e.g., Shanas, 1979) have given much effort to the task of demonstrating the involvement of family, friends, and neighbors in the support of elderly people. It has only been in recent years that investigators have considered negative aspects of close relationships (Broderick, this volume; Eckels, 1981; Ingersoll & Antonucci, 1983; Rook, 1984; Turkington, 1985). Additional exploration of problems and stresses associated with close relationships, as such problems intersect with the developmental changes that adults experience, would further enhance our understanding of the roles of close relationships in the second half of life.

Research is also needed into age-related changes in the broader social context or social network of aging people. What are the implications of the "graying of America" for social relationships or, more specifically, of large numbers of retirement community or nursing home residents growing increasingly old and frail? How do people who relocate in advanced years develop new friendships either with age peers or others?

Recent reviews of family gerontology literature (Bengtson & DeTerre, 1980; Blieszner, 1986; Mancini, 1984; Streib & Beck, 1980) identified many other research questions which should be addressed, particularly in terms of the quality and psychological meaning of middle-age and late-life close relationships. The practical application of empirical information about close relationships, in terms of enhancing the quality of life or alleviating problems of adults, remains to be explored more thoroughly. Given that so much of adult life is shaped by ongoing interactions with close persons (Plath, 1984), these are crucial challenges for future research.

REFERENCES

Arling, G. (1976). The elderly widow and her family, neighbors and friends. *Journal of Marriage and the Family, 38,* 757-768.

Baruch, G., Barnett, R., & Rivers, C. (1983). *Lifeprints: New patterns of love and work for today's women.* New York: New American Library.

Bengtson, V. L., & DeTerre, E. (1980). Aging and family relations. *Marriage and Family Review, 3,* 51-76.

Bengtson, V. L., & Kuypers, J. L. (1985). The family support cycle: Psychosocial issues in the aging family. In J. M. A. Munnichs, P. Mussen, E. Olbrich, & P. G. Coleman

(Eds.), *Life-span and change in a gerontological perspective* (pp. 257-273). Orlando, FL: Academic Press.

Blau, Z. S. (1973). *Old age in a changing society.* New York: New Viewpoints.

Blieszner, R. (1986). Trends in family gerontology research. *Family Relations, 35,* 555-562.

Brown, B. B. (1981). A life-span approach to friendship: Age-related dimensions of an ageless relationship. In H. Z. Lopata & D. R. Maines (Eds.), *Research in the interweave of social roles, vol. 2: friendship* (pp. 23-50). Greenwich, CT: J.A.I.

Cobb, S. (1976). Social support as a moderator of life stress. *Psychosomatic Medicine, 38,* 300-314.

Cytrynbaum, S., Blum, L., Patrick, R., Stein, J., Wadner, D., & Wilk, C. (1980). Midlife development: A personality and social systems perspective. In L. W. Poon (Ed.), *Aging in the 1980s* (pp. 463-474). Washington, DC: American Psychological Association.

Dickens, W. J., & Perlman, D. (1981). Friendship over the life-cycle. In S. Duck & R. Gilmour (Eds.), *Personal relationships 2: Developing personal relationships* (pp. 91-122). London: Academic Press.

Eckels, E. T. (1981, November). *Negative aspects of family relationships for older women.* Paper presented at the 34th Annual Scientific Meeting of the Gerontological Society of America, Toronto, Canada.

Erikson, E. H. (1963). *Childhood and society (2nd ed.).* New York: Norton.

Farrell, M. P., & Rosenberg, S. D. (1981). *Men at midlife.* Boston: Auburn House.

Finch, C. E., & Hayflick, L. (Eds.). (1977). *Handbook of the biology of aging.* New York: Van Nostrand Reinhold.

Fischer, C. S. (1982). *To dwell among friends.* Chicago: University of Chicago Press.

Gambria, L. M. (1979-80). Sex differences in daydreaming and related mental activity from the late teens to the early nineties. *International Journal of Aging and Human Development, 10,* 1-34.

Gilford, R. (1984). Contrasts in marital satisfaction throughout old age: An exchange theory analysis. *Journal of Gerontology, 39,* 325-333.

Gould, R. M. (1978). *Transformations.* New York: Simon & Schuster.

Gruen, W. (1964). Adult personality: An empirical study of Erikson's theory of ego development. In B. L. Neugarten (Ed.), *Personality in middle and late life* (pp. 1-14). New York: Atherton.

Gutmann, D. (1977). The cross-cultural perspective: Notes toward a comparative psychology of aging. In J. E. Birren & K. W. Schaie (Eds.), *Handbook of the psychology of aging* (pp. 302-326). New York: Van Nostrand Reinhold.

Havighurst, R. J. (1972). *Developmental tasks and education* (3rd ed.). New York: David McKay.

Hochschild, A. R. (1973). *The unexpected community: Portrait of an old age subculture.* Berkeley: University of California Press.

Huston, T. L., & Robins, E. (1982). Conceptual and methodological issues in studying close relationships. *Journal of Marriage and the Family, 44,* 901-925.

Huyck, M. H. (1982). From gregariousness to intimacy: Marriage and friendship over the adult years. In T. M. Field, A. Huston, H. C. Quay, L. Troll, & G. E. Finley (Eds.), *Review of human development* (pp. 471-484). New York: John Wiley.

Ingersoll, B. & Antonucci, T. (1983, November). *Non-reciprocal social support: Another side of intimate relationships.* Paper presented at the 36th Annual Scientific Meeting of the Gerontological Society of America, San Francisco.

Johnson, C. L. (1985). The impact of illness on late-life marriages. *Journal of Marriage and the Family, 47,* 165-172.

Kahn, R. L., & Antonucci, T. C. (1981). Convoys of social support: A life-course approach. In S. B. Kiesler, J. N. Morgan, & V. K. Oppenheimer (Eds.), *Aging: Social Change* (pp. 383-405). New York: Academic Press.

Keating, N. C., & Cole, P. (1980). What do I do with him 24 hours a day? Changes in the housewife role after retirement. *Gerontologist, 20,* 84-89.

Kelley, H. H. (1981). Marriage relationships and aging. In R. W. Fogel, E. Hatfield, S. B. Kiesler, & E. Shanas (Eds.), *Aging: Stability and change in the family* (pp. 275-300). New York: Academic Press.

Levinson, D. J., Darrow, C. N., Klein, E. B., Levinson, M. H., & McKee, B. (1978). *The seasons of a man's life.* New York: Ballantine.

Lopata, H. Z. (1973). *Widowhood in an American city.* Cambridge, MA: Schenkman.

Lowenthal, M. F., & Haven, C. (1968). Interaction and adaptation: Intimacy as a critical variable. *American Sociological Review, 33,* 20-30.

Lowenthal, M. F., Thurnher, M., Chiriboga, D., & Associates. (1975). *Four stages of life.* San Francisco: Jossey-Bass.

Maas, H. S., & Kuypers, J. A. (1974). *From thirty to seventy: A forty-year longitudinal study of adult life styles and personality.* San Francisco: Jossey-Bass.

Mancini, J. A. (1980). Friend interaction, competence, and morale in old age. *Research on Aging, 2,* 416-431.

Mancini, J. A. (1984). Research in family life in old age: Exploring the frontiers. In W. H. Quinn & G. A. Hughston (Eds.), *Independent aging: Family and social systems perspectives* (pp. 265-284). Rockville, MD: Aspen.

Neugarten, B. L. (1968). The awareness of middle age. In B. L. Neugarten (Ed.), *Middle age and aging* (pp. 93-98). Chicago: University of Chicago Press.

Neugarten, B. L. (1977). Personality and aging. In J. E. Birren & K. W. Schaie (Eds.), *Handbook of the psychology of aging* (pp. 626-649). New York: Van Nostrand Reinhold.

Neugarten, B. L., & Gutmann, D. L. (1968). Age-sex roles and personality in middle age: A thematic apperception study. In B. L. Neugarten (Ed.), *Middle age and aging* (pp. 58-71). Chicago: University of Chicago Press.

Plath, D. W. (1984). Of time, love, and heroes. In V. Rogers (Ed.), *Adult development through relationships* (pp. 16-27). New York: Praeger.

Reisman, J. M. (1981). Adult friendships. In S. Duck & R. Gilmour (Eds.), *Personal relationships 2: Developing personal relationships* (pp. 205-230). London: Academic Press.

Rook, K. S. (1984). The negative side of social interaction: Impact on psychological well-being. *Journal of Personality and Social Psychology, 46,* 1097-1108.

Rosow, I. (1970). Old people: Their friends and neighbors. *American Behavioral Scientist, 14,* 59-69.

Rubin, L. B. (1979). *Women of a certain age.* New York: Harper & Row.

Ryff, C. D., & Heincke, S. G. (1983). Subjective organization of personality in adulthood and aging. *Journal of Personality and Social Psychology, 44,* 807-816.

Shanas, E. (1979). Social myth as hypothesis: The case of the family relations of old people. *Gerontologist, 19,* 3-9.

Shock, N. W. (1977). Biological theories of aging. In J. E. Birren & K. W. Schaie (Eds.), *Handbook of the psychology of aging* (pp. 103-115). New York: Van Nostrand Reinhold.

Shulman, N. (1975). Life-cycle variations in patterns of close relationships. *Journal of Marriage and the Family, 37,* 813-821.

Skolnick, A. (1981). Married lives: Longitudinal perspectives on marriage. In D. Eichorn, J. A. Clausen, N. Haan, M. P. Honzik, & P. H. Mussen (Eds.), *Past and present in middle life* (pp. 269-298). New York: Academic Press.

Sorell, G. T., Smyer, M. A., & Hooker, K. A. (1984, November). *Age-related and context-related differences in women's personalities during adulthood.* Paper presented at the 37th Annual Scientific Meeting of the Gerontological Society of America, San Antonio, TX.

Spanier, G. B., & Lewis, R. A. (1980). Marital quality: A review of the seventies. *Journal of Marriage and the Family, 42,* 825-839.

Stinnet, N., Carter, L. M., & Montgomery, J. E. (1972). Older persons' perceptions of their marriages. *Journal of Marriage and the Family, 34,* 665-670.

Streib, G. A., & Beck, R. W. (1980). Older families: A decade review. *Journal of Marriage and the Family, 42,* 937-956.

Stueve, C. A., & Gerson, K. (1977). Personal relations across the life-cycle. In C. S. Fischer & Associates, *Networks and places* (pp. 79-98). New York: Free Press.

Szinovacz, M. E. (1980). Female retirement: Effects on spousal roles and marital adjustment. *Journal of Family Issues, 1,* 423-440.

Tamir, L. M. (1982). *Men in their forties: The transition to middle age.* New York: Springer-Verlag.

Tesch, S. A. (1983). Review of friendship development across the life span. *Human Development, 26,* 266-276.

Thompson, L., & Walker, A. J. (1982). The dyad as the unit of analysis: Conceptual and methodological issues. *Journal of Marriage and the Family, 44,* 889-900.

Troll, L. E. (1975). *Early and middle adulthood.* Monterey, CA: Brooks/Cole.

Turkington, C. (1985, February). What price friendship? The darker side of social networks. *APA Monitor,* pp. 38, 41.

Vaillant, G. E., & Milofsky, E. (1980). Natural history of male psychological health: IX. Empirical evidence for Erikson's model of the life cycle. *American Journal of Psychiatry, 137,* 1348-1359.

Weiss, L. J. (1977, November). *Intimacy: An intervening factor in adaptation.* Paper presented at the 30th Annual Scientific Meeting of the Gerontological Society, San Francisco.

Weiss, R. S. (1973). *Loneliness: The experience of emotional and social isolation.* Cambridge: MIT Press.

Weiss, R. S. (1974). The provisions of social relationships. In Z. Rubin (Ed.), *Doing unto others* (pp. 17-26). Englewood Cliffs, NJ: Prentice-Hall.

Weiss, R. S. (1975). *Marital separation.* New York: Basic Books.

Wood, V., & Robertson, J. F. (1978). Friendship and kinship interaction: Differential effect on the morale of the elderly. *Journal of Marriage and the Family, 40,* 367-375.

Zube, M. (1982). Changing behavior and outlook of aging men and women: Implications for marriage in the middle and later years. *Family Relations, 31,* 147-156.

7

Relationships Among Family Members and Friends in Later Life

Colleen Leahy Johnson

Until recent years, research on the family has focussed primarily on earlier stages of the life cycle. Those researchers specifically interested in the problems of old age have looked at the family as the major source of support to an age group in which large numbers have depleted resources. Their findings have convincingly documented the viability of the family, finally setting to rest the widespread myth of family abandonment of its elderly (Shanas, 1979b). Although no one doubts the efficacy of the family, no one further suggests that public programs of assistance be abandoned because they duplicate the functions of the family.

The limitations of the late-life family lie mainly in its structure. Unlike in earlier stages of life, most elderly have abbreviated family units in which children and other relatives rarely share households or cooperate in economic activities. Moreover, individuals who live to advanced old age often experience mounting social losses, and many simply outlive their families. As a consequence of these depletions in family and friendship circles, the networks of many elderly are small and inconsequential. With the onset of illness and debility, when support is

AUTHOR'S NOTE: The research on which much of this article was based was funded by the National Institute of Mental Health 1R01 MH 31907. The author wishes to acknowledge the help of Barbara Barer and Donald Catalano, whose research assistance was invaluable in the empirical phase of this research.

needed these needs are generally met by one individual at a time rather than a network of family and friends who function together to provide support. In keeping with these realities, research questions revolve on what family members are available and sufficiently motivated to meet the needs of older relatives. At the theoretical level, we need to study dimensions of dyadic relationships rather than the family or the social network as functioning units.

This article analyzes the major dyadic relationships in old age in an attempt to identify those dimensions which are associated with the provision of social supports. Comparisons will be made between marital, parent-child, friendship and kinship dyads in order to single out those elements of the dyadic relationship that facilitate supportive behaviors when one partner must respond to the needs of the other. In addition to the research literature on the late life family, I will draw upon my research on family support to 167 elderly who were studied shortly after being discharge from a hospital.

It is proposed that with the typical dependence of old age, more is potentially expected from family and friends. With the higher incidence of chronic illness, decreased functioning, widowhood, and economic decrements, heavy demands are placed upon members of the primary group. In the process, a relationship changes because of the revised expectations for ego, who is in need of help, and alter, who is in the position to respond. Essentially these relationships are put to a test when expectations need to be redefined. I assume that the responses of family and friends are determined not only by situational factors but also by generic characteristics specific to each type of relationship (Blieszner, Larson & Bradney, this volume).

AGE-SPECIFIC CHARACTERISTICS
OF DYADIC RELATIONSHIPS

Demographic evidence identifies major changes in social situations of the elderly, many of which entail social losses. Retirement and widowhood entail the loss of major social roles, which are accompanied by loss of relationships peripheral to these roles (Rosow, 1974). As noted above, however, the family appears to compensate for these losses. National surveys have found that only 3% of the elderly have no relatives. Almost 80% have children, and over three-quarters of these see one child at least weekly. Moreover, of the bedfast elderly over half are cared for by a spouse or child, and only 8% used hired help

(Shanas, 1979a; 1979b). There are large gender differences, however, in the individuals available to the elderly as assessed by marital and household status. A large proportion of women are unmarried, particularly after age 75, and in most cases, they are vulnerable by virtue of living alone. For example, with the gender-linked discrepancy in longevity, only 46% of the women, ages 65-74, are married in comparison to 78% of the men, and a scant 22%, 75 years and older are married in comparison to 68% of the men. Thus, significantly fewer men live alone, 12% of the younger group and 18% of the older men, proportions one-third that of women (Soldo, 1980).

Changes in the family in this century have also affected the potential supports from children (Treas, 1977). Older women today have an average of 1.2 daughters, in comparison to 3.0 in 1900. Today, these daughters are more likely to be married and subject to the competing commitments of their families of procreation. Also, the percentage of middle-aged women working today has more than quadrupled since 1940, a situation that impedes daughters from providing support despite their best intentions. Not surprisingly, then, it has been found that children actually provide little support, although they tend to express "filial anxiety" at the prospect of these demands being place upon them (Cicirelli, 1981).

Other family relationships also risk becoming attenuated in old age. Although the grandparent-grandchild relationship might be important emotionally, there is little evidence that grandchildren are a source of support in old age (Bengtson and Robertson, 1985; Johnson, 1983a). Also, less than one-half of older people are in frequent contact with siblings or other relatives (Shanas, 1979a). Thus kin relationships might be important to the elderly, but for all intents and purposes, few individuals are available to function on a daily basis. Health and functional status are major factors affecting the social involvement of older people (Shanas and Maddox, 1985). Those elderly with declining capacities are more likely to experience a shrinkage of their social environment; healthier and functionally active individuals are more likely to have a functioning social network. In their social interactions, not only is their increased preference for contacts with age-peers in old age over younger individuals, but also interactions with age-mates has been associated with higher levels of life satisfaction (Laing et al., 1980; Rosow, 1967). In fact, there is some evidence of ambivalence in intergenerational relationships (Arling, 1976; Hess and Waring, 1978; Wood and Robertson, 1978). The rapid growth of age-segregated communities reflects this preference for age-peers who are more likely than younger people to provide the psychological rewards of self-validation and enhancement of one's self-esteem.

While there is evidence that some relationships are willingly sloughed off with an attitude of "good riddance" (Lowenthal and Robinson, 1976), older persons benefit from having at least one intimate relationship. The presence of a confidant has been associated with higher morale (Lowenthal and Haven, 1968). The individual most likely to function in that capacity is an age-peer, either a spouse or a friend. It could be that it is age-similar relationships, not necessarily family and kin, that compensate for social losses in later life. Because age-peers also risk illness and dependency, however, their viability as sources of support is unstable.

Using results of national surveys, Ethel Shanas (1979a) has formulated the principle of substitution, which suggest that family members are available to older relatives in serial order. If one is married, a spouse provides support; if one is widowed, a child steps in to help; and if one is childless, another relative provides supports. It is likely, however that with increasing kinship distance, the support becomes more perfunctory and consequently less reliable over a prolonged period of time. Rather than substitution, other researchers such as Eugene Litwak (1985) suggest that kinship relationships are specialized and thus vary in their support potential, depending upon the strength of the commitment, their proximity, and other qualitative variables. For example, kin might not be in proximity, but they are likely to have a strong commitment. While they cannot assist in daily care, they can take over such tasks as money management. In this conception, there is a specialization of function rather than interchangeable functions among family members and relatives. Some relatives may specialize in emotional functions, and others in instrumental functions.

If various types of dyadic relationships are not characterized by overlapping or interchangeable functions, one needs to single out the dimension of support associated with each type of relationship. Then one can go on to study the quantity and quality of specific types of support. Instrumental supports are the objective types of tasks needed on a daily basis—transportation, household help, meal preparation, shopping, and financial help. Emotional supports are those less easily measured dimensions that have been associated with well-being in later life and perhaps throughout the life course. These functions include provisions for pleasurable sociability, advice, comfort, and self-validation. Ritualized supports are usually those that take place at distance. Members of these dyads maintain contact through letters, telephone calls and sporadic contacts, activities that might intermittently boost one's morale but not necessarily handle the practical aspects of daily living. Some dyads are multifunctional, providing instrumental and expressive supports, while others may be specialized, providing but one type of support.

Those individuals who experience dependency place more demands on their social relationships. When loyalties are tested, dyadic relationships can be expected to change. How they change, I maintain, depends upon underlying dimensions of specific relationships. These changes that are of both practical and theoretical significance are analyzed in the following sections. They include not only the study of objective manifestations of change but also those dimensions of relationships that are more likely to convey qualitative benefits to those in need of help.

Three patterns of change were observed in a longitudinal study of posthospitalized elderly and their primary caregivers (Johnson, 1983b; Johnson, 1983c; Johnson, 1985b; Johnson & Catalano, 1983). First, some caregivers established greater physical or psychological distance from the patient, whose needs were then met more by other family members or the formal support network in the community. Second, others became more enmeshed in the relationship, usually shedding other involvements and concentrating energies on caring for the older person. Third, in still other dyads, the relationships ceased to function as contact became sporadic or nonexistent. Children generally took the first alternative; they were more likely than spouses to establish more distance from the parent by enlisting the help of other relatives or the formal support network. Spouses, on the other hand, tended to become more enmeshed in the relationship, often to the point of regressing socially, withdrawing from other contacts. Finally, other relatives and friends significantly decreased their contacts with the patient over this time period.

From these findings, it is logical to assume that when dyadic relationships are challenged by one partner's illness and dependency, they are redefined, in turn resulting either in reinforcement of the relationship, a distancing between partners, or a breakdown or dissolution of the relationship. Through a content analysis of open-ended responses, three dimensions of relationships emerged that account for the variations in the caregivers' responses. These dimensions focus on the degree of normative regulation specific to the relationship, the type of reciprocity operating, and the changing power structure in the dyad as dependency needs change.

DIMENSIONS OF RELATIONSHIPS

Obligatory and optional norms. The American family and kinship system are noted for the relative flexibility granted to individuals in forming and dissolving relationships (Furstenberg, 1981; Hagestad, 1981). The element of personal choice permits one to select out those relatives with whom to form enduring relationships. These decisions are usually made on the basis of personal attraction and mutual interests. Relationships are more likely to be molded by optional and flexible rules in contrast to more traditional kinship systems where obligations among kin are buttressed by specific rules on rights and obligations. Given these characteristics, the boundaries between kinship and friendship relationships are often blurred.

There are exceptions to the operation of the voluntaristic principle. While it has been pointed out that it also applies to the parent-adult child dyad (Hess and Waring, 1978), this dyad differs from other dyads in the strong emotional commitment of both partners. For example, irrespective of how much support a child might be able to provide a parent, the norm of obligation undoubtedly has some influence over the parent's expectations and the child's perceived need to comply. Thus at the implicit level at least, obligatory rather than optional norms color interactions. The marital dyad also might be voluntary in earlier stages of the family cycle when divorce is a frequent option. In later life, however, few individuals select the option of divorce (Treas and Van Hilst, 1976). Most research findings indicate that spouses are the primary source of support, and their presence is the major factor associated with a number of measures of well-being (Johnson, 1983b; Troll, 1986; Verbrugge, 1979). The fact that the divorce rate is low among older people suggests that a marriage persists even with the pressures that illness and dependency impose. Thus the norm of obligation is also likely to operate here (Johnson, 1985c).

The norm of reciprocity. In the analysis of how late-life dyadic relationships function when social support are needed, theories on reciprocity provide useful analytic concepts. In contrast to exchange theory that suggests social relationships are motivated largely by the maximation of self-interest (Dowd, 1980; Emerson, 1976), processes of reciprocity suggest the diffuse exchanges observed in primary relationships. The norm of reciprocity has been described by Gouldner (1960) as the principle of "give and take" that provides the all-purpose moral cement underpinning the stability of the social system. It is a universal norm that defines, regulates and harmonizes social relationships and, in the process, provides the primary basis of social conformity. The directive is to help others who help one and not harm them, so relationships regulated by the norm of reciprocity are typically nonexploitive. In this broad scheme, the time dimension is also incorporated. The norm integrates past events and engenders motives for returning benefits. There is a future orientation also, because in the operation of the norm, egoistic motivation is channeled to maintain orderly social life, preventing exploitation of others. Nevertheless, there is egoism in altruism, because long-term personal benefits are expected to accrue. As Gouldner notes, because of the comparative indeterminancy of debts and credits, the norm does not require specific or uniform performance or direct calculations of the exchange. Thus individuals are often uncertain of who is in whose debt. In the absence of time-bound and equivalent exchanges, the resulting indebtedness potentially creates a strong and enduring interdependence, for such debts are not easily discharged. The underlying assumption is that abrogation of this norm leads to a breakdown of the relationship.

In order to operationalize these concepts for empirical study, it is useful to use Sahlins's (1965) distinction between three types of reciprocity. Generalized reciprocity portrays the altrusitic and solitary extreme. It is the "pure gift" (Mauss, 1967), whereby hospitality and aid are given without conscious consideration of an equal or time-bound return. A gives to B and has only indefinite expectations for a return. In such dyads, perpetual indebtedness is more likely to develop, because debts are not repaid promptly. Such a situation sets the basis for future status differentiation, because unpaid debts place the debtor in a more dependent situation.

Balanced reciprocity, on the other hand, is a more direct and equitable form of reciprocity, where A gives to B expecting a time-bound, equivalent return. In this more precise accounting, there is less tolerance of a one-way flow of benefits, so relationships are more easily disrupted if the flow becomes inequitable. Since individuals are expected to discharge their debts, the burden of obligation is minimized. Nevertheless, the relationship is inherently less stable. If inequities arise, failure to reciprocate not only violates social expectations, but also provides the rationale for dissolving the relationship.

Negative reciprocity, in marked contrast, is the unsociable extreme where A gives to B, but there is no return benefit. Such situations of utilitarian advantage are infrequent in primary relationships, for normative sanctions are usually imposed to prevent such exploitations. The relationship would break down or, if it persisted, interaction would be characterized by constant negotiation and haggling to maintain one's interests.

One can propose, as Sahlins does, that these types of reciprocity reflect concentric rings of social integration. At the core are the most intimate relationships, where generalized reciprocity operates to create relationships that endure without continual evaluation of debts and credits. In later life, the parent/child and marital dyad are usually at the core of the support system, although it is conceivable that other dyads also exhibit this pattern of reciprocity. At the next ring, relationships might be intimate with high sociability, but the course of the relationships rests upon operation of balance reciprocity. Examples of these dyads are the sibling and close friendship dyads where sociability rests upon the continuing exchange of benefits to both partners. At the periphery of the circles, less intimate relationships are prone to negative reciprocity in the event of illness and dependency. Since one partner is unable to reciprocate, the relationships often cease to function on a day-to-day basis.

Autonomy, power, and dependency. The balancing between individual and group interests can form opposing components of relationships in all cultures. Van der Veen (1971) identifies oppositions between the need to interrelate and be dependent versus the need to express oneself and be autonomous. One could go on to add further oppositions between the obligation to give versus the desire to hold, altruism versus egoism, and group interests versus individual interests. Some cultures accentuate one over the other, such as in the United States, where independence and autonomy are more highly valued than dependence on others. Because older people are likely to experience various forms of dependency (economic, physical, or psychological), their status is often incongruent with our major value orientation. They, too, are projects of our culture, however, so they are placed in an unenviable situation in which they either deny their dependency or recriminate themselves for being dependent (Clark, 1969). While certainly some ethnic groups in our society do not follow these cultural mandates (Johnson, 1985b), the dominant value orientation is one of autonomy from one's family of origin in order to pursue personal interests.

Since our kinship system has only vague normative guidelines on the form and content of relationships, personal options often determine who does what for whom. Without specific rules, however, individuals can experience confusion and uncertainty. Core relationships where generalized reciprocity operates are particularly prone to ambivalence, for they are cemented by obligatory ties that can be in direct conflict with an individual's wish for autonomy. Such debts are not easily discharged, yet the relationship cannot be broken off. Consequently, both the donor and recipient are likely to experience reservations that ultimately will affect the quality of their interactions.

The balance between interdependence and autonomy is disturbed when one partner of the dyad becomes more dependent. As exchange theorists have pointed out (Emerson, 1962), with dependency ego transfers power to alter, resulting in asymmetry in formerly egalitarian dyads or increased asymmetry or reversals of status in already hierarchical dyads. These asymmetries change the quality of the relationships. In dyads regulated by voluntary norms, balanced reciprocity is expected. If inequities arise that increase the costs and conflict with one's autonomy, the relationship can be dissolved. Where the dyad is an obligatory one, however, balancing mechanisms are required to resolve inequities and maintain reciprocity and harmony in the relationship itself (Lebra, 1969). If one partner in the dyad requires help from the other, reciprocity is difficult to maintain. Costs to the donor may outstrip the rewards and subsequently cause the relationship to deteriorate. Yet with obligatory dyads, one should not expect a precise accounting of debts and credits, nor can one leave the relationships without normative sanctions.

Consequently, power relationships change; as ego becomes dependent, alter, the caregiver, becomes more powerful. If partners in the dyad are to continue interaction without excessive costs or conflicts, some balancing mechanisms are required. For example, both parties can arrive at the recognition that ego has the right to be dependent. The dependent partner is permitted to regress to a more childlike status, where his or her needs are satisfied. In such cases, alter can reduce the costs and accrue rewards from the caregiving, such as the enhancement of status achieved through his or her increased power. Or altruism and self-sacrifice in themselves can accrue rewards if such actions are congruent with social expectations. If so, caregiving can result in substantial benefits.

Other means might be found to enhance the status of the dependent one or diminish the status of the more powerful one. The dyad might achieve a level of interdependence, with each having some degree of power over the other. To accomplish this end, the dependent partner must have some resources with which to bargain and some means to increase the rewards to the donor. In other situations, a perpetual donor might find other means to reduce personal costs. Donors can enlarge the support network to include other individuals, an option that lessens the tension in the dyadic relationship. Or the donor may withdraw subjectively and motivationally while at the same time continuing to perform instrumental services. In other words, costs are reduced by reinterpreting one's actions as less onerous.

Relationships regulated by obligatory rather than optional norms would be better able to withstand the challenges of illness. The quality of the relationship that affects mostly the expressive component of supports might suffer, however, if reciprocity becomes inequitable, if the power balance becomes too asymmetrical, or if one's autonomy is threatened. Obviously the situation is complex and dynamic as multiple dimensions interact and change over time. Nevertheless, in the following sections these dimensions serve to discriminate between types of dyadic relationships as they respond to the predictable problems of old age.

THE MARITAL DYAD

Marital status is a key variable in a number of findings on the physical and psychological well-being of older people. Married individuals generally have better health and suffer from less disability than the unmarried (Verbrugge, 1979). Being married is the single most significant factor in preventing institutionalization of the elderly (Health Care Financing Agency, 1981). With illness and the need for social supports, the spouse is the major provider of services (Shanas, 1979a; Palmore et al., 1979; Johnson, 1983b). The presence of a spouse is also associated with high morale and greater social integration among older people (Larson, 1978; Longino and Lipman, 1981). Given their instrumental and emotional significance, old-age marriages rarely end in divorce (Treas & Van Hilst, 1976). In fact, marital satisfaction tends to increase in the later stages of the family cycle, although communication declines and health problems are the most frequent topic of conversation (Rollins & Feldman, 1970).

Marriages at all stages in the family cycle are the key family relationship for fulfilling psychological and emotional needs (Berger and Kellner, 1964; Weiss, 1974). Marital satisfaction, however, changes at various stages of the cycle (Gilford and Bengtson, 1977; Skolnick, 1981; Troll, 1986). After a decline during the child-rearing years, it increases with children's maturity. Marital satisfaction in old age appears to differ in more subtle dimensions of the relationship. Troll (1982) describes late-life marriage as passively congenial having progressed from attraction to loyalty and from ardor to attachment. In my research the sources of satisfaction in the marriage also include a sense of survivorship in which a strong bond resulted from a sense of survivorship and the long-term sharing of experiences (Johnson, 1985c). As a result, the marriages were noted for a low level of conflict, egalitarian structure, and shared interests.

A high level of interdependence is also evident in most marriages. In my research, spouses fulfilled the role of caregiver more adequately than children and provided comprehensive care with less help from either the formal or informal support system (Johnson, 1983b). Not surprisingly, there was a significantly lower likelihood of institutionalization among the marrieds. Moreover, the spouse as caregiver was less likely than a child to experience ambivalence, conflict, or strain in the performance of the caregiving role. The interdependence of spouses often was magnified, because children were relatively uninvolved when both parents were alive, irrespective of how much help was required. Thus when a partner became ill these couples were likely to be more isolated from relatives than were the widows who also participated in the study. Social isolation was a particular problem if the caregiver also had a health problem, for the couple's withdrawal left them with few substitutes for each other.

Marriages in old age closely approximate the situation where generalized reciprocity operates. First, the relationship is more permanent and likely to be viewed as obligatory at this stage in life, contrasting with earlier stages, when divorce is a widespread option currently. Second, in the generalized, reciprocal exchanges, a spouse gives to his or her partner usually without consideration of time-bound and equivalent returns. In fact, the precise calculation of debts and credits is virtually nonexistent, because over the long term costs and benefits are viewed as having equalled out (Schaffer & Keith, 1981).

Third, ambivalence over the responsibilities of caregiving is less likely to occur, because personal interests and dyad interests often coincide. The provider of care also has a strong identification with the ailing spouse because of having shared a variety of experiences together over a long period of time and because of the similarity in status and interests. Neither exploitation of a spouse nor abandonment of the marriage is likely, because of the high interdependence and mutual-need fulfillment that is often achieved in later years. Generalized reciprocity represents a delayed repayment for the benefits received in the past.

Fourth, with the equalization in status between husband and wife, power issues are less likely to be subject to negotiation (Holahan, 1984). The dyad is more amenable to balancing mechanisms because of its structure. With the dependency of a husband, which is more common than a wife's dependency, a wife gains power and in the process the marriage becomes more symmetrical (Gutman, 1979). This situation in itself can bestow rewards, particularly because her previous social and economic dependence on her husband becomes reversed. This change in status also provides the opportunity for altruism, where self-sacrifice bestows rewards as an end in itself. Because the dependency from illness in old age is viewed as inevitable and usually irreversible, it usually is a socially recognized and nonsanctioned form among age peers.

The risks of dependency can affect everyone in this age group. A wife who is caring for a husband following a heart attack recognizes that she too can be vulnerable to debilitating illness in the future. It is in her interest to build up a store of credits in case the situation becomes reversed and she should then need his support. In other words, in keeping with the tenets of generalized reciprocity, her efforts are motivated not only by altruism but also by egoism stemming from her potential needs in the future. Inequities are tolerated with the expectations of future rewards that will restore balance to the dyad.

Older couples usually have fewer options to the marriage because there has been declining involvement with work, raising children, and voluntary associations (Rosow, 1974). Thus there are potentially fewer alternative sources of rewards. Wives, who are more likely to be the caregivers because of gender-linked differences in longevity, have even fewer alternatives than men to form new unions. A spouse as caregiver could enlist help from others to reduce the costs, but here too evidence suggests that children maintain intimacy at a distance in such situations, while friends generally withdraw with prolonged dependence (Johnson, 1983b). Thus when inequities develop, the major means of reducing costs and increasing rewards comes through the use of altruism and self-sacrifice, which in turn will enhance one's status. Since the marital dyad is the central one in the American family system, emphasis is placed on such sacrifices that accrue outside social approval.

Interdependence in the marital dyad is often strengthened with the challenges of illness and dependency. Since the older marital couple is often more isolated from other social ties than the younger couples, social isolation can be a problem. In fact, social regression or a withdrawal from larger social aggregates can occur, resulting in an exclusion of outside contacts and an intensified investment in the marriage. Unlike social mechanisms that prevent dyadic withdrawal among younger couples (M. Johnson and Milardo, 1984; Milardo, 1983; Slater, 1963), there are fewer mechanisms in later life that propel individuals back into the social system. One outcome is role enmeshment, where the caregiver takes on the role as a full-time one, sheds other responsibilities and contacts, and intensifies the commitment to the marriage (Johnson & Catalano, 1983).

THE PARENT-CHILD DYAD

Much emphasis has been placed on an offspring's capacity to function as a caregiver for disabled parent, but many impediments arise when such responsibilities are thrust upon them (Shanas, 1979a). Because of social mobility, living in separate households, and having to respond first to the competing commitments to their families of procreation and their work, children generally have difficulty functioning as supporters on a daily basis. Moreover, having children is not associated with happiness in later life (Glenn & McLanahan, 1982). Hess and Waring (1978) identify numerous constraints to a smooth-functioning parent-child relationship in later life, which they trace in part to changes from obligatory to optional norms. Sacrifices are neither expected nor preferred by either generation. Children are permitted to maintain distance, particularly from a married parent, although they might be a last resort for a widowed parent who has no other sources of support.

Although the voluntaristic principle might govern the parent-adult child dyad during normal times, there is no evidence that large numbers of children abandon a parent who is ill and in need of help. While there are no cultural mandates on filial sacrifices, people generally disapprove of children who are inattentive to a needy parent. Parent-child relationships, differ qualitatively from other kinship relationships in terms of the psychological underpinnings (Cicirelli, 1981; Bengtson & Robertson, 1985; Troll, 1986). The explicitly voluntary nature of the relationship expressed in the commonly heard statement, "I never want to be a burden on my child," is accompanied by an implicit norm of obligation. Psychotherapists speak of the internalization of moral norms that have strong psychological effects (Boszormenyi-Nagy and Spark, 1973). If the norm of obligation operates only at the implicit level, and if rights and duties are unspecified, specific responses are left to individual choice. In any case, it is likely that the abrogation of the norm can cause guilt internally and risk externally imposed sanctions.

Not surprisingly, we usually find a fear of dependency among older people at the possibility that they might become burdens to their children (Clark and Anderson, 1967) and filial anxiety among the adult children that such a situation might arise (Cicirelli, 1981). Children follow cultural expectations by placing priority on their own autonomy from parents as they fulfill the needs of their nuclear families. Nevertheless, when illness and perhaps dependency appear, the norm of obligation usually is expressed at least implicitly by members of both generations. Yet the resulting expectations are incongruent with broader cultural values on independence and the high priority one should allot to the family of procreation. This situation can produce ambivalence and resentment on the part of children when they meet their obligations, or guilt if they should reject their obligations. Few rewards of approval come if one meets a parent's needs at the expense of one's husband and children, yet subtle social sanctions are imposed on any child who abandons a parent.

When necessity activates the norm of obligation, certain dimensions of the offspring's relationship with parents can be expected to change. First, a unilateral dependent relationship is created out of necessity; parents become more dependent upon a child. Here, too, generalized reciprocity usually operates. Rather than a precise accounting, children view their services as a repayment for past benefits received from parents over the years of child rearing. However, they are not expected to repay these debts if their own children might suffer. Thus when parents require comprehensive supports, the incongruence is most apparent between the expectations for their independence and their diffuse obligations. Such actions are in conflict with our values and likely to create ambivalence in both generations, a situation that can be expected to undermine the quality of the relationship.

Second, inevitably there is an inequity in exchange values, for in most cases the parents are unable to reciprocate because typically their resources have diminished. With the exception of wealthy parents who will have large estates to bequeath, the exchanges in most dyads are asymmetrical. In keeping with the principles of generalized reciprocity, however, social debts and credits of past supports given and received are not always discernible or quantifiable, nor should they be, according to the diffuse moral values underlying the relationship (Lebra, 1969).

Third, the relationship is asymmetrical, but having parents in the dependent role and the child in the power role reverses the hierarchy of the childhood situation. Implicitly, the parent has the power to command help from the child because of past services rendered. Although few Americans voice explicit expectations, as noted above, the norm of obligation becomes a social mandate when parents can no longer care for themselves. With incapacity and dependence, some power is transferred to the child. Because the power base is fluid and dynamic due to the changing dependency of the parent, it is quite difficult to retain equity in the relationship in a semblance of the earlier power structure. Blenkner (1965) has described an additional stage in psychosocial development, filial maturity, to describe a healthy stage of psychosocial development. In her view, there should be no reversal of the parent-child roles; a child should not become a parent as a rock of support. The developmental task is one of achieving emancipation from the parent, so that he or she is then free to help the parent as a mature adult.

In many cases, however, these processes undermine the parent-child relationship. With the loss of resources accompanying dependency in old age, there is considerable ambiguity as to how much a child should sacrifice, and without assistance from others, children can easily become overburdened. Also, the hierarchical relationship that this situation creates is usually less intimate and less capable of fulfilling emotional needs. Such a turn of events can explain why incapacitated parents are less likely to be satisfied with the assistance they receive from a child than what they receive from a spouse (Johnson, 1983b). Since a child accumulates more costs than rewards, it is also understandable that he or she also experiences considerable conflict and stress in the role of caregiver.

Anthropological literature points out that most cultures provide mechanisms to ameliorate the tensions generated in asymmetric relationships (Lebra, 1969). In other words, reciprocity is seen to underlie all relationships, so there is usually a strain toward symmetry (Gouldner, 1960). For those children who experience inordinate strain in caring for a parent, two compensatory mechanisms are available in order to reduce tensions. They can establish more social distance from the parent by decreasing social contact or they can form triads by enlisting support from others, usually from formal agencies outside the family.

OTHER PRIMARY RELATIONSHIPS

Only in rare cases do other dyadic relationships in the primary network function as sources of comprehensive support to dependent elderly. While siblings, cousins, and friends of long standing might continue to be a source of sociability and emotional satisfaction, there is little evidence that these individuals take over the more burdensome aspects of day-to-day care. In my research, only 15% of the older people identified a relative other than a spouse or child as their primary caregiver (Johnson, 1983b; 1985a). In half of these cases, the caregiver was from a younger generation, a niece, nephew, or grandchild. Upon interviewing either the patient or the caregiver, however, it was found that these individuals in reality did little more than perfunctory duties, usually acting as an intermediary between the patient and service bureaucracy. If the older persons needed daily help, he or she resorted to formal community supports or they relied on a close friend (Johnson and Catalano, 1981).

Some age-similar dyads among siblings or close friends tended to function somewhat like the marital dyad. The partners expressed a long-term commitment to each other, exhibited relatively little strain and ambivalence, and were less concerned with the day-to-day reckoning of costs and rewards. In general, they shared households or adjacent apartments. Most activities were joint and they tended to rely primarily on each other for their emotional needs, in some cases to the point of isolation from other social contacts. It would seem that support potentials are more likely to be found in age-similar dyads, although relationships like the marital one are the exception rather than the rule. Most relationships are not likely to withstand the demands for long-term support.

In our second contact, the involvement of siblings, other relatives, and friends declined significantly with those patients who remained in need of help. In fact, friends were virtually invisible for the highly impaired individuals, except in those cases where they functioned more like a spouse. Those siblings who were not primary caregivers did remain in contact, although they, too, provided little support over time. These patterns reflect the blurring between kinship and friendship in our society. Both types of dyads share at least three characteristics (Johnson, 1985b; Suttles, 1970). First, both ties rest upon the voluntaristic principle and are thus outside the boundaries of normatively based obligations. Relationships are formed and maintained on the basis of attraction and mutual interests. In our society, friendship and kinship can be interchangeable categories because any actions rest upon personal choices. Second, where these optional relationships are formed, one can predict that the affective component is emphasized over the instrumental component, with the major function ·being the conveyance of a sense of worth (Paine, 1974). Third, these kinship and friendship dyads are likely to be based upon equivalence in status and equitable exchanges.

Given the similarity between friendships and more distant kin relations, it is useful to consider the conditions under which siblings or close friends actually serve as primary caregiver. There are, for example, cases where widowed sisters are the primary relatives for each other, because children are not in the area. In other cases, childless individuals form intimate friendship dyads and make strong commitments to help each other. Such substitutes for a spouse or child only take place in the absence or unavailability of primary relatives, a situation that suggests that core family relations are sought out first. Since these relationships lie outside those regulated by the norm of obligation, they are inherently unstable and, not surprisingly, such potential sources of support are rarely utilized (Cicirelli, 1982).

CONCLUSIONS

Using findings from research on social supports to the elderly, I have attempted to clarify the support potentials of their family. Evidence from various sources generally indicates that neither the contemporary family nor the informal network functions as a unit in meeting the needs of older people. Instead, caregivers are available in serial order. Because family members generally substitute for each other rather than cooperate in the care, the dyadic relationship is the most productive unit of analysis. Since research has found that the amount and types of supports vary depending upon the category of dyadic relationship, however, it is useful to identify how dimensions of each major relationship varies.

The marital dyad functions more adequately in old age than other dyads as a source of social supports because of status similarities, mutual identification, and long-term interdependence. Children, on the other hand, are rarely able to provide comprehensive supports because of the many competing commitments typical in middle age. Moreover, when they are placed in such situations, they are likely to find some means to spread the responsibilities. In any event, they often express resentment and conflict if they must provide extensive support, or they experience guilt if they should not live up to parental expectations. Other relatives and friends are less involved, particularly when the dependency of the older person persists over a period of time. If these individuals must assume the role of caregiver, the services are generally perfunctory and center mainly on helping the older person find access to formal community supports. Those individuals who provide comprehensive supports were invariably age peers whose relationship with a dependent partner shared characteristics with the marital dyad.

In some respects, there is a leveling process among age peers in old age when the risk of illness, social and economic losses, and declining functioning act as equalizers irrespective of previous differentiation. Old age is also a time when other commitments decrease, leaving few alternatives to one's existing primary relationships. Since the well-being of older people has been positively associated with age-dense environments, age peers are more likely to offer self-validation and enhanced self-esteem than are younger persons.

These factors alone, however, cannot account for the support potentials in a dyadic relationship when high needs demand responses on a day-to-day basis. Therefore, I have identified three dimensions of relationships that can account for variations in the provision of social supports. The analysis is based upon the assumption that the event of illness and the attendant dependency creates a need for social supports that, in turn, places a demand on an individual's primary relationships. Commitment to the dyad is challenged when the increased dependency of one partner changes mutual expectations. These processes result in redefinitions of the relationship and ultimately differing outcomes, depending upon the characteristics specific to each type of relationship.

Expectations and the responses are in large part determined by the normative regulation of the relationship. Whether one should provide supports is often vaguely stated in our society because much is left to personal choice. Nevertheless, obligatory norms at least implicitly govern relationships between husbands and wives and parents and children. Rejection or abandonment in times of need elicits social disapproval and often brings feelings of guilt to individuals. Thus one can assume that where obligatory norms are present, responses will vary considerably from those where personal options are permitted to influence one's responses.

A second dimension in dyadic relationships is variation in the type of reciprocity. It is proposed here that generalized reciprocity characterizes marital and parent-child dyads. In these dyads, one should exchange goods and services without direct calculation of debts and credits because it is expected that such actions take into account past and future benefits. Without precise accounting, however, one is never sure who is in whose debt. Such a process differs greatly from balanced reciprocity, where exchanges are more equitable and debts are to be paid promptly. If the exchanges become inequitable, the relationship becomes unstable and risks breakdown, because both donor and recipient suffer from the failure to perform as expected.

Third, related to the patterns of reciprocity is the changing structure of the dyad when one partner becomes dependent. Invariably, dependency of ego transfers power to alter. At the same time, alter is giving more than receiving, which increases the costs unless the relationship can be dissolved or some balancing mechanism compensates for the inequities. For optional dyads, the relationship often breaks down, because unpaid debts determine the quality for both the debtor and the creditor. In contrast, obligatory relationships cannot be dissolved, yet their changing structure and inequitable exchanges are likely to undermine the quality. Without balancing mechanisms, the perpetual donor is likely to experience ambivalence, for any dedicated efforts are in conflict with our cultural mandates of personal autonomy and self direction. Since American culture places high value on independence and personal autonomy, such dilemmas between the need to help and the need for independence can become magnified with those primary relationships that cannot be dissolved.

These conclusions apply to the dominant model of family and kinship in our society. In some ethnic groups, obligatory norms exist that cement the bond with kin. Moreover, not all subgroups in our society so enthusiastically endorse values of independence. Not only do these group differences need to be taken into account, but also specific aspects of dyadic relationships warrant further research. Studies of social networks often do not distinguish between members of the family or between the family and other relationships even though, at least in old age, support usually comes from one individual at a time. Moreover, studies of social supports do not always consider the complex interpersonal environment that influences the extent and quality of the aid. Hopefully, this analysis offers a productive mode for future inquiry.

REFERENCES

Arling, G. (1976). The elderly widow and her family and friends. *Journal of Marriage and the Family, 38,* 757-768.

Bengtson, V. & Robertson, J. (Eds.). (1985). *Grandparenthood.* Newbury Park, CA: Sage.

Berger, P. & Kellner, H. (1964). Marriage and the construction of reality. *Diogenes, 46,* 1-25.

Blenkner, M. (1965). Social work and family relationships in later life with some thoughts on filial maturity. In E. Shanas and G. Streib (Eds.), *Social structure and the family: Intergenerational relations.* (pp. 46-61). Englewood Cliffs, NJ: Prentice-Hall.

Boszormenyi-Nagy, I. & Spark, G. (1973). *Invisible loyalties.* New York: Harper & Row.

Cicirelli, V. (1981). *Helping elderly parents: The role of adult children.* Boston: Auburn House.

Cicirelli, V. (1982). Sibling influence throughout the life span. In M. Lamb & B. Sutton-Smith (Eds.), *Sibling relationships* (pp. 455-462). Hillsdale, NJ: Lawrence Erlbaum.

Chown, L. (1981). Friendship in old age. In S. Duck & R. Gilmour (Eds.), *Personal Relationships 2: Developing personal relationships* (pp. 231-246). New York: Academic Press.

Clark, M. (1969). Cultural values and dependency in later life. In R. Kalish (Ed.), *The dependencies of older people,* pp. 59-72. (Occasional Papers in Gerontology, no. 6.) Ann Arbor: Institute of Gerontology, University of Michigan.

Clark, M. & Anderson, B. (1967). *Culture and aging.* Springfield, IL: Charles C Thomas.

Dowd, J. (1980). Exchange rates and older people. *Journal of Gerontology, 35,* 596-602.

Emerson, R. (1962). Power and dependency. *American Sociological Review, 27,* 31-40.

Emerson, R. (1976). Social exchange theory. In A. Inkeles & J. Coleman (Eds.), *Annual review in sociology, 2,* 335-362.

Furstenberg, F. (1981). Remarriage and intergenerational relations. In R. Fogel et al. (Eds.), *Aging: stability and change in the family* (pp. 115-142). New York: Academic Press.

Gilford, R. & Bengtson, V. (1977). Measuring marital satisfaction in three generations: Positive and negative dimensions. *Journal of Marriage and the Family, 41,* 15-25.

Glenn, N. & McLanahan, S. (1982). Children and marital happiness: A further specification of the relationship. *Journal of Marriage and the Family, 44,* 63-72.

Gouldner, A. (1960). The norm of reciprocity: A preliminary statement. *American Sociological Review, 25,* 161-178.

Gutman, D. (1979). Individual adaptation in the middle years: Developmental issues in masculine mid-life crisis. *Journal of Geriatric Psychiatry, 9,* 41-59.

Hagestad, G. (1981). Problems and promises in the social psychology of intergenerational relations. In R. Fogel, et al. (Eds.), *Aging: Stability and change in the family* (pp. 11-46). New York: Academic Press.

Health Care Financing Agency. (1981). *Long term care: Background and future directions.* Washington, DC: U.S. Department of Health and Human Services.

Hess, B. & Waring, J. (1978). Parent and child in later life: Rethinking the relationship. In R. Lerner & G. Spanier (Eds.), *Child influences on marital and family interaction* (pp. 241-273). New York: Academic Press.

Holahan, C. (1984). Marital attitudes over 40 years: A longitudinal cohort analysis. *Journal of Gerontology, 39,* 49-57.

Johnson, C. (1983a). A cultural analysis of the grandmother. *Research on Aging, 5,* 547-567.

Johnson, C. (1983b). Dyadic family relations and social support. *Gerontologist, 23,* 377-383.

Johnson, C. (1983c). Fairweather friends and rainy day kin. *Urban Anthropology, 12,* 103-124.

Johnson, C. (1985a). *Growing up and growing old in Italian American families.* New Bruswick, NJ: Rutgers University Press.

Johnson, C. (1985b). The impact of illness on late-life marriages. *Journal of Marriage and the Family, 47,* 165-172.

Johnson, C. & Catalano, D. (1981). The childless elderly and their family supports. *Gerontologist, 21,* 610-618.

Johnson, C. & Catalano, D. (1983). A longitudinal study of family supports. *Gerontologist, 23,* 612-618.

Johnson, M. P. & Milardo, R.M. (1984). Network influence on pair relationships: A psychological recasting of Slater's (1963) theory of social regression. *Journal of Marriage and the Family, 46,* 893-899.

Keating, N. & Cole, P. (1983). What do I do with him 24 hours a day? *The Gerontologist, 22,* 84-89.

Larson, R. (1978). Thirty years of research on the subjective well-being of older Americans. *Journal of Gerontology, 33,* 109-125.

Laing, J., Dvorkin, L., Kahana, E. & Maxian, F. (1980). Social integration and morale: A re-examination. *Journal of Gerontology, 35,* 746-757.

Lebra, T. (1969). Reciprocity and the asymmetric principle: An analytical reappraisal of the Japanese concept of *on. Psychologia, 12,* 129-138.

Lee, G. (1978). Marriage and morale in later life. *Journal of Marriage and the Family, 40,* 131-139.

Litwak, E. (1980). Research patterns in the health of the elderly: The community mental health center. In E. Borgatta and N. McCluskey (Eds.), *Aging and Society,* (pp. 78-130). Beverly Hills: Sage Publications.

Litwak, E. (1985). *Helping the elderly.* New York: Guilford.

Longino, C. & Lipman, A. (1981). Married and spouseless men and women in planned retirement communities: Support network differentials. *Journal of Marriage and the Family, 43,* 169-177.

Lowenthal, M. & Haven, C. (1968). Interaction and adaptation: Intimacy as a critical variable. *American Sociological Review, 33,* 20-30.

Lowenthal, M. & Robinson, B. (1976). Social networks and isolation. In R. Binstock & E. Shanas (Eds.), *Handbook of aging and the social sciences,* (pp. 432-456). New York: Van Nostrand Reinhold.

Mauss, M. (1967). *The gift: Forms and functions of exchange in archaic societies.* New York: Norton.

Milardo, R. (1983). Social networks and pair relationships: A review of substantive and measurement issues. *Sociology and Social Research, 68,* 1-18.

Paine, R. (1974). Anthropological approaches to friendship. In E. Leyton (Ed.), *The compact: Selected dimensions of friendship* (pp. 1-14). Toronto: University of Toronto.

Palmore, E., Cleveland, W., Nowlin, J., Ramm, D., & Siegler, I. (1979). Stress and adaptation in later life. *Journal of Gerontology, 34,* 841-851.

Rollins, B., & Feldman, H. (1970). Marital satisfaction over the family life cycle. *Journal of Marriage and the Family, 32,* 20-28.

Rosow, I. (1967). *Social integration of the aged.* New York: Free Press.

Rosow, I. (1974). *Socialization to old age.* Berkeley: University of California Press.

Sahlins, M. (1965). On the sociology of primitive exchange. In M. Banton (Ed.), *The relevance of models in social anthropology* (pp. 139-236). New York: Praeger.

Schaffer, R. & Keith, P. (1981). Equity in marital roles across the family cycle. *Journal of Marriage and the Family, 43,* 359-367.

Shanas, E. (1979a). The family as a social support system in old age. *Gerontologist, 19,* 169-174.

Shanas, E. (1979b). Social myth as hypothesis: The case of the family relations of old people. *Gerontologist, 19,* 3-9.

Shanas, E. & Maddox, G. (1985). Health, health resources, and the utilization of care. In E. Shanas & R. Binstock (Eds.), *Handbook of Aging and the Social Sciences* (pp. 697-726). New York: Van Nostrand Reinhold.

Sinnott, J. (1977). Sex-role inconstancy, biology, and successful aging: A dialectical model. *Gerontologist, 17,* 450-463.

Skolnick, A. (1981). Married lives: Longitudinal perspectives on marriage. In D. Eichorn, J. A. Clausen, N. Haan, M. P. Honzik, & P. H. Mussen (Eds.), *Past and present in middle life* (pp. 269-298). New York: Academic Press.

Slater, P. (1963). On social regression. *American Sociological Review, 28,* 339-364.

Soldo, B. (1980). America's elderly in the 1980s. *Population Bulletin, 35,*(4).

Suttles, G. (1970). Friendship as a social institution. In G. McCall et al. (Eds.), *Social relationships* (pp. 96-135). Chicago: Aldine.

Treas, J. (1977). Family support system for the aged: Some social and demographic considerations. *Gerontologist, 17,* 486-491.

Treas, J. & Van Hilst, A. (1976). Marriage and remarriage rates among old Americans. *Gerontologist, 16,* 132-136.

Troll, L. (1986). Introduction. In L. Troll (Ed.), *Current Gerontology: Family Issues.* New York: Springer-Verlag.

Troll, L. (1982). *Continuations: Adult development and aging.* Monterey, CA: Brooks-Cole.

van der Veen (1971). Ambivalence, social structure and dominant kinship relationships. In F. Hsu (Ed.), *Kinship and culture,* pp. 377-408. Chicago: Aldine.

Verbrugge, L. (1979). Marital status and health. *Journal of Marriage and the Family, 41,* 267-285.

Weiss, R. (1974). The Provision of Social Relationships. In Z. Rubin (Ed.), *Doing onto Others* (pp. 17-26). Englewood Cliffs, NJ: Prentice-Hall.

Wood, V. & Robertson, J. (1978). Friendship and kinship interaction: Differential effect on the morale of the elderly. *Journal of Marriage and the Family, 40,* 367-375.

8

Loneliness: A Life-Span, Family Perspective

Daniel Perlman

Our relationships with other people are among life's most important experiences. We love, we embrace, we mourn, and we hate. As a result of this, we sometimes feel elated and we sometimes feel lonely. Life is a continuous process of growth, transition, and deterioration. The purpose of this chapter is to chart some of the fluctuations in loneliness that occur in conjunction with human development and the family life cycle. A life-span perspective and concerns have been implicit in several popular (Gordon, 1976; Hritzuk, 1982; Rubenstein & Shaver, 1982) and scholarly (Hartog, Audy, & Cohen, 1980; Peplau & Perlman, 1982) treatments of loneliness. Yet to date, no one has synthesized the growing empirical literature on loneliness to provide a data-based portrait of loneliness over the life cycle. This chapter will paint such a picture. First, however, considering a few general points about loneliness will provide a framework for the main body of the chapter.

LONELINESS:
DEFINITION, DEMOGRAPHICS AND CAUSES

What is loneliness? Many definitions have been offered (see Peplau & Perlman, 1982, p. 4) but their essence can be captured in the following statement. *Loneliness* is the unpleasant experience that occurs when a person's network of social relationships is deficient in some important way, either qualitatively or quantitatively. This definition shares three points of agreement with the way most other scholars view loneliness. First, loneliness results from a deficiency in a person's social relationships. Loneliness occurs when there is a mismatch between a person's actual social relations and the person's needs or desires for social contact. Sometimes loneliness results from a shift in an individual's social needs rather than from a change in their actual level of social contact. Second, loneliness is a subjective experience; it is not synonymous with objective social isolation. People can be alone without being lonely, or lonely in a crowd. Third, the experience of loneliness is aversive. Although loneliness may be a spur to personal growth, the experience itself is unpleasant and distressing.

As concepts are developed and elaborated, a common step is to identify various subtypes. Three dimensions have been used in differentiating types of loneliness (de Jong-Gierveld & Raadschelders, 1982). These include: time (loneliness as a trait versus a state), the domain in which interpersonal deficits occur (i.e., romantic, friendship network, etc.), and whether loneliness is a positive or negative experience.

Research on types of loneliness is only now beginning to accumulate. Two points about this thrust are worth noting. First, Schmidt and Sermat (1983) have developed a differential measure which provides scores for loneliness in four specific interpersonal domains (including the areas of romantic and family relationships). Second, Weiss (1973) has argued that loneliness stemming from a lack of intimate ties is more aversive than loneliness stemming from deficiencies in one's broader social network.

Roughly 25% of respondents in representative samples of the U.S. population report that they have recently felt lonely or remote from others (Weiss, 1973). That means that over 50 million Americans experience loneliness each week. Women are more apt than men to label themselves as lonely, although gender differences are rarely found when the UCLA Scale, the most popular measure of loneliness, is administered to males and females (Borys & Perlman, 1985).

Although popular culture depicts youth as a time of sociability and old age as a time of loneliness, several large-scale surveys challenge this stereotype (Fidler, 1976; Parlee, 1979; Rubenstein & Shaver, 1982). As shown in Table 1, self-reports of loneliness are highest among adolescents. (This is true despite the validity of conventional wisdom that adolescents are a highly sociable group—see Dickens & Perlman, 1981.) As people get older, self-reported loneliness declines. Thus in Parlee's

TABLE 1
Age Trends in Loneliness

Age Group

Percentage of Respondents Reporting Loneliness

Study								
NIMH (Radloff, 1982)	18-24 39%	25-44 24%	45-64 21%	65+ 25%				
Andersson (1982)	16-24 40%	25-34 32%	35-54 31%	55-74 40%				
Parlee (1979)	<18 79%	18-24 71%	25-34 69%	35-44 60%	45-54 53%	55+ 37%		
Dean (1962)						50-59 26%	60-69 35%	70-79 29%	80+ 53%

Mean Loneliness Scores (Max. = 20)

Study							
Rubenstein et al. (1979)	18-25 +12.8	26-30 +9.5	31-39 +8.9	40-49 +2.9	50-59 -3.8	60-69 -9.4	70+ -22.5
Revenson & Johnson (1984)	18-24 15.2	25-34 14.6	35-44 13.8	45-54 14.0	55-64 12.8	65-74 11.4	75+ 6.7

NOTE: Comparisons between studies should be done with caution. Each study provides a curve for the relationship between age and loneliness. But the results are not fully equivalent: The age groupings, the questions themselves, and the response categories varied across studies. The NIMH and Andersson studies used representative samples in the US and Sweden, respectively. Parlee, Rubenstein et al., and Revenson and Johnson's data came from interested newspaper and magazine readers who voluntarily completed published questionnaires.

survey (see Table 1), 79% of respondents under age 18 said they were sometimes or often lonely, compared to only 53% of 45-54 year olds, and 37% of those 55 and over. The one possible exception to this pattern is some evidence that among the very old, those over 80, loneliness is very common. For example (see Table 1), Dean (1962) found fairly similar levels of loneliness among adults ages 50 to 79, but a sharp increase in loneliness among those 80 and over (compare Blieszner, this volume).

Many factors can contribute to the experience of loneliness. As a way of thinking about causal factors and organizing the existing literature, Anne Peplau and I (Perlman & Peplau, 1984) have formulated a discrepancy model of loneliness (shown in Figure 1). We find it helpful to distinguish between *predisposing* factors that make people vulnerable to loneliness and *precipitating* events that trigger the onset of loneliness. Predisposing factors can include characteristics of the person (e.g., shyness, lack of social skills), characteristics of the situation (e.g., competitive interaction, social isolation), and general cultural values (e.g., individualism). Among the most important predisposing factors for the purposes of this chapter are the individual's early parent-child relations.

Precipitating events are factors such as the breakup of a love relationship or moving to a new community that in turn change a person's social life in some significant way. Precipitating events create a mismatch between the person's actual social relations and the person's needs or desires; a change in one of these two factors without a corresponding change in the other can produce loneliness. More so, perhaps, than some other scholars, we believe that cognitive processes can intervene between social deficits and the experience of loneliness. Attributions and a sense of control can moderate the intensity of one's loneliness. Finally, people react and cope with loneliness in a variety of ways. Rubenstein and Shaver (1982) have empirically identified four such responses: doing nothing (sad passivity), active solitude, spending money, and trying to promote social contact.

In thinking about loneliness in a family and life cycle perspective, several questions come to mind. Are there certain times in life or certain family life roles that are especially linked to loneliness? How do parent-child and marital relations contribute to loneliness? Do family life transitions such as parenthood or becoming widowed alter levels of loneliness? As we go through the life cycle, do the predictors of loneliness wax and wane in importance (i.e., do the set of predictors change)?

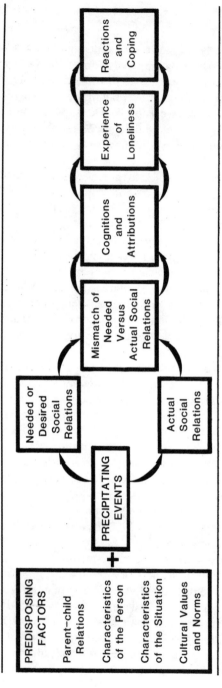

Figure 1.

In the present chapter, I will attempt to answer these questions. The chapter is organized in a manner parallel to the life course. Starting with childhood, it moves through major life stages from infancy to old age. In the final section of the chapter, I will make suggestions, taking into consideration family factors, on how loneliness can be avoided and alleviated.

CHILDHOOD

The Importance of Intergenerational Transmission and Early Attachment

Common sense suggests that parents and their children tend to be alike. To test this notion, Judith Lobdell and I (Lobdell & Perlman, 1986) administered questionnaires to 130 female undergraduates and their parents. As expected, the parents' loneliness scores were modestly correlated with those of their daughters. (The correlations were $r(128) = .25, p < .01$ form mother-daughter pairs and $r(128) = .19, p < .05$ for father-daughter pairs). Naturally, either biological or social factors could account for these correlations. I am most concerned with how social factors contribute to loneliness.

Psychodynamic theorists stress the crucial importance that early childhood experiences have on our later social lives. Bowlby (1977), for example, emphasizes the significance of parent-child attachment during infancy. He believes the nature of the parent-child bond establishes an orientation to others. It influences the way we approach and interpret later relationships, as well as our ability to form friendships and intimate bonds. Bowlby claims that frustration of our natural propensity to form strong, secure emotional attachments in infancy leads to various forms of emotional distress and personality disturbances. These include anxiety, depression, emotional detachment, and by implication, loneliness.

A few studies examining loneliness have been cast in an attachment frame-work. For example, Shaver and Rubenstein (1980) postulated that the forms of psychological distress associated with poor early attachment would be found as a cluster of characteristics manifest by lonely people. They also hypothesized that children whose *early* attachment bonds were threatened by parental divorce would be especially likely to experience loneliness. Both these predictions proved correct. Lobdell and Perlman (1986) reviewed and provided new evidence consistent with an attachment model showing the links between parent-child relations and the sociability of children with their peers. Childhood peer relations were, in turn, correlated with adolescent loneliness.

Thus the evidence fits with what one would expect from an attachment position. The evidence must, however, be taken as merely suggestive rather than as definitive support. Unfortunately, research of this sort depends on retrospective recall; direct measures of attachment are rarely feasible. Alternate explanations of the results are clearly possible.

Parent-Child Relations

A related developmental perspective suggests that the predisposition to loneliness is acquired during childhood through one's relationships with one's parents. Here less emphasis is placed on the very early formation of attachment bonds. Instead, more emphasis is placed on parental child-rearing practices and interpersonal qualities as they were manifest during a broader span of childhood.

Based on a number of studies, one can generally conclude that lonely people had (or at least report that they had) cold, less nurturant parents (Bergenstal, 1981; Brennan & Auslander, 1979; Franzoi & Davis, 1985; Hojat, 1982; Paloutzian & Ellison, 1982; Goldenberg & Perlman, 1984; Rubenstein, Shaver, & Peplau, 1979). For instance, in one large-scale study (Rubenstein et al., 1979), lonely respondents remembered their parents as being remote, less trustworthy, and disagreeable. Nonlonely respondents remembered their parents as warm, close, and helpful. Similar findings have been reported by Brennan and Auslander (1979, p. 200). They summed up their evidence by stating that lonely adolescents come from families manifesting "An absence of emotional nurturance, guidance or support. The climate is cold, violent, undisciplined, and irrational." Among other findings, lonely adolescents reported higher levels of punishment and greater parental dissatisfaction with their choice of friends. Lonely offspring, furthermore, felt their parents gave them little encouragement to strive for popularity. In a third study (Bergenstal, 1981), loneliness was positively related to past (real or threatened) separations from one's father, and inversely related to the number of hours per week fathers were available to interact with their sons.

Lobdell and Perlman (1986) also had women at a university rate their parents' child-rearing practices. A lack of positive parental involvement with their children was associated with the loneliness of the offspring. The child-rearing practices increased the predictability of daughters' loneliness scores even when the strongest known correlates of loneliness were also used as predictors. Collectively, these studies demonstrate that parent-child relations are important in identifying who is lonely.

When Do Children First Experience Loneliness?

The age at which children first experience loneliness is subject to debate. Sullivan (1953) believed that a new kind of intimacy emerges in preadolescence. Children of this age (9-12) engage in self-disclosure and begin to validate their self-worth through relationships. Chumships emerge. Sullivan argued that it is only when such intimacy can be achieved that it can be missed. Therefore, he suggested that it is not until preadolescence that the child can experience loneliness.

Others believe that loneliness can occur at a much earlier age. Ellison (1978, p. 7) goes so far as to argue that "the first signs of loneliness appear during the first three months of life." Zick Rubin (1982, p. 266) writes:

> Children as young as three, and, I suspect, children even younger than that, can feel what Robert Weiss (1973) calls "the loneliness of social isolation." Although the loneliness of children may differ in its details from the loneliness of adolescents or adults, I believe that we are talking about the same basic experience. Like adults who lack a satisfying social network, children without friends can experience painful feelings of malaise, boredom, and alienation.

While I am not as extreme as Ellison, I tend to side with those emphasizing the earlier onset of loneliness. One reason for my leaning in that direction is because children as young as seven or eight can meaningfully complete scales assessing loneliness (Asher, Hymel, & Renshaw, 1984, Asher & Wheeler, 1985). Their answers to various items in the scale show internal consistency, are reliable, and correlate with sociometric data. Rejected children are especially apt to be lonely. It is unlikely that youngsters could provide such valid, reliable scores if they had not yet experienced loneliness.

Further discussions of the age at which children first experience loneliness may benefit from making careful distinctions among terms. My hunch is that children can experience separation anxiety at a very early age, yet are not able to accurately label the experience of loneliness until considerably later. This raises the question of the relationship between separation anxiety and loneliness, plus the question of whether people can be lonely without recognizing it. Whatever answers one gives, I believe children are capable of experiencing loneliness before preadolescence.

ADOLESCENCE

Factors Contributing to Adolescent Loneliness

We are especially apt to be lonely during adolescence and young adulthood, as demonstrated in Table 1. Brennan (1982) and others (e.g., Ostrov & Offer, 1978) have suggested developmental and social factors that contribute to adolescent loneliness. Five such factors are worth noting. First, teenagers frequently have excessive expectations. They feel they should be popular, have dates, and experience success. Few youths, however, have fully developed their social skills. Many experience rejection and other forms of social failure. Second, as Brennan quips, the adolescent's social role is fairly clear—s/he hasn't got one! Such a sense of marginality is a component of loneliness. Third, along with this sense of marginality adolescents' self-concepts are often confused and poorly formed; in Erikson's terms, they experience a sense of *identity diffusion*. Identity diffusion is associated with high levels of loneliness (Goldenberg & Perlman, 1984). Fourth, the cognitive development of adolescents is more advanced than that of children. The adolescent gives up an egocentric view of the world, and can take the other person's perspective. With these developments comes an awareness of the self as separate. Existential loneliness becomes possible.

Finally, during adolescence, youths reorganize their social worlds. They separate from their parents as their primary attachment figures and they become increasingly involved with same- and opposite-sex peers. As Brennan (1982, p. 274) notes, "this readjustment almost certainly disrupts the important interpersonal relationships of the adolescent." Such disruptions, presumably, lead to loneliness.

Not only do such changes contribute to the level of loneliness, they may also alter which interpersonal domains contribute the most to loneliness. To explore this idea, Goldenberg and Perlman (1984) administered measures of family and peer relations to 480 Winnipeg students in grade 8, grade 11, and the first year at a university. As expected, family deficits were more closely associated with the loneliness

TABLE 2
Age-Related Correlates of Loneliness

| | School Level | | |
Predictor	Grade 8	Grade 11	University
Closeness to mother	.50	.23	.20
Mother's help	.48	.26	.23
Closeness to father	.41	.17	.20
Quality of family relations	.52	.46	.35
Total frequency of contact with friends	.18	.27	.38

NOTE: As indicated by one-tailed z-tests, the magnitude of the correlation for each variable was different among eighth graders than it was among university students. For the first three variables, the correlations for grade 8 students also differed significantly from the correlations for grade 11 students.

of grade 8 students, while deficits in peer relationships were more closely linked to the loneliness of university students (see Table 2). In this study, incidentally, the overall level of loneliness was comparable for all three age groups.

In a related study, Russell, Steffen, and Salih (1981) used satisfaction with relationships to predict loneliness. Regression analyses were performed separately for students aged 18 to 19 and for those 24 and older. For younger students, loneliness was best predicted by satisfaction with friendships, while for older students loneliness was primarily determined by satisfaction with romantic relationships. Taken together (compare Franzoi & Davis, 1985), these studies suggest that ties, first with the family, then friends, and later romantic ties, are crucial to experiencing or avoiding loneliness in one's teens and twenties.

Courtship and Loneliness

Two findings pertaining to courtship are worthy of note because of their relevance to the model of loneliness introduced earlier (see Figure 1). First, with the help of a paging device, Larson, Csikszentmihalyi, and Graef (1982) monitored the activities and feelings of 75 high school students for a week. While these students didn't particularly mind being alone during the daytime on weekends, they were especially apt to feel lonely if they were alone on Friday or Saturday evenings. In terms of the conceptual model offered earlier, it appears that Friday and Saturday evenings are times of the week when adolescents have particularly high expectations for social contact. When these expectations are not realized, they feel lonely (see Larson & Bradney, this volume).

Second, Hill, Rubin, and Peplau (1976) studied the end of 103 dating relationships. As these relationships ended, both partners presumably experienced a decline in their social environments. But in most break-ups there are two sides: that of the person who initiates the break-up and that of the person who is rejected. Hill et al. found that the initiators suffered significantly less loneliness than the partners who were rejected. In terms of the aforementioned conceptual model, one can say that the initiators had greater control over the situation. This sense of control presumably plays a buffering role, reducing the negative effect of losing a partner. Of course, it is also possible that the individuals who initiated the break-ups had less to lose from the termination of the relationships and/or had alternative relationships pending. But then, either or both these circumstances may be associated with having greater control.

The Transition to College

The transition to college has important ramifications for the loneliness of both the students themselves and their parents. I will start with the evidence on the children. Two noteworthy studies (Shaver, Furman, & Buhrmester, 1985; Cutrona, 1982b) have been done.

In the first study, Shaver et al. collected data from students (N = 166) at four separate times: the summer before they entered the University of Denver and again in the fall, winter, and spring of their first year. The results showed that the quality of their relationships plunged after they entered the university and rose again by the spring. State loneliness showed a similar, but reverse, pattern. It was greatest in the fall. The increase in state loneliness was considerably greater for males than for females. Thus not everyone reacted to starting college with the same intensity of loneliness. Besides gender, Shaver et al. emphasized the role that social skills, especially initiation skills, played. Students who had the courage to use active coping strategies, who introduced themselves to strangers, who attended group meetings, who called new acquaintances for a date, and so on were more likely to avoid the loneliness frequently associated with starting college.

Cutrona (1982b) examined which UCLA students (N = 162) overcome loneliness. She collected data twice within the first seven weeks of the new students' arrival on campus, and again in the spring after they had been there for seven months. During their first two weeks at UCLA, 75% of the new students reported feeling lonely. By the end of the spring term, only 25% of the respondents reported having felt lonely in the previous two weeks. Most students overcame their loneliness, but a few

(13% of the total sample) did not. Students who remained lonely initially believed that their loneliness was their own fault. They generally had low expectations for improving their social lives, and pinned their hopes on finding a boyfriend or girlfriend. The key factor identified for recovering from loneliness was increasing the satisfaction students obtained from their friendships. The students' romantic attachments were not so crucial, although later in life they may serve as an important buffer against loneliness.

MIDLIFE

Marriage

Marriage, when successful, can provide adults with intimacy, affection, identity, and care. A good deal of research (see Fehr & Perlman, 1985) shows the protective effect marriage has on both physical and mental well-being. Thus one might anticipate an association between marital status and loneliness.

This is indeed the case. Several data sets (see Table 3) document that loneliness is least common among married people. When the unmarrieds are divided into various more specific groups, the results vary somewhat by sample. The general tendency appears to be for single (never-married) people to be moderately lonely, with the widowed and the divorced being the most lonely. At least in one Dutch sample (de Jong-Gierveld, 1986a), single parents were also a group very high in loneliness.

Naturally, marriage is no guarantee that one can avoid loneliness. In examining individual cases, several authors (Seidenberg, 1980; Rubenstein & Shaver, 1982; Weiss, 1973) have noted the loneliness that can occur within marriage. Interestingly, both Seidenberg and Weiss describe housewives married to successful organizational men. In the case of Mrs. Phillips, described by Weiss, loneliness was triggered by an occupationally dictated move to a new community. Seidenberg depicts the suburban housewife's role as filled with menial, boring, and uncreative tasks. For the corporate wife, says Seidenberg (1980, p. 187), "loneliness means being left behind in knowledge, participation, mental growth, and influence." Complementing this analysis, survey research shows that homemakers are twice as likely as employed women to report feelings of loneliness (Gove & Geerken, 1977).

Even in the initial stages of marriage, partners can experience

TABLE 3
Loneliness as a Function of Marital Status

Study	Sample Size	Marital Status			
		Married	Single (Never Married)	Divorced	Widowed
		Percentage of Respondents Reporting Loneliness			
NIMH (Radloff, 1982)	2835	18	38	43	41
Berg et al. (1981)	1007	10	16	16	43
Gubrium (1974)	210	49	41	67	72
Edmonton-Winnipeg Survey[a]	727	22	41	44	41
Harvey & Bahr (1974)	2005	17	–	–	34
Parlee (1979)	4000+	56	72	69	59
		Loneliness -Scale Scores			
de Jong-Gierveld (1986b)	392	.56	2.23	3.33	3.17

NOTE: Because of differences in question wording and so forth, between-study comparisons of loneliness levels is not possible. Most of the investigations presumably selected representative samples; Parlee did not. Two of the samples (Gubrium and Berg et al.) consisted only of older adults. Harvey and Bahr did not report levels of loneliness for single and divorced individuals.
a. Edmonton-Winnipeg data provided by the Winnipeg Area Study and the Population Research Laboratory, University of Alberta, R.F. Currie, L. W. Kennedy, and C. Thacker, Principal Investigators.
b. In de Jong-Gierveld's study, higher scores reflect greater loneliness. "Married" respondents include all individuals living with a partner.

loneliness. Sadava and Matejcic (1987) studied 38 recently married couples. Several of these respondents reported high levels of loneliness. Furthermore, the respondents' loneliness was associated with other aspects of their marriages. Compared with nonlonely men, lonely husbands had more apprehension about communicating with their wives. Lonely wives liked their husbands less than did nonlonely wives. Turning to the impact of one's loneliness on one's spouse, the husbands of lonely wives engaged in less self-disclosure within their marriages. The wives of lonely husbands experience less liking for and less intimacy with their partners. In essence, the marriages of lonely people appear to be in jeopardy from the start.

Not surprisingly, the marital satisfaction of lonely people tends to be low. This is true for newlyweds (Sadava & Matejcic, 1987) as well as for senior citizens (Perlman, Gerson, & Spinner, 1978). Furthermore, lonely people tend to be dissatisfied with their sex lives (Rubenstein & Shaver, 1982, p. 82).

An interesting, but obscure, study by John Woodward (see Gilger, 1976) related marital status to the timing of loneliness experiences. Apparently, Woodward collected data from people over the course of the Christmas holidays. According to the report of this study, never-married and divorced people were the most lonely during the holidays themselves. Married housewives, on the other hand, felt most lonely after the holidays. For housewives, who were typically surrounded by family during the holidays, the aftermath may be a letdown and period of interpersonal loss. For divorced and single individuals, the Christmas holidays themselves may increase an awareness of their isolation and create a longing for more intimate social bonds.

In sum, then, marriage generally protects people from loneliness. But when it fails, marriage can become a prison in which the plight of loneliness becomes all the more painful.

Networks and the Family

With regard to the two themes of this volume, families and social networks, de Jong-Gierveld's work (1986b) is relevant in that she connects networks, gender, and loneliness. She found that

> the loneliness of male respondents was *strongly* associated with the perceived quality of only one relationship, namely that with their female confidant/partner. In contrast, the loneliness of female respondents was *strongly* associated with the subjective evaluation of their network-in-general. For women in her study, intimacy with their romantic partner was *non*-significantly correlated with loneliness.

Incidentally, very little research has been done linking networks factors, per se, with loneliness. (There is, of course, work relating the quantity and quality of various types of relationships with loneliness.) In one of the few published studies focused on network characteristics, Stokes (1985) demonstrated that people with more interconnected, dense networks tend to be less lonely. Complementing Cutrona's (1982b) view that quality is more important than quantity, Stokes failed to find a significant relationship between network size and loneliness.[1] Thus these findings suggest the importance of network structure in insulating people from loneliness.

Because kin-dominated networks are likely to be dense (i.e., the kin are all likely to know one another), one might expect individuals with family oriented networks to be less lonely. Stokes asked respondents what proportion of their network members were relatives. His data provide support for the assumption that kin-oriented networks tend to be high in density. But, contrary to expectation, in his data set, kin orientation was not associated with the amount of loneliness respondents experienced. In another study, however, Jones (1981) found that individuals who had a higher proportion of their interactions with family members were less lonely. Thus, there is at least partial support for the view that kinship bonds enhance network density and network density in turn reduces loneliness.

Parenthood: The Birth and Departure of Children

In Chapter 3 of this volume, Saulnier discusses network changes during the transition to parenthood. She found that the number of network members decreases, and marital satisfaction declines. Given these changes, one might expect loneliness to increase. Somewhat surprisingly, she did not find any significant changes in loneliness between the early stages of pregnancy and the time of the last data collection, 14 months after delivery. In another study, however, Cutrona (1982a) found that loneliness during pregnancy was a strong predictor of women's postpartum depression.

In a piece aptly titled, "The loneliness of the long distance mother," Pauline Bart (1980) discussed how the launching of children affects middle-aged women. Bart interviewed a small sample of women (n = 22) and examined the case records of many more (n = 533). Based on this analysis, Bart concluded that women who adopt the traditional feminine role of being homemakers devoted to their children are more apt to experience loneliness and depression when their children leave than are women less invested in a maternal, homemaker role.

Divorce

Separation and divorce are both experiences which can be stressful and reduce our social ties (Rands, this volume). As already discussed (see Table 3), divorced individuals tend to have high loneliness scores. Thus it is not surprising that in one study of recently divorced men (see Bloom, White, & Asher, 1979, p. 194), 60% of those interviewed considered loneliness a major emotional problem.

Woodward, Zabel, and Decosta (1980) asked 59 divorced persons when and under what circumstances they felt lonely. These respondents were more apt to experience their period of greatest loneliness before (rather than after) the divorce decree became final. Both men and women felt lonely when they were left out or rejected by others or when they felt out of place at a particular event. For women, loneliness was also triggered when they felt stigmatized by being divorced, when finances became a problem, when they had no one with whom to share decision-making responsibilities and daily tasks, and when they wanted to join in an activity but were unable to do so.

Jones and Adams (1978) examined the relationship between loneliness and the divorce experiences of 74 men and women. Significant correlations were obtained in terms of blame, the relationships between exspouses, and coping. Lonely subjects blamed more of the marriage's problems on their former partners. They also had more difficulties in their relationships with their exspouses. They felt less affection, they argued more frequently over child-rearing, and they had less friendly interactions. In terms of adjusting to separation, lonely respondents felt more cut-off from their friends, drank more, and experienced greater depression. They spent more time with their children and were less likely to become romantically involved with a new partner.

OLD AGE

Several studies of loneliness among seniors have been conducted. I have been struck with how this research differs from research on younger adults in two, interrelated ways. First, the most commonly investigated correlates of loneliness seem to differ. In studies of adolescent and adult loneliness, considerable attention has been focused on personality traits, social skills, and cognitive processes. Much less attention has been focused on such variables in studies of seniors. (Even among seniors, however, such personality characteristics as depression, anxiety, low self-esteem, and self-consciousness are reasonably strong predictors of loneliness; see Schultz & Moore, 1984; Hansson, Jones, Carpenter, & Remondet, 1986). Second, in most studies with adults the investigators are concerned with loneliness per se; they seem oblivious to developmental concerns. In studies with seniors, authors seem more sensitive to life-span issues. Often the variables they select to correlate with loneliness implicitly have special significance in the lives of seniors.

A comprehensive review of the literature on loneliness among the elderly is beyond the scope of the present chapter. Instead, I will first address the question of the general level of loneliness among seniors.

Then I will turn to the predictors of loneliness in old age. I will selectively examine a few predictors that appear to have special significance in the lives of seniors, and then I will look at the role of kin versus friends. Finally, I will examine the death of a spouse as a trigger of loneliness.

Why Aren't Seniors Lonelier?

As indicated in the beginning of the chapter, seniors are not as lonely a group as widely held stereotypes would suggest. Two factors help to explain why seniors aren't lonelier. A first explanation stems from Peplau and Perlman's aforementioned discrepancy framework. It is probably true that the amount of social contact declines with age (see Larson, Zuzanek, & Mannell, 1985). But, according to a discrepancy formulation, actual levels of contact are not the key. One must consider the gap between achieved and desired or needed levels of contact. It may be that the desired level of contact drops as rapidly as actual levels of contact, thus protecting older adults from loneliness.

Two multigenerational studies (Perlman, Locke, & Bond, 1985; Revenson & Johnson, 1984) provide another clue concerning how seniors avoid greater loneliness. In both these studies, respondents were asked about the quality of their relationships. In both studies, seniors rated the quality of their relationships as higher than did younger people. Having satisfying, intimate relations is, of course, associated with lower levels of loneliness. Thus the generally higher quality of those contacts seniors do have appears to be a crucial factor in explaining seniors' protection from severe loneliness (compare Johnson, this volume).

Correlates of Loneliness Among the Elderly

Empirical surveys and popular stereotypes suggest that a variety of changes occur as we age. The stereotypes generally paint a gloomy picture. Health problems can emerge; most seniors in the United States have relatively low incomes; transportation can be a difficulty, and so on. Among those in their late 70s and beyond, 18% of men and 41% of women live alone (see Peplau, Bikson, Rook, & Goodchilds, 1982). Many observers equate being alone with being lonely. Finally, old age is seen as a time when we are apt to lose our social power and become increasingly dependent upon others. Thus for loneliness researchers an important question become: Are these, or similar, factors related to loneliness? The answer, with qualifications, of course, is yes.

Studies have generally found an association between poor health and greater loneliness (Berg, Mellstrom, Persson & Suanborg, 1981; Dooghe, Vanderleyden, & van Loon, 1980, Kivett, 1979; Perlman, Gerson, & Spinner, 1978). In one study, this association was stronger among seniors than it was among college-aged women (Schmitt & Kurdek, 1985). Most of these studies use self-report, rather than objective, measures of health. Thus critics might claim that the poor health of lonely people is primarily due to their tendency to see the world negatively rather than real differences in their actual physical condition. Two new lines of work, however, appear to rebut this criticism. In studies using physiological measures to assess the body's immune system, Kiecolt-Glaser and her associates (1984) obtained evidence showing that lonely medical students were less able to fight off infectious diseases (see Kiecolt-Glaser et al., 1984). And, in a longitudinal study of the rural elderly, those seniors who were the most lonely at the initial testing had the poorest health outcomes two years later. Among the most lonely group, 22% moved to an institution; among the least lonely people, only 4% moved from their own home to a nursing facility. Even more striking was the finding that the loneliest people were four times more likely to die during the two-year follow-up period than were the least lonely.

Available research generally confirms that having trouble getting transportation and limited access to using a car are related to greater loneliness (Berg et al., 1981; Kivett, 1979; Perlman et al., 1978). The evidence on income and the loneliness of seniors is less conclusive. Perlman et al. reported that greater loneliness went hand in hand, especially among men, with having a lower income. In their study of Swedish seniors, Berg et al. did not find a significant association between income and loneliness. Perhaps because of that government's strong commitment to providing benefits for retired people, economic differences among Swedish seniors are relatively small and less important.

Schulz (1976) has provided an experimental demonstration of the importance of control. He had college students visit residents of a retirement home for a two-month period. In half of these dyads the seniors could decide on the frequency and duration of these visits. In the other half of the dyads the seniors did not have this control. Although the total contact was the same in both conditions, seniors who could decide on the contacts reported themselves as lower in loneliness. They were also higher in hope and happiness. Non-experimental indications of the importance of control are also available. For example, in Perlman et al. 's data, loneliness was greater among respondents who had moved to their present residence because of circumstances rather than choice.

Turning to living arrangements, adults who live alone are generally more lonely than those who live by themselves (de Jong-Gierveld, 1986; Revenson & Johnson, 1984). This appears also to be true among seniors (Berg et al., 1981; Tunstall, 1967); although among those over 64 in Revenson and Johnson's data set, this trend did not reach statistical significance. Several loneliness scholars have cautioned against giving findings such as these too much importance (see Peplau et al., 1982). In part, they have argued that it is desolation (i.e., changes or discontinuities in social engagement) rather than isolation per se that leads to loneliness (Gubrium, 1974; Revenson, 1986).

To sum up, the correlates of loneliness among senior citizens include poor health, low income, difficulties getting transportation, a lack of perceived control, and living along. All of these may be age-related "causes" of loneliness. But certainly this is not the only possibility. Living alone, income, and perceived control are all associated with loneliness at other stages of the life cycle, and the direction of causality is not altogether clear. It may well be that loneliness causes seniors to rate their health poorly or that both loneliness and health assessments stem from some underlying third factor.

Nonetheless, the available evidence does paint a fairly clear picture of who tends to be lonely in old age. A couple of final factors are worth adding to this picture. In particular, lower levels of loneliness are associated with having a confidant and feeling the quality of one's own social relationships are as good as those of one's peers. Both these are fairly strong predictors (Clark & Anderson, 1980; Perlman, Locke, & Bond, 1985).

The Importance of Children Versus Friends

The importance of kin in old age is frequently mentioned. For example, two noted gerontologists (Riley & Foner, 1968, p. 561) claimed:

> Friends and neighbors play an important part in the lives of many older people. . . . They are, however, generally less important to people than children and relatives.

Consistent with this view, older adults do interact with their relatives, especially their children, on a fairly frequent basis. Also, family members exchange various forms of aid and support (Fehr & Perlman, 1985). I, however, tend to resist arguments about the greater importance of children. Data on this point come from at least three studies. Arling (1976) asked elderly widows (n = 409) about the frequency of their contacts with children, other relatives, and friends. Arling found that contact with children was unrelated to loneliness, but greater contact with friends and neighbors was associated with low levels of loneliness. Perlman and associates (1978, 1985) obtained similar results in two separate studies—once using frequency of contact measures and once using quality of relationships measures.

While contact with family members may persist, this is no guarantee that it is enjoyable. Rosnow (1967) has argued that frequent contact between the elderly and their children often becomes ritualistic—based on obligation rather than on warmth or closeness. At the end of the life-cycle, contact with children may have little importance as a causal factor preventing loneliness. Instead, such contact may be the result of the older person's frailty, increasing needs, and the lack of alternative sources of support (see Johnson, this volume). Consistent with this view, in a study by Scharlach (in press), the more daughters perceived their aging mothers to be a burden, the more the mothers tended to be lonely.

Widowhood

As indicated earlier in Table 3, widowed individuals tend to be lonely. Roughly half of respondents in one survey (Lopata, 1969) reported loneliness as their major problem in widowhood. Loneliness is usually inversely related to how long people have been widowed (Hansson et al., 1986; Revenson & Johnson, 1984; Lopata, Heinemann, & Baum, 1982). Feelings of loneliness are greatest shortly after the loss of a spouse and subside over time.

In her studies of Chicago widows, Lopata (1969) analyzed the components or forms of loneliness, and the situations in which respondents felt lonely. Based on this, she formulated a list of 11 ways in which widows missed their husbands. For example, when their husbands die, widows lose

a partner who made them feel important,
a companion with whom they shared activities,
an escort to public encounters as well as a partner in couple-based socializing, and
a financial provider who enabled them to participate in more costly activities and enjoy a more expensive lifestyle.

Both Lopata (1980, Lopata et al., 1982) and Hansson (Hansson et al., 1986) have investigated the correlates of loneliness among widows. Lopata et al. (1982) found greater loneliness among widows whose husbands had died unexpectedly. Consistent with the pervasive negativism of lonely people, Lopata (1980) also found that lonely widows had more negative attitudes toward their late husbands[2] (Lopata, 1980). In Hansson et al.'s study, greater loneliness was associated a with maladaptive orientation toward widowhood. Prior to the death of their husbands, the lonely widows engaged in less behavioral rehearsal (e.g., finding jobs, getting around on their own) for widowhood and instead engaged in more rumination about the largely negative consequences of their spouse's impending death. At the time of their spouse's death, subsequently lonely widows experienced more negative emotions and felt less prepared to cope. Lonely widows were also less likely to engage in social comparison with widowed friends. In both these studies, other factors, not related to the widows' marriages, were also correlated with loneliness. These included such familiar variables as the respondents' health, personality attributes, and the strength of their social support systems.

OVERCOMING LONELINESS

Having provided an empirically based picture of loneliness, it is obvious that loneliness varies in severity from person to person and at different points in the life cycle. While people often gradually overcome their loneliness, a variety of programs have been developed to prevent loneliness or alleviate the discomfort associated with it. Rook (1984a, 1984b) examines three kinds of interventions: facilitating social bonds, promoting better coping strategies for dealing with loneliness, and preventing loneliness. While my comments on overcoming loneliness are not as detailed or as comprehensive as Rook's excellent analysis, my suggestions are rooted specifically in a family life cycle perspective. I will cover three topic: ways of dealing with loneliness at various points in the life cycle, transition programs for coping with social loss, and therapy outcome studies. First, however, a comment is in order concerning the role of the family in alleviating loneliness.

Some research has been done to identify the significant others to whom lonely people turn for help. This research serves as one gauge of the importance of the family in alleviating loneliness (Lopata et al., 1982). In trying to overcome loneliness, a high proportion of widows

(61%) turned to friends. Right after this in importance came children (55%) and siblings (40%). Neighbors were mentioned by a moderate number of respondents (33%). A small proportion of widows turned to such formal supports as the church (31%) or voluntary organizations (22%). In Cutrona's (1982b) UCLA study, very few students (9%) turned to psychotherapists or counselors. Thus it appears that family members are mentioned moderately often as persons who can help alleviate loneliness. What they can do to help may depend upon where the lonely (or potentially lonely) person is in the life cycle.

Alleviating Loneliness: Life-Cycle Considerations

From a life-cycle perspective, several suggestions can be offered for preventing or alleviating loneliness. A key ingredient in preventing loneliness appears to be positive parental involvement with children. Parents need to spend time with their sons and daughters. They need to be affectionate, trustworthy, and sounding boards with whom their children can talk over problems. The retrospective recall data suggest parents should be approving of their children's choice of friends and encourage their children to strive for popularity. To help isolated younger children, parents often play matchmaker, trying to find their son or daughter a suitable playmate. A similar approach recommended by experts (compare Rubin, 1982, p. 258) is to foster cross-age friendships. Often a child who has difficulty relating to peers can form meaningful bonds with children who are slightly younger. In these relationships, the older child can develop social skills and enjoy the benefits of both respect and childhood intimacy.

Children whose parents divorce are at risk of being lonely in adulthood, and they are apt to experience loneliness in the aftermath of their parents' separation (Wallerstein & Kelly, 1980). Early intervention with such high risk groups is warranted. Traditional social support and skill training methods might be used.

In adolescence and young adulthood, two strategies may have particular relevance. First, it often seems that adolescents have unrealistically high expectations for their relationships. They look around at peers, aggrandizing the interpersonal success others achieve. Meanwhile, data suggests that adolescents as a group have poorer quality relations, at least in comparison with seniors. Thus it follows that students should constrain their aspirations, avoid interactions that contribute to conflicted, low quality relationships, and more realistically assess how their personal ties compare with those of their peers.

Second, in adolescence and young adulthood, dating becomes very important. Unfortunately, for many individuals, this is fraught with fear, awkwardness, and disappointment. Various social skill programs are available for heterosexual anxiety. These should be of value for individuals with dating difficulties.

As people get into their 20s and beyond, they are apt to become targets of what have been called "loneliness businesses." These include dating services, singles bars, cruises, clubs, religious retreats, and the like. What these all share in common is that, either explicitly as a primary goal or implicitly as a secondary benefit, they offer people the hope of developing satisfying relationships. This hope promotes business. The effectiveness of such ventures is, however, a matter of speculation. Sometimes they produce short-lived romances which cannot stand the test of time. I suspect that in the long run they are most successful when they capitalize on fundamental principles of attraction such as the importance of attitude similarity.

Since marital satisfaction is associated with loneliness, in midlife couples might want to participate in marital enrichment activities. There are various special programs designed to enhance marital satisfaction. Many of these advocate that couples engage in higher levels of self-disclosure and mutual reinforcement. These are behaviors which can usually be increased without professional help. Based on Bart's analysis, one might suggest to traditional women that they develop new interests and activities prior to their children's departure from home.

Looking at the correlates of loneliness in old age, several ways of helping people come to mind. As one of the more mundane, efforts should be made to provide seniors with good transportation systems. This can be done informally through carpools, or by increasing the availability and range of services provided by mass transit systems. Another obvious step is letting seniors maintain the maximum feasible level of control and autonomy in their lives. Schulz (1976) and others have described ways of empowering people, even those in poor health in institutional settings. Such strategies are worth exploring. Lopata's data also suggest the value of doctors informing husbands and wives of the terminal nature of their spouses' illnesses.

Two themes in the gerontology literature are the tendency of older adults to disengage and the benefits for well-being of remaining active (see Revenson & Johnson, 1984). Seniors, especially older men, should be encouraged to continue to develop new friendships. Networking, which is popular in many communities, can be helpful with promoting social relationships among seniors (see Rook, 1984b). The existence of a confidant is beneficial, so seniors should be encouraged to sustain or strive for intimate bonds. Finally, it appears seniors should keep active. Even if activities are solitary, if they bolster self-esteem they may prevent loneliness.

Transition Programs for Dealing with Divorce and Bereveament

Weiss (1976) has developed programs for helping individuals deal with the loss of a spouse. The goals of Weiss' sessions are to provide information about the crises, to provide support, and to help people find a place in a temporary community. The format used is to have a series of eight weekly meetings plus a reunion about six weeks later. The meetings mix lectures with small-group discussion. They tend to be of a more educational and supportive nature than traditional therapeutic sessions.

The programs were first developed for individuals going through marital separation. Adjustments had to be made for helping widows deal with bereavement. In contrast to people getting separated, the widowed view their loss as irrevocable and without compensation. Rather than finding mixed-sex discussion of the nature of the separation helpful, the bereaved find discussion of the nature of grief painful. The experience of widows and widowers (but not of men and women getting divorced) is sufficiently different that same-sex bereavement groups work best.

Weiss indicates the benefits that he believes accrue from his seminars and gives clinical evidence of their success. Empirical evaluations have documented the effectiveness of other, similar, professional programs for the bereaved (see Rook, 1984b).

Outcome Research

There is a growing body of outcome research on the treatment of loneliness (see Perlman & Peplau, 1985). To date, the results have been uniformly encouraging. Three studies are noteworthy. Andersson (1985) designed a short intervention program consisting of four meetings to help Swedish seniors overcome their loneliness. The program was based on three psychological concepts including control. Individuals randomly assigned to the treatment group experienced less loneliness after participating in the program than they had before. No change was observed in the no-treatment group. Ancillary data showed that the program changed the participants' sense of perceived control, and that perceived control correlated with posttreatment loneliness scores. Presumably, these changes in perceived control were a key ingredient in the intervention's success in alleviating loneliness. Besides the development of personal control, another key component of this program was getting seniors to engage in realistic social comparisons. Thus the results of this project tie in nicely with the conceptual model of loneliness presented at the beginning of the chapter.

Jones and his associates (1982) conducted another noteworthy therapy outcome study in which the treatment had its roots in loneliness research. Jones et al. identified three unique characteristics of the way lonely people interact in conversations: (1) they make fewer other-references and ask fewer questions of their partner; (2) they change the topic more often; and (3) they delay longer in filling gaps in the conversation. Jones et al. therefore developed a short social skills training program to help students overcome these interpersonal deficits, incorporating explanation, modelling, practice with prompting, and feedback on the students' performance of target behaviors. Compared with a no-treatment and a placebo treatment (conversation only) control group, the skills training produced desired changes in the participants' interactional styles. The intervention also reduced students' loneliness. Indeed, the magnitude of the reduction in loneliness was appreciable compared to that reported in most psychological research.

Finally, Scharlach (in press) designed a brief cognitive behavioral intervention to help middle-aged women reduce their unrealistic feelings of responsibility for their aging mothers. Indirectly, this program was also designed to increase the mothers' sense of personal control. As expected, data collection six weeks after the end of the intervention showed that the daughters perceived their mothers as being less burdensome. But more striking and germane to the present chapter, the aging mothers became less lonely after the intervention. Presumably by creating greater mother-daughter autonomy, both parties benefited.

CONCLUSION

The basic premise of this chapter has been that loneliness is intertwined with human development and the family life cycle. The evidence testifies to the merits of this premise. Parent-child relations are associated with loneliness. Lonely adults remember their parents as being remote, disagreeable, and untrustworthy. Adolescence is a period in the life cycle when loneliness is especially common. In terms of family roles, housewives and single parents are at risk. Although marital partners can be intimate strangers, being married is typically associated with being less lonely. Divorced and widowed individuals experience high levels of loneliness. Such transitions as going away to college, breaking up, or becoming widowed increase loneliness. At least with the transition to college, men's loneliness increased more than did women's.

Several authors have obtained the correlates of loneliness separately for different age groups (Goldenberg & Perlman, 1984; Lobdell & Perlman, 1986; Perlman, Gerson, & Spinner, 1978; Perlman et al., 1985; Russell et al., 1981; Schmitt & Kurdek, 1985; Schultz & Moore, 1984). Three kinds of correlates consistently appear. First, personality variables such as self-esteem, depression, and anxiety are associated with loneliness in all age groups. Second, regardless of the age of respondents, those people who think they have poorer social relations than their peers tend to be lonely. Third, the quality of people's relationships matter.

But it is here that variation enters the picture. At least in the first third of life, the key interpersonal domain leading to loneliness appears to shift. It starts with the family, moves first to friends and later to romantic attachments. Similarly, the importance of health appears to be stage specific, having its greatest importance in old age.

The ebb and flow of loneliness over the life cycle underscores the importance of both predisposing and precipitating factors. Some people are always lonely, others are rarely so. Personality characteristics and situational factors both contribute to the prediction of loneliness. An interesting question is whether the people who succumb to loneliness at one life transition are the same as those who succumb at other crisis points. Presumably, the predisposing factors are relatively enduring, thus creating some degree of cross-crises responsivity.

With reference to the life cycle, a series of interventions were recommended to help the lonely. Such strategies as making realistic social comparisons and gaining control may be relevant to all stages of the life cycle. Other interventions such as Seminars for the Separated have value for specific groups.

While loneliness is a fact of human existence, its likelihood and intensity is greater at some points in life than others. As it says in Ecclesiastes, "for everything there is a season." There is a time to be lonely, and a time to savor the joys of friendship. A key question is how much time one spends in each season. In January some people prefer the warmth of Florida to the bluster of winter. Its unlikely that we will ever be able to totally eliminate loneliness—even Florida occasionally gets frost. But, armed with a better understanding of the phenomenon and by realizing the therapeutic implications of what is known, people should gain greater control over how much of their lives are spent in each season. Hopefully, the research described in this chapter is blazing a trail to the sunbelt!

NOTES

1. In a Manitoba data set, however, Dufton and Perlman (1986) found network size to be a moderately strong predictor of loneliness.

2. This finding runs counter to the idea that people in successful marriages have more to lose and it was not replicated in Lopata et al.'s (1982) analyses. In that report, however, a composite measure of loneliness was used. It included items on the respondents' desire for more friends and life satisfaction. Spousal sanctification was associated with greater loneliness. To reconcile these differences, Lopata (personal communication, June 14, 1985) comments: "If she [the widow] has poor health, lacks friends and is dissatisfied with her life now, she could easily idealize the past. . . . If asked only about loneliness, a different type of woman comes forth—one who has probably always been lonely and does not have good memories of her late husband."

REFERENCES

Andersson, L. (1985). Intervention against loneliness in a group of elderly women: An impact evaluation. *Social Science and Medicine, 20*, 355-364.

Arling, G. (1976). The elderly widow and her family, neighbors and friends. *Journal of Marriage and the Family, 38*, 757-768.

Asher, S. R., Hymel, S., & Renshaw, P. D. (1984). Loneliness in children. *Child Development, 55*, 1457-1464.

Asher, S. R., & Wheeler, V. A. (1985). Children's loneliness: A comparison of rejected and neglected peer status. *Journal of Consulting and Clinical Psychology, 53*, 500-505.

Bart, P. (1980). The loneliness of the long-distance mother. In J. Hartog, J. R. Audy, & Y. A. Cohen (Eds.), *The anatomy of loneliness* (pp. 204-219). New York: International Universities Press.

Berg, S., Mellstrom, D., Persson, G., & Suanborg, A. (1981). Loneliness in the Swedish aged. *Journal of Gerontology, 36*, 342-349.

Bergenstal, W. K. (1981). The relationship of father support and father availability to adolescent sons' experience of loneliness and separation anxiety. (Doctoral dissertation, California School of Professional Psychology.) *Dissertation Abstracts International, 42*, 2024B-2025B.(University Microfilms No. 8124394.)

Bloom, B. L., White, S. W., & Asher, S. J. (1979). Marital disruption as a stressful event. In G. Levinger & O. C. Moles (Eds.), *Divorce and separation: Context, causes, and consequences* (pp. 184-200). New York: Basic Books.

Borys, S., & Perlman, D. (1985). Gender differences in loneliness. *Personality and Social Psychology Bulletin, 11*, 63-74.

Bowlby, J. (1977). The making and breaking of affectional bonds: Aetiology and psychopathy in the light of attachment theory. *British Journal of Psychiatry, 130*, 201-210.

Brennan, T. (1982). Loneliness at adolescence. In L. A. Peplau & D. Perlman (Eds.), *Loneliness: A sourcebook of current theory, research and therapy* (pp. 269-290). New York: Wiley-Interscience.

Brennan, T., & Auslander, N. (1979). *Adolescent loneliness: An exploratory study of social and psychological predispositions and theory* (Vol. 1). Washington, DC: National Institute of Mental Health, Juvenile Problems Division. (ERIC Document Reproduction Service No. ED 194 822.)

Clark, M., & Anderson, B. G. (1980). Loneliness and old age. In J. Hartog, J. R. Audy, & Y. A. Cohen (Eds.), *The anatomy of loneliness* (pp. 259-283). New York: International Universities Press.

Cutrona, C. E. (1982a). Depressive attributional style and nonpsychotic postpartum depression. *Dissertation Abstracts International, 42*, 3413-B.

Cutrona, C. E. (1982b). Transition to college: Loneliness and the process of social adjustment. In L. A. Peplau & D. Perlman (Eds.), *Loneliness: A sourcebook of current theory, research and therapy* (pp. 291-309). New York: Wiley Interscience.

Dean, L. R. (1962). Aging and the decline of affect. *Journal of Gerontology, 17*, 440-446.

de Jong-Gierveld, J. (1986a). Loneliness and the degree of intimacy in personal relationships. In R. Gilmour & S. Duck (Eds.), *The emerging field of personal relationships* (pp. 241-249). Hillsdale, NJ: Erlbaum.

de Jong-Gierveld (1986b). Men and loneliness. In R. Lewis & R. E. Salt (Eds.), *Men in families*. Newbury Park, CA: Sage.

de Jong-Gierveld, J., & Raadschelders, J. (1982). Types of loneliness. In L. A. Peplau & D. Perlman (Eds.), *Loneliness: A source book of current theory, research and therapy* (pp. 105-119). New York: Wiley Interscience.

Dickens, W. J., & Perlman, D. (1981). Friendship over the life cycle. In S. W. Duck & R. Gilmour (Eds.), *Personal Relationships 2: Developing personal relationships* (pp. 91-122). London: Academic Press.

Dooghe, G., Vanderleyden, L. & van Loon, F. (1980). Social adjustment of the elderly residing in institutional homes: A multivariate analysis. *International Journal of Aging and Human Development, 11*, 163-176.

Dufton, B. D., & Perlman, D. (1986). Loneliness and religiosity: In the world but not of it. *Journal of Psychology and Theology, 14*, 135-145.

Ellison, C. W. (1978). Loneliness: A social developmental analysis. *Journal of Psychology and Theology, 6*, 3-17.

Fehr, B., & Perlman, D. (1985). The family as a social network and support system. In L. L'Abate (Ed.), *Handbook of family psychology and therapy* (Vol. 1, pp. 323-356). Homewood, IL: Dow-Jones Irwin.

Fidler, J. (1976). Loneliness: The problems of the elderly and retired. *Royal Society of Health Journal, 96*, 39-41, 44.

Franzoi, S. L., & Davis, M. H. (1985). Adolescent self-disclosure and loneliness: Private self-consciousness and parental influences. *Journal of Personality and Social Psychology, 48*, 768-780.

Gilger, K. (1976). *Loneliness and the holidays*. Lincoln: University of Nebraska, Department of Agricultural Communications.

Goldenberg, S. & Perlman, D. (1984). *Social relations and loneliness during adolescence.* Unpublished manuscript, University of British Columbia, Division of Family Science, Vancouver.

Gordon, S. (1976). *Lonely in America.* New York: Simon & Schuster.

Gove, W. R., & Geerken, M. R. (1977). The effect of children and employment on the mental health of married men and women. *Social Forces, 56,* 66-76.

Gubrium, J. R. (1974). Marital desolation and the evaluation of everyday life in old age. *Journal of Marriage and the Family, 36,* 107-113.

Hansson, R. O., Jones, W. H., Carpenter, B. N., & Remondet, J. H. (1986). Loneliness and adjustment to old age. *International Journal of Aging and Human Development, 24,* 41-53.

Hartog, J., Audy, J. R., & Cohen, Y. A. (Eds.) (1980). *The anatomy of loneliness.* New York: International Universities Press.

Hill, C. T., Rubin, Z., & Peplau, L. A. (1976). Breakups before marriage: The end of 103 affairs. *Journal of Social Issues, 32*(1), 147-168.

Hojat, M. (1982). Loneliness as a function of parent-child and peer relations. *Journal of Psychology, 112,* 129-133.

Hritzuk, J. (1982). *The silent company: How to deal with loneliness.* Englewood Cliffs, NJ: Prentice-Hall Spectrum.

Jones, W. H. (1981). Loneliness and social contact. *Journal of Social Psychology,* 113, 295-296.

Jones, W. H., & Adams, L. (1978, April). *Loneliness and Divorce.* Paper presented at the meeting of the Southwestern Psychological Association, New Orleans.

Jones, W. H., Hobbs, S. A., & Hockenbury, D. (1982). Loneliness and social skill deficits. *Journal of Personality and Social Psychology, 42,* 682-689.

Kiecolt-Glaser, J. K., Garner, W., Speicher, C., Penn, G. M., Holliday, J., & Glaser, R. (1984). Psychosocial modifiers of immunocompetence in medical students. *Psychosomatic Medicine, 46,* 7-14.

Kivett, V. R. (1979). Discriminators of loneliness among the rural elderly. *Gerontologist, 19,* 108-115.

Larson, R., Csikszentmihalyi, M., & Graef, R. (1982). Time alone in daily experience: Loneliness or renewal? In L. A. Peplau & D. Perlman (Eds.), *Loneliness: A source book of current theory, research and therapy* (pp. 40-53). New York: Wiley Interscience.

Larson, R., Zuzanek, J., & Mannell, R. (1985). Being alone versus being with people: Disengagement in the daily experience of older adults. *Journal of Gerontology, 40,* 375-381.

Lobdell, J., & Perlman, D. (1986). The intergenerational transmission of loneliness: A study of college females and their parents. *Journal of Marriage and the Family, 48,* 589-596.

Lopata, H. Z. (1969). Loneliness: Forms and components. *Social Problems, 17,* 248-261.

Lopata, H. Z. (1980). Loneliness in widowhood. In J. Hartog, J. R. Audy, & Y. A. Cohen (Eds.), *The anatomy of loneliness* (pp. 237-258). New York: International Universities Press.

Lopata, H. Z., Heinemann, G. D., & Baum, J. (1982). Loneliness: Antecedents and coping strategies in the lives of widows. In L. A. Peplau & D. Perlman (Eds.), *Loneliness: A sourcebook of current theory, research and therapy* (pp. 310-326). New York: Wiley Interscience.

Ostrov, E., & Offer, D. (1978). Loneliness and the adolescent. In S. Feinstein (Ed.), *Adolescent psychology* (pp. 34- 50) Chicago: University of Chicago Press.

Paloutzian, R. F., & Ellison, C. W. (1982). Loneliness, spiritual well-being and quality of life. In L. A. Peplau & D. Perlman (Eds.), *Loneliness: A sourcebook of current theory, research and therapy* (pp. 224-237). New York: Wiley-Interscience.

Parlee, M. B. (1979, October). The friendship bond. *Psychology Today*, pp. 43-54, 113.

Peplau, L. A., Bikson, T. K., Rook, K. S., & Goodchilds, J. D. (1982). Being old and alone. In L. A. Peplau & D. Perlman (Eds.), *Loneliness: A sourcebook of current theory, research and therapy* (pp. 327-347). New York: Wiley-Interscience.

Peplau, L. A., & Perlman, D. (Eds.) (1982). *Loneliness: A sourcebook of current theory, research and therapy*. New York: Wiley-Interscience.

Perlman, D., Gerson, A. C., & Spinner, B. (1978). Loneliness among senior citizens: An empirical report. *Essence, 2*, 239-248.

Perlman, D., Locke, J., & Bond, J. (1985, August). *Loneliness among university students and their grandparents*. Paper presented at the meeting of the American Psychological Association, Los Angeles.

Perlman, D. & Peplau, L. A. (1984). Loneliness research: A study of empirical findings. In L. A. Peplau & S. E. Goldston (Eds.), *Preventing the harmful consequences of severe and persistent loneliness* (DHHS Publication No. ADM84-1312, pp. 13-64). Washington, DC: U.S. Government Printing Office.

Radloff, L. S. (1982). [Data from the Center for Epidemiologic Studies, National Institute of Mental Health]. Analysis of unpublished data.

Revenson, T. A. (1986). Debunking the myth of loneliness in late life. In E. Seidman & J. Rappaport (Eds.), *Redefining social problems* (pp. 115-135). New York: Plenum.

Revenson, T. A., & Johnson, J. L. (1984). Social and demographic correlates of loneliness in late life. *American Journal of Community Psychology, 12*, 71-85.

Riley, M. W., & Foner, A. (1968). *Aging and society: Vol. 1. An inventory of research findings*. New York: Russell Sage.

Rook, K. S. (1984a). Interventions for loneliness: A review and analysis. In L. A. Peplau & S. E. Goldston (Eds.), *Preventing the harmful consequences of severe and persistent loneliness* (DHHS Publication No. ADM 84-1312, pp. 47-79). Washington, DC: U. S. Government Printing Office.

Rook, K. S. (1984b). Promoting social bonding: Strategies for helping the lonely and socially isolated. *American Psychologist, 39*, 1389-1407.

Rosnow, I. (1967). *Social integration of the aged*. New York: Free Press.

Rubenstein, C., & Shaver, P. (1982). *In search of intimacy*. New York: Delacorte Press.

Rubenstein, C. M., Shaver, P., & Peplau, L. A. (1979, February). Loneliness. *Human Nature, 2*, 59-65.

Rubin, Z. (1982). Children without friends. In L. A. Peplau & D. Perlman (Eds.), *Loneliness: A sourcebook of current theory, research and therapy* (pp. 255-268). New York: Wiley-Interscience.

Russell, D., & Cutrona, C. E. (1985). *Loneliness and physical health among the rural elderly*. Paper presented at the meeting of the American Psychological Association, Los Angeles.

Russell, D., Steffen, M. & Salih, F. A. (1981, August). Testing a cognitive model of loneliness. In L. A. Peplau (Chair), *New directions in loneliness research*. Symposium presented at the annual meeting of the American Psychological Association, Los Angeles.

Sadava, S. W., & Matejcic, C. (1987). Generalized and specific loneliness in early marriage *Canadian Journal of Behavioural Science, 19*, 56-66.

Scharlach, A. E. (in press). Relieving feelings of burden among women with elderly mothers. *Psychology and Aging.*

Schmidt, N., & Sermat, V. (1983) Measuring loneliness in different relationships. *Journal of Personality and Social Psychology, 44*, 1038-1047.

Schmitt, J. P., & Kurdek, L. A. (1985). Age and gender differences and personality correlates of loneliness in different relationships. *Journal of Personality Assessment, 49*, 485-496.

Schultz, N. R., & Moore, D. (1984). Loneliness: Correlates, attributions, and coping among older adults. *Personalty and Social Psychology Bulletin, 10*, 67-77.

Schulz, R. (1976). The effects of control and predictability on the physical and psychological well-being of the institutionalized aged. *Journal of Personality and Social Psychology, 33*, 563-573.

Seidenberg, R. (1980). The lonely marriage in corporate America. In J. Hartog, J. R. Audy, & Y. A. Cohen (Eds.), *The anatomy of loneliness* (pp.186-203). New York: International Universities Press.

Shaver, P., Furman W., & Buhrmester, D. (1985) Transition to college: Network changes, social skills, and loneliness. In S. Duck & D. Perlman (Eds.), *Understanding personal relationships: An interdisciplinary approach* (pp. 193-219). London: Sage.

Shaver, P., & Rubenstein, C. (1980). Childhood attachment experience and adult loneliness. In L. Wheeler (Ed.), *Review of personality and social psychology* (Vol. 1, pp. 42-73). Newbury Park, CA: Sage.

Stokes, J. P. (1985). The relation of social network and individual difference variables to loneliness. *Journal of Personality and Social Psychology, 48*, 981-990.

Sullivan, H. S. (1953). *The interpersonal theory of psychiatry.* New York: Norton.

Tunstall, J. (1967). *Old and alone.* New York: Humanities Press.

Wallerstein, J. S., & Kelly, J. B. (1980). The effects of parental divorce: Experiences of the child in later latency. In J. Hartog, J. R. Audy, & Y. A. Cohen (Eds.), *The anatomy of loneliness* (pp. 148-169). New York: International Universities Press.

Weiss, R. S. (1973). *Loneliness: The experience of emotional and social isolation.* Cambridge: MIT Press.

Weiss, R. S. (1976). Transition states and other stressful situations: Their nature and programs for their management. In G. Caplan & M. Killilea (Eds.), *Support systems and mutual help: Multidisciplinary explorations* (pp. 213-232). New York: Grune & Stratton.

Woodward, J. C., Zabel, J., & Decosta, C. (1980). Loneliness and divorce. *Journal of Divorce, 4*, 73-82.

9

Healing Members and Relationships in the Intimate Network

Carlfred B. Broderick

It is becoming increasingly clear that as the natural immune system is to the body, so the kin-friend network is to the individual and the family. Medical researchers are finding that too often their interventions, intended to fight a disease entity, actually suppress the body's own capacity to cure itself. Just so, we psychotherapists are beginning to suspect that, too often, our therapeutic interventions may result in insulating our clients from the healing potential of their intimate networks. Our medical colleagues are beginning to believe that the cure for cancer or the common cold will be found *not* in the development of more sophisticated serums and inoculations from without, but in the enablement of the natural immune system. Just so, we may discover that in many cases our most effective interventions will be to potentate the healing powers of the intimate network rather than to administer directly to the observed dysfunction.

Lest I be misinterpreted, let me make it very clear that I am not suggesting that direct intervention is never effective. Neither am I recommending that the chief role of the therapist is to activate the kin-friend network. I *am* suggesting that if one ignores this powerful and impactful social matrix the results may be a further disabling of the individual's or family's ability to cope successfully in their real world.

Before proceeding to consider how the therapist may function more effectively in the context of the natural network, it is important to understand how these elusive structures function in support of or in opposition to the well-being of individuals and families.

THE INTIMATE NETWORK AS A MATRIX FOR THE SURVEILLANCE AND SUPPORT OF INDIVIDUAL AND FAMILY WELL-BEING

There are many ways of categorizing networks, but for our purposes it may be sufficient to consider three main types: (a) those which are *effective* in monitoring, maintaining and when necessary, restoring the well-being of its members and their families, (b) those which are *ineffective* in this function for a variety of reasons, and (c) those which can be shown to be actively *destructive* of the well-being of individuals and their families.

Effective Networks

Some therapists and their clientele feel that nearly everyone needs therapy. It should be pointed out, however, that human beings have been surviving without therapy for thousands of years. Even today a small fraction of all individuals or families with problems elect to include a professional therapist in the process of resolving problems. Most mental illness is handled within the family and its circle of intimates. Most marital problems are worked out within the same matrix. When that resource is insufficient, the next most common response is to reach out to a still broader circle of informal resources. Typically, we "network" our way to church, encounter groups, or voluntary associations for those with special problems, Alcoholics Anonymous being the prototype. Indeed, even the decision to go to a therapist is likely to be initiated in the intimate network and facilitated through the extended network.

The point is that families and their intimate and extended networks have been handling the problems of their members independent of professional help since the dawn of time. But it is equally clear that networks are not all equally effective. For example my own work with Carle Zimmerman years ago was able to demonstrate that in one fairly large sample of urban families the effectiveness of the immediate network was a function of its size and its homogeneity. Of the 1791 target families with high school age children, only 19 reported that they never visited or were visited by anyone. Both in that study (Zimmerman and Broderick, 1954, 1956) and in the larger studies that followed (Zimmerman and Cervantes 1960; Cervantes, 1965), it was these totally unconnected families that were the most unstable, and whose children were most likely to have difficulty in school and with the law. Other, more recent studies have shown that isolated families are prone to violence (Straus, Gelles and Steinmetz, 1981) and a substantial variety of other dysfunctions. Moreover, in the work by Broderick, Zimmerman and Cervantes there was a clear regular increase in the effectiveness of these networks as their size increased from one to five close families.

The mechanism of this effectiveness became evident when the issue of homogeneity was taken into account. Each bond between target and friend family was evaluated as to whether the two families shared the same core status and values, such as social class, religious denomination and regional background. When examining only those people who listed five or more other families as friends, we discovered that in some cases all shared core background characteristics—the networks were entirely homogeneous—while in other cases the target families and network members shared very few similarities and occasionally none— the networks were entirely heterogeneous. The effectiveness of the network as measured by the target family's stability, problems with juvenile delinquency or problems associated with school performance was directly proportional to the homogeneity of the network. In terms of surveillance and support, families with five friends who were from different religious, political and social backgrounds were no better off than those with no friends at all.

Destructive Networks

In clinical practice one becomes aware that some networks are not only ineffective in sponsoring a family's well-being, they are actively destructive. Presumably there are a variety of destructive styles possible but I will mention two which clinicians run into with some frequency. Most blatant is the network that has crime, violence, incest or some other antisocial practice or value at its core. In our experience the only salvation for families or individuals caught up in such webs is to flee from them and establish an altogether separate and independent life in a more constructive web of associations.

A second type of destructive network is the result of a painful explosion of some sort in a close, richly interconnected network such that some elements are cut off from or actively feuding with other elements. These tensions can continue for years without resolution taking their individual destructive tolls over the entire period.

In considering the various types of effective, ineffective and destructive networks, it seems that, in addition to the issues of sufficient size and homogeneity, at least two other dimensions must be taken into account in any attempt at therapeutic intervention. They are the degree of *cohesion* and *flexibility* of the network. Olson and his colleagues (1983) have identified these same dimensions as of central importance in the family's internal structure and function, although Olson prefers the term "adaptability" to flexibility. There are a number of strong parallels between the ways in which families differ in their operation and the ways in which social networks differ in theirs.

Cohesiveness

Networks that anchor the high end of this dimension are very tightly organized. Members visit each other often and permit little privacy or autonomy for the individual families. As a result, surveillance and conformity to group norms is high and independence or rebellion is costly. External boundaries are well maintained. It is not easy to gain entrance to such a network and equally difficult to get disengaged from one.

At the other end of the continuum we find networks that are so loosely connected that all of the members may not know each other. The bonds are not very intense or influential and may, in some cases, be quite transitory.

Flexibility

At the more structured end of this dimension we have rigid networks. The reciprocal obligations among members may be defined precisely and the interactions almost ritualistic, with services, visits, phone calls and letters at specified intervals and with expectable content. At the opposite end of this dimension are "chaotic" networks. The relationships of members are ad hoc and ephemeral, shaped to the present need or impulse.

A Fourfold Typology of Networks

Cohesiveness and flexibility may be thought of as orthogonal dimensions forming a fourfold typology. Networks which are both cohesive and rigidly structured may be labeled "tight" networks. They are typically homogeneous in their values and effective in enforcing those values among their members. They exclude outsiders and are very intrusive into the lives of their members. They are the most effective of all types in providing emotional and material support for members and are the most ruthless in punishing members who violate group norms. They are not well designed to sponsor innovations or independence in their members.

Networks which are highly cohesive but also highly flexible may be called "engaged" networks. They are the type most valued by members. Olson and his colleagues found that among families these structured qualities were associated with the highest morale among members by a large margin (Olson and McCubbin, 1983, p. 184). This type of network provides the support level typical of "tight" networks, but permits more individual independence and creativity. It is more adaptable to changing times and circumstances.

A third type of network features weak bonding and few rules or specifications regarding the nature or frequency of interactions between members. The boundaries are highly permeable, the structure elusive and often unstable, and consequently such networks are viewed as "loose" in their structure. They may be thought of as highly adaptable in times of rapid change. They are the least intrusive, and therefore the least reliable in times of extended crisis or need.

Finally, the forth type of network—"disengaged"—is also the least appreciated, if we extrapolate from Olsen's findings on morale in families with these structural features. It features loose bonds which are inflexibly defined and typically negative in content. These rigid and often conflicted networks are held together by obligations to kin or other formal relationships (such as neighborhood or work situation), but the content of the interaction is competitive or even hostile. These are among the networks that in an earlier section we characterized as destructive.

THE OUTSIDER AS WOULD-BE HEALER

Outsiders have always played a role in healing individuals and families. Long before there were professional psychotherapists or family therapists there were priests and princes, medical practitioners and prostitutes. Literature and life are replete with physicians called upon to heal the spirit or mend a breach between family members.

The outsider can be cast in various roles. He or she can be the deus ex machina (God from the machine), the one lowered onto the stage by a crane in second rate Greek dramas to magically resolve impossible plot dilemmas. At the last possible moment the actor would remove the love spell from the ensorced heroine or raise the fallen hero back to life. Networks also may bring in a therapist at the last minute to save the terminally ill marriage, to redeem the wayward member, or to untangle an impossible knot of stubborn antipathies. Recently, for example, I received several telephone calls from the network of a man who had finally decided to leave his wife and three children and "come out" as a gay. His pastor phoned, his wife came in to see me, his new lover's girlfriend came in, and eventually the two men arrived. All wanted magic. My assignment was to make both of the men straight and rapturously sexually attracted to their wife and girlfriend, respectively. The real challenge of course was to disclaim any such power and to redefine myself as a mere resource to help them deal with their own problems as best they might. The would be healer must face a variety of hazards depending on the type of network the client maintains.

INTERVENTION IN A TIGHT NETWORK

If a client is enmeshed in a tight network, one of two problems almost inevitably intrudes into the therapist-client relationship. In the commonest case the client casts the therapist into the role of coconspirator in rebellion against the main body of the network. Nothing is more common than for therapists, especially those working with troubled youths, to fall into this trap and become the enemy of the network and the champion of the rebelling member. Every experienced clinician has discovered, however, that it is not possible to free an enmeshed member from a rigid, overconnected system. In the long run the strong bonds and connective energies of the system will prevail over the far weaker and more transient bond between the therapist and client. The client will be reclaimed as a troubled and troublesome prodigal member.

The more profitable intervention is focused on helping the client and the network accept a more differentiated, and less destructive, definition of the relationships between them. In order to accomplish this the therapist must maintain credibility with the system even as he or she works with the rebellious person to differentiate from it.

This brings us to an equally challenging but distinct problem therapists sometimes face when working with members of a tight network. Oftentimes, far from being defined as the enemy of the system we find ourselves being defined as its agent and retainer. In such cases, representatives of the network have counseled together and sought out a professional to aid them in assisting a troubled member. Often enough they set up the appointment and offer to pay the bills. As might be expected, they also expect to oversee the therapeutic process and to receive regular progress reports from the therapist, without which they will surely debrief the member unit after each session about what went on, how the therapy is going and so on. Network representatives will attempt to influence the course of the therapy (with only the best of motivations) through letters, phone calls, and even through separate appointments with the therapist. If these overtures are resisted, it is instructive to see a well-structured system martial its resources. I have been contacted by network members and affiliates from a great distance, some with impressive credentials or influence. If one resists being a fully cooperative agent of the system, one will be pressured to become, at least, a double agent who reports to both parties on conversations with the other.

Clearly the therapist's job is to resist every such pressure to become an enmeshed unit in the system. One of the goals of the therapy surely will be to help the client maintain his or her (or their) status in the system, but on a new, more differentiated basis with more privacy and more control over their own destinies. In the process of achieving these goals, representatives of the larger network may meet with the therapist and with the client unit and therapist. Each school of therapy has its own approaches to integrating therapeutic goals with network values, and space does not permit us to review each method. Rather, my concern here is that the solution take into account that the clients will still be connected in some important fashion, however happily or contentiously, with their networks long after the therapy relationship has terminated. If the clinical experience has only served to alienate the client further from the network, as often occurs, it may be that more long-range harm than good will be the final result of the intervention. The therapist will merely have succeeded in converting a tight into a disengaged network.

Intervention in a Disengaged Network

A disengaged network is one in which the members have very little interaction with each other because of long-standing grudges, and yet they are very much in one another's consciousnesses. From time to time one is called upon to perform the role of fence-mender or conciliator in such a network, in much the same way as the prince was called upon in Romeo and Juliet. Lacking the prince's political clout, this is likely to be a very difficult task. One is far more apt to succeed if the estranged parties are each privately looking for some face-saving mechanism for reconciliation. When the motivation is all on one party's side, the chances for success are much reduced. Presumably every professional would avoid the third logically possible situation, where only the intervener is motivated to get the members of the network back into comfortable communication with each other.

As with every mediation, the main job of the therapist in these cases is to maintain careful symmetrical rapport with both (or all) sides while searching for a premise for reconciliation. This is more difficult if, as often happens, one party has already established a relationship with the therapist through earlier work with him or her. Such a circumstance calls for separate sessions with the alienated parties until good rapport has been established with all concerned. Only then can the modality profitably shift to conjoint work.

One special feature of such systems may complicate the efforts of reconciliation if it is unsuccessfully resolved. Typically, the estranged members of a disengaged network keep track of each other through a linking party. If the estranged parties are parent and child, it may be another sibling of the parent or of the child that keeps each informed of the other. If the estranged members are former friends, it may be a mutual friend or kin/friend (i.e., kin to one and friend to the other) who provides the link. The interconnections of network members can only be ignored at substantial risk to the mediation enterprise. At the very least, a therapist should seek the support of the linking party, else he or she may be tempted to undermine the conciliation effort.

Intervention in Engaged and Loose Networks

In many ways, working with an individual or family from an engaged network is facilitated because in the typical case they are supportive of any positive changes that occur. The special case when the values of the network clash with those of the therapist or even with the Therapeutic Establishment will be discussed below.

Therapy with units from a loose network is also relatively uncomplicated because there is, by definition, little opposition. On the other hand, there may be little reliable support to depend on when necessary. In the most extreme cases there may be little to differentiate between the client with a very loose network and the client with no network at all. In this case there are special therapeutic challenges to consider.

Interventions with an Isolated Person or Family

The goal of therapy, when working with an isolated unit, is to teach individuals to construct a workable network from the social opportunities available. This may be difficult under the best of circumstances, but here are two particular hazards in need of scrutiny. The first is to avoid allowing the client to cast the therapist into the role of surrogate network. In this role the therapist is encouraged to participate with the client in social settings and to take responsibility for surveillance, support, and repair on an ongoing basis. This inappropriate level of dependency is seductive and sometimes difficult to replace with the more challenging task of teaching a client how to construct a separate network.

One of the most appropriate treatment modalities for isolated individuals is to place them in a group with others like themselves. This method is useful, but not without the hazard of overattachment. In mutual support groups, members find companionship and develop social skills in a sheltered environment. The problem arises when the group becomes enmeshed. Like overconnected families it may forget that its prime function is to launch members, not to keep them. When leaving such a group becomes an act of disloyalty rather than a "graduation with honors," the technique has backfired.

The above examples are illustrative of how therapists may interact with various types of networks. Therapists may find themselves cast into roles as disparate as consultant to a network or as interloper into forbidden avenues. The point is that virtually every therapeutic encounter is also an encounter with a network. Rarely can that reality be ignored to the benefit of clients.

SPECIAL CASES AND THEIR IMPLICATIONS FOR SUCCESSFUL THERAPEUTIC INTERVENTION

Elsewhere I have made the case that the therapeutic profession is based on a particular set of existential values that amount to a secular religion (Broderick, 1983). For example, they value individual growth and freedom over loyalty or sacrifice, the forthright expression of feelings over their suppression, full disclosure over discretion or diplomacy and egalitarian over traditional role structure.

When clients come from other value premises, one of several things may occur. First, the therapist may come to understand the client's value system and work within it. This is the textbook solution, and in my observation almost never occurs unless the therapist shares some of those same core values in his or her own private life. Second, the clients can perceive that their values are being undermined and leave therapy. Third, the client can gradually assume the values of the therapist and in effect become a therapeutic convert. This is probably the most common outcome, at least if the therapist has any measure of charisma, which many successful clinicians do.

But while the client may be gradually adopting the faith of his or her therapist, the network may be proselytized by the client with books, tapes, articles, workshops and even parallel therapy. More often, however, the network becomes alarmed to see their relative or friend losing his or her way by falling under the baleful influence of this libertine guru. This is particularly likely to be the reaction if the network has a unifying religious or ethnic commitment to traditional values.

Whereas the culture of therapy holds that seeking professional help is the quintessence of responsibility, prudence, and resourcefulness, the very idea of seeking help outside of one's network is anathema to many and contrary to traditional wisdom. Individuals who are competent, capable, and responsible solve their own problems. If personal resources are insufficient, it is appropriate to take the problem to wise relatives or close friends. In some cultures counsel from clergymen may be sought without violating the prime value system, but to seek the help of an outsider, with all that implies in terms of alien values, is tantamount to declaring moral bankruptcy.

One of the premises of the therapeutic subculture is that one tells a therapist everything, withholding nothing. No subject is too sacred or too private or too disgraceful to be pried into. Indeed, resistance is seen as playing games, being dishonest, defensive, counterproductive and self-defeating. By contrast, in traditional culture it is a virtue to be discrete, to keep confidences, to refrain from mentioning unmention-ables, to maintain the boundaries of privacy and to defend the sacred against the profane exposure. To do otherwise is "washing your dirty linen in public" or at worst disloyal, impious and reprobate.

In the therapeutic subculture we place a premium on expressivity of feelings. We treasure every color of emotional revelation; lust, hate, fear, despair and weakness are all grist for the therapeutic mill. The chief sin is withholding or denying one's feelings. The chief virtue is emotional honesty and authentic self-revelation. But a core value within many traditional networks is that strength is most admirably demonstrated by stoicism, and self-control is the chief virtue. Only the weak and childish, only the self-indulgent and incompetent "wear their feelings on their sleeves." The strongest and most virtuous do not indulge themselves in entertaining such feelings in their own hearts, and only the least admirable lose control in front of others. It is a matter of corporate as well as personal pride.

Therapists spend a great deal of their time and energy teaching their clients to become assertive, to ask for what they want, to refuse to let others walk all over them or constrain their choices. We want our clients to become *self-actualized* with all that implies in terms of freedom from social constraints and external moral authority. But traditionally oriented networks are quite likely to honor those who sacrifice their own needs for others and are uncomplaining in their conformity to social expectations and obligations. "Assertiveness" is apt to translate as "willfulness" and "self-actualization" as mere "selfishness" or "rebelliousness."

Therapists are almost without exception committed to the principle of equality between the sexes and of governance by negotiation. Most traditional networks retain loyalty to a patriarchal paradigm within which women exert influence through time-honored strategies of manipulation and subversion but without challenging the legitimacy of male authority. Moreover, this is not viewed as a tradition or cultural artifact but as God-given and intrinsic in the natural fabric of biology and society.

The very premise of all therapeutic intervention is that problems are meant to be solved, obstacles removed and resistances overcome. It is proactive in its core. By contrast, at least some traditional networks have a strong fatalism in their approach to life. God or the fates have allotted to each of us tests and trials. Our task is to suffer them well.

Finally if there is a single byword of therapists it is "differentiate." Enmeshment is a villainous term that evokes imagery of smothered individuality and oppressive intrusiveness by kin and friends. Yet, in many circles what we call "enmeshment" is called "togetherness," and it is highly prized. What we call "differentiated" is seen as "not caring," or "forgetting who really loves you." In fact, Olson and McCubbin (1983) found in their sample of 1,000 midwestern Lutheran families that the happiest individuals, marriages, and families were those who were clearly the most enmeshed.

The point, however, is not whether one or the other set of values is right. In the nature of values, that question is objectively indeterminable. The therapeutic establishment frequently finds itself at odds with its own clients and with their networks in these and many other areas. It is a small wonder we are often viewed as libertine seducers and corrupters.

Therapists will continue to respond to this value discrepancy in a variety of ways. Most will doubtless choose to restrict their practice to true believers or to those willing to convert. For some, this choice may be forced upon therapists by the unwillingness of others to place themselves in the hands of a professional helper, or to see members of their network so placed. I would encourage members of our professional community to experiment with a variety of more conciliatory approaches and challenge only those values which seem to be so destructive in their consequences in a particular case that they must yield or no good can be accomplished.

A traditional world view, for example, may not be converted to the therapeutically approved egalitarian model, but it may be transformed in part. Typically a rigid, oppressive tyrant may be encouraged to become a more sensitive and considerate husband and father without attacking the entire belief system within which the family operates. Or, to take another example, couples from a conservative network can be helped with the solving of their sexual problems without violating their highly developed sense of sexual modesty and privacy. Rather than using the usual approaches complete with desensitization, an intrusively detailed sex history, and sensate homework assignments, I have found it possible to accomplish the same goals within the couple's value framework. A key factor is to diagnose the problem in terms that the clients can fully understand and to draw from their own system of values solutions which can be applied latter in the privacy of their home. To my considerable amazement this actually works about as well as the more conventional therapies with less conservative couples as well.

THE PLACE OF FORMAL NETWORK THERAPY

It may seem anomalous to leave for this final section of the chapter an evaluation of the already well-established therapeutic intervention which has been called Network Therapy. This approach, pioneered by Speck and others (1973), developed as an expansion of family therapy. One of the foundational insights of early family therapists was the observation that if individual therapy wasn't working it might very well be because the fault lay in the family system of which the client was a unit. The remedy was to bring in the larger system and work on it as a system. In a similar fashion some family therapists have found that the family may get stuck if the problem is rooted in a larger system—the network. The solution is to bring the entire network into the therapeutic arena.

Network therapy is a production with as many as 80 to 100 individuals involved. First, there are the immediate relatives and friends of each member of the family, including the friends of each of the children and sometimes their families. Members of other network sectors may be involved as well: School teachers and guidance personnel, other therapists, social workers and perhaps the business associates of spouses.

A team of therapists divides the network into smaller groups with the challenge to work on the target family's problem as constructively as they are able. Some hours later they may reassemble and provide progress reports. This is a major event, and a powerful one. For the family members, there is nowhere to hide. The kids are unable to rebel against the parents by fleeing to their friends' homes and complaining about being badly treated at home. Those friends and their parents are here, coopted into becoming allies of the family in finding solutions. The father is unable to hide at work, pleading an unsympathetic and demanding boss. He is here, helping to work out the family's problem. The mother accustomed to revealing problems to her own mother and siblings finds they to have been coopted into the therapeutic environment. When this massive intervention is well choreographed, it is virtually irresistible. Probably the only reason it has not replaced family therapy is that few people who have ever sponsored one of these therapeutic extravaganzas lust after the opportunity to do another one the following evening. It remains and will remain the ultimate clinical intervention into a network, but it is destined to remain a relatively uncommon remedy due to its high cost.

What I urge, rather, is a more modest proposal. Therapists of every shade of doctrine can hope to do better therapy if they are aware of their clients' networks and how they figure as part of the daily life and enduring values of family members. Through a detailed knowledge of the "network connection" it may be possible (1) to more accurately diagnose where a particular problem is rooted, (2) to avoid expensive and unnecessary power struggles with an aroused and possibly hostile network, (3) to work within the value framework of the network to achieve therapeutic gains, and (4) to potentate the network to participate in and eventually assume responsibility for the healing process.

REFERENCES

Broderick, C. B. (1983). *The therapeutic triangle*. Newbury Park, CA: Sage.

Cervantes, L. F. (1965). *The drop outs: Causes and curses*. Ann Arbor: University of Michigan Press.

Kantor, D., & Lehr, W. (1975). *Inside the family: Toward a theory of family process*. San Francisco: Jossey-Bass.

Olson, D. H., & McCubbin, H. I. (1983). *Families: What makes them work*. Newbury Park, CA: Sage.

Olson, D. H., Sprenkle, D. H., & Russell, C. S. (1979). "Circumflex model of marital and family systems: 1; cohesion and adaptability dimensions, family types, and clinical applications." *Family Process, 18:* 3-28.

Speck, R., & Attneave, C. (1973). *Family Networks*. New York: Vintage.

Straus, M. A., Gelles, R. J., & Steinmetz, S. K. (1980). *Behind closed doors: Violence in the American family*. Garden City, NY: Doubleday.

Zimmerman, C. C., & Broderick, C. B. (1954). Nature and role of informal family groups. *Marriage and Family Living, 16,* 107-110.

Zimmerman, C. C., & Broderick, C. B. (1956). The family self protective system. In C. C. Zimmerman & L. Cervantes (Eds.), *Marriage and the family* (pp. 101-117). Chicago: Regnery.

Zimmerman, C. C., & Cervantes, L. (1960). *Successful American families*. New York: Pageant.

About the Contributors

Rosemary Blieszner is Associate Professor in the Department of Family and Child Development, and Associate Director of the Center for Gerontology, at Virginia Polytechnic Institute and State University. She received her doctorate in human development and family studies from Pennsylvania State University. Rosemary's research interests focus on family and friend relationships in adulthood and old age, and she is currently coediting a book on adult friendships.

Nancy Bradney is a graduate student in the Committee on Human Development at the University of Chicago. Her research interests center on adolescent and adult development.

Carlfred B. Broderick is Professor of Sociology and Director of the Marriage and Family Therapy Doctoral Program at the University of Southern California. His degrees are from Harvard (social relations) and Cornell (child development and family relations); at both places his research was on the friend-family network. More recently his interests have focused on family process and on the structure of therapeutic intervention.

Colleen Leahy Johnson is Professor of Medical Anthropology, University of California, San Francisco. She received her doctorate in anthropology from Syracuse University and remained there on the human development faculty for five years. In addition to numerous articles on the family, aging, and ethnicity, she has recently published two books, *Growing Up and Growing Old in Italian American Families* (Rutgers University Press, 1985) and *The Nursing Home in American Society* (with Leslie Grant; Johns Hopkins University Press, 1985). She is currently engaged in research on the relationships of kin with divorced and remarried individuals.

Reed W. Larson is Associate Professor in the Division of Human Development and Family Ecology at the University of Illinois in

Urbana/Champaign. He is also the Director of the Laboratory for the Study of Adolescence at Michael Reese Medical Center in Chicago. Along with Mihaly Csikszentmihalyi and others at the University of Chicago, Reed is responsible for the development of the Experience Sampling Method. His research is aimed at describing and analyzing daily experience across the life span, with special interest in the time people spend alone and the time they spend with family members and friends.

Kathryn McCannell is Associate Professor of Social Work, University of British Columbia. She has researched and written about social networks, the ecological approach to practice, and feminist contributions to family therapy. Recently she guest edited a special issue of the *Canadian Journal of Community Mental Health* on "Women and Mental Health." Her clinical work focuses on violence in families.

Robert M. Milardo is Associate Professor of Family Relationships at the University of Maine. He received his doctorate in Human Development and Family Studies from Pennsylvania State University, specializing in the social psychology of close relationships. He is currently engaged in research on social networks in distressed and nondistressed marriages. His clinical interests concern violent families and the treatment of male batterers.

Daniel Perlman is Director of the School of Family and Nutritional Sciences, and Lecturer in Psychology at the University of British Columbia. Having received his doctorate in social psychology from the Claremont Graduate School, he is a Fellow of both the American and the Canadian Psychological Associations. He has edited two recent Sage volumes: *Understanding Personal Relationships* and *Intimate Relationships: Development, Dynamics, and Deterioration.* Since the mid-1970s, his research has focused on loneliness. He has also contributed a chapter on the editorial review process to Ruston and Jackson's book, *Scientific Excellence: Origins and Assessment.*

Marylyn Rands is Assistant Professor of Psychology at Wheaton College in Norton, Massachusetts. A graduate of the social psychology program at the University of Massachusetts, Amherst, she has authored and coauthored research articles and chapters on close relationships. Her interests include social networks, conflict and compatibility, social stress, relationships across the life span, and women's experience. She served as department coordinator to integrate the new scholarship on women into the curriculum and has served as a consultant on this subject.

Catherine A. Surra is Assistant Professor of Family Relationships, Division of Child Development and Family Relations, University of Arizona. She received her doctorate in Human Development and Family Studies from Pennsylvania State University and was the 1979 recipient of the National Council on Family Relations Outstanding Graduate Student Award. Her research focuses on the development of close romantic relationships, especially changing patterns of interdependence between partners and between partners and their social networks. Based on variations in the development of commitment to wed, she identified a typology of courtships. She also has devised a scheme for coding people's reasons for marrying, which are related to commitment and later marital satisfaction.

NOTES

NOTES

NOTES